JOHN HOWARD,

AND

THE PRISON-WORLD OF EUROPE.

FROM ORIGINAL AND AUTHENTIC DOCUMENTS.

BY HEPWORTH DIXON.

WITH

AN INTRODUCTORY ESSAY,

BY RICHARD W. DICKINSON, D.D.

"He lived an Apostle, and died a Martyr." BENTHAM (*trans.*)

SLIGHTLY ABRIDGED.

WEBSTER, MASS.
PUBLISHED BY FREDERICK CHARLTON
1852.

BAZIN AND CHANDLER, PRINTERS,
37 Cornhill, Boston.

CONTENTS.

CHAPTER I.

THE PRISON-WORLD BEFORE THE DAYS OF HOWARD.

CHAPTER II.

YOUTH---EDUCATION---SUFFERING.

CHAPTER III.

HOME LIFE AT CARDINGTON..

CHAPTER IV.

DISCIPLINE OF A WOUNDED SPIRIT.

CHAPTER V.

THE CRUSADE COMMENCED.

CHAPTER VIII.

THEORIES OF CRIME.

CHAPTER IX.

PERILS BY SEA AND LAND.

CHAPTER X.

AN EUROPEAN PILGRIMAGE.

CHAPTER XI.

THE CITIES OF THE PLAGUE.

INTRODUCTORY ESSAY.

AMONG the various works recently issued from the Press, we have noticed with especial interest the lives of eminent men, whose names are associated with existent creeds and institutions. The past seems to have been explored with a distinct reference to the personal history of those, who, though dead, yet speak in the views which they advanced, or in the movements which they projected. To us, this is a favorable sign, indicating a more philosophical scrutiny of such theories and systems as owe their origin to individual minds — a generous desire to do justice to men who in their generation were doomed to encounter prejudice or suffer neglect; and to perpetuate, by holding up to the contemplation of youth, the influence of names which stand as symbols of all that is scriptural in faith, pure in personal religion, or heroic in good deeds. No secular study can be more important than that of the lives of men, who, having directed the minds of their contemporaries, left an impress of themselves on succeeding generations. He, therefore, who brings us into a more intimate communion with any one of the master spirits of the past, by presenting his personal history in a clearer and stronger light, writes not in vain.

The period, which our Author's pages embrace, was not wanting in men who did signal service for the highest interests of society. There were Blackstone, whose masterly "Commentaries" have grounded so many minds in the principles of law and justice; and Price, whose profound treatise on Morals, revived the true theory of moral obligation, which seemed to have been exploded by Hume and Hutcheson. There were Butler and Lardner, who, uniting erudition with thought and sagacity, vindicated revealed religion from the attacks of all assailants. There was Watts, a name not to be lightly spoken by any lover of pure Christianity; and the amiable Curate of Olney, whose labors were prominently instrumental in the revival of evangelical piety. There was Wesley, who having travelled three hundred thousand miles, and preached forty thousand times, lived to witness the wide-spread influence of his polity, and the fruits of his labors; and Whitefield, whose eloquence swayed his immense auditories at will, and whose apostolic preaching was unparalleled in its effects. Then, too, commenced that series of missionary labors which have resulted in the establishment of Christian Churches, where Schmidt preached Christ amid the styes of the Hottentot, and Swartz amid the idols of the Hindoos.

But though these men have in turn claimed and rewarded our attention, no one has interested us more than John Howard. There is a peculiarity in his life, and an originality in his labors of love and mercy, which elicit sympathy, win affection, and command our reverence.

Great and good men there were in that age, — men who contended earnestly for the faith, and served God faithfully to the extent of their abilities, in their respective spheres of duty; men, too, whose voice, when raised in behalf of justice and humanity, "shook the Senate" with the resistless appeals of their eloquence; but in comparison with the labors of Howard, neither Burke, impeaching Warren Hastings for "high crimes and misdemeanors," nor even the aged Chatham, rising from his bed to protest against the employment of the merciless Indian in "the defence of disputed rights," seems other than an ordinary man.

It were a pleasant task to descant on the merits of the Statesmen, Divines, and Writers of the last century. The influence of not a few who then lived and toiled, may still be traced in our halls of legislation, in our seminaries of learning, in our pulpits, and in our walks of literature. We need hardly go farther back in history for all that is profound in thought, eloquent in utterance, or admirable in style. In our view, they were men then who may be regarded as models in debate, in controversy, in preaching, and in writing. But be this as it may:

there can be no doubt that the past age has bequeathed to us, in the life and labors of Howard, a model in benevolence. His history deserves, and will reward, our study. It will benefit as well as interest us to place ourselves, in imagination, in his circumstances, — to see as he saw, and feel as he felt. Mr. Dixon is right; another history was needed; and he is entitled to credit for having brought such a man to the more distinct knowledge of the reading community. In the prosecution of his work, he has displayed a commendable diligence in his researches, and a laudable desire to do justice to his subject. And if at times his remarks border on hyperbole, it is to be ascribed rather to the *Furor Biographicus*, than to any inherent defect in judgment; or, if an occasional remark seems to be exceptionable, or must be received with some qualification, it is not that he did not aim to imbue his own mind with "Howardian ideas," but that he has an imperfect apprehension of the moving springs of Howard's course. In his researches, he has left but little if anything to reward any future inquirer; and, in his comments on the facts in Howard's life, he has advanced far enough to answer his prominent design — to wit, that Howard was the father of Prison Science, and that the present advanced state of prison discipline is owing to a return to those very views which, when first advanced by the Philanthropist, were ignorantly spurned. The work, moreover, is interspersed with anecdote, and some important observations; while the whole is conducted in such a manner, that, (with the exception of an occasional page that might better have been referred to an Appendix,) our interest in its perusal increases, until we become painfully anxious as we approach the conclusion, and, at last, involuntarily drop a tear over the good man's foreign grave.

In one respect, however, it is not such a work as we could have wished to see, or such as the material, for his life amply warrant. If Brown, in our author's judgment, could not write a suitable life, because he was a mere "Barrister," nor Aikin because he was a "Physician," something more is necessary than an acquaintance "with prisons and prison discipline," to understand and appreciate Howard's character; nothing short, indeed, of such a knowledge of the Bible as Howard had, if not so marked a sympathy with the genius of Christianity as he evinced. His character is to be interpreted in the light of Christian truth and duty; and it is with a special reference to this defect in our author's work, and if possible to remedy it, so that the work itself may be the means of greater good — that in introducing it to the American public, we would call the readers attention to the character of Howard as a *Christian.*

From the multiplied details of this work, it is evident that he was a man of physical as well as moral courage, of indomitable strength of purpose, quick in his perceptions, rapid in his conclusions, instant and firm in his decisions, whom no evasions could blind, no perplexities embarrass, no difficulties deter. He was indefatigable in his exertions, expeditious in his movements, yet scrupulously attentive to all points of order and minor arrangements. To the completest self-command over his appetites and passions, he added an extraordinary control over the minds of others. Though strong and ardent in his domestic affections, yet was he generous and expansive in his sympathies. Though most sensitive to the wants and woes of humanity, yet was he exactly, critically just. No man ever had a keener sense of right in union with so great love of mercy — none ever freer in charity, and at the same time, more discriminating and judicious. In these respects, he is eminently worthy note. We have been forcibly struck by some particulars, illustrative of these traits in his character, and especially by his manner of life at Cardington. How much good might be done, it gentlemen who have retired from commercial pursuits, made their residences the centres of such influences in their respective neighborhoods!

These habits he brought with him from his father's store ; and, whatever difference of opinion may arise in relation to the mode and extent of his academic culture, it is obvious, that with such habits and qualifications he would have been respected and useful in any sphere, or even adorn the highest stations in society. But neither his natural qualities nor personal habits, — neither his domestic arrangements nor his interest in improving his neighborhood, will furnish us with an explanation of his subsequent career. Men will encounter great hardships and perils for the sake of gain; but Howard left behind him the home which avaricious men sedulously aim to secure, and not only refused all recompense, but in the prosecution of his object expended his own means. Men will deny themselves the delights of home and country, and even submit to years of toil, for the sake of fame; but Howard shunned display, rebuked every demonstration of applause, and was filled "with poignant distress" when told of the honor which his countrymen designed to pay him. Men will go on perilous errands when clothed with official dignity and promised an ample pecuniary recompense; but Howard went forth at his own suggestion, of his own accord, with none of the insignia of rank and power — a plain man, at first accompanied by a single servant, at last, alone! So may many be found who will incur great expense and great risks in order to see men and manners, to survey the ruins of ancient cities, and gratify a classic taste; but Howard went forth "to dive into the depths of dungeons, to plunge into the infection of hospitals, to survey the mansions of sorrow and pain, to take the gauge and dimensions of misery, depression, and contempt; to remember the forgotten, to attend to the neglected, to visit the forsaken, and compare and collate the distresses of all men in all countries."

His course is the more remarkable, when we consider that, though a man of delicate constitution and feeble health, he voluntarily encountered perils which other men are so eager to avoid, and that through scenes of the greatest danger he would allow no one to accompany him. How happened it, then, that a life which might have been pleasantly and by no means uselessly spent at Cardington, became a life of extraordinary toil and peril? That, while the benevolence of such men as Dutze and Bulgarkow was confined to their respective countries, his took the circuit of the world? That, while other men, not deficient in humanity and courage, shrunk from encountering the horrors of Newgate, or the infection of the "Lazarettos," he calmly persevered?

It is true, that the vessel in which he had taken passage to visit Portugal — the capitol of which lay buried in the ruins of the terrible earthquake of 1755 — was captured by privateers; that he was carried into the port of Brest, cast into a dungeon, and treated with the utmost barbarity; yet he was only one of many subjected to the like treatment; and why should he, more than any other, have been led to reflect on the treatment which prisoners of war then received at the hands of their enemies?

So, while tossed to and fro on the Mediterranean, and prevented from landing on either side, through the dread which he everywhere encountered that the vessel in which he sailed was infected, he was led to reflect on the Plague; but how many had been similarly situated; and why should such a circumstance have suggested to him an errand of mercy? Circumstances can afford no rational explanation of Howard's course, for many before him had been in the same circumstances. In these, however, we may discern the Providences of that God "who shapes our ends."

There was a special work of mercy to be done in that age, and Howard was the selected agent,—as God had raised up Luther to expose the corruptions of the Romish Church, or Washington to secure to his country the blessings of civil and religious liberty. Howard's belief in a wise and overruling Providence was strong and clear. He had been accustomed to observe and defer to Providences; while in the light of God's dealings with him he was wont to decide his duty. This, by itself, would sanction the inference that he was a religious man; but this is far from being the only evidence. We know that he made the Bible the man of his counsel, and from the testimony incidentally furnished by our author, it is clear that he had been brought under the influence of its great truths. His was no theoretic knowledge, no speculative faith, no formal acknowledgment of its authority, or merely outward conformity to its requirements. By its illuminations he had been led to see and know himself, to feel his need of a Saviour from the guilt and power of sin, and to cast himself on the mercy and grace of God through Jesus Christ. We have no means of ascertaining his early exercises on the subject of religion; but whatever they were, it is evident, from his occasional letters, and from the fragments of his private journal, that he had awaked to a sense of his high relations, had imbibed much of the spirit of his blessed Lord, and was deeply, prayerfully anxious to adorn the doctrine of God his Saviour. This will be admitted by all who have "so learned Christ;" but whatever doubt may exist in other minds, or however some may attempt to explain his mission on the ground of "his physical organization," or of "certain occult forces which, from the depth of ages, had been working themselves up to the surface of European civilization" — thus imitating the German fashion of theorizing on events and persons — we maintain, there is but one way philosophically to account for the essential traits — the radical elements — of his character. And what were these? Not his decision, though this is the feature which John Foster has elaborately depicted; not his indifference to all works of art and all objects of curious research in comparison with his visits of mercy, though this formed the web of Burke's splendid eulogium on his character; not that humanity and zeal which led him to visit the several gaols of the kingdom, though these constituted the ground on which the supreme legislature of his country passed in his favor a vote of thanks; but that he was so humble in his piety, so devout in his affections, so circumspect in his walk, so conscientious in his manner of living and in the improvement of his time. His *responsibility* to God, was the one deep and irrepressible sentiment of his being—his *obligation* to his Divine Redeemer, lay at the basis of all his works of love and mercy. It was, therefore, his grand desire to glorify God and do good to man.

"So, O my soul! keep close to Him in the amiable light of redeeming love. Remember thou art a candidate for eternity! Daily, fervently, pray for wisdom. Lift up thine heart and eyes to the rock of ages,—and then look down on the glory of this world! A little while longer, and thy journey will be ended. Be thou faithful unto death. Duty is thine, though the power is God's. O compassionate and divine Redeemer! save me from the dreadful guilt and power of sin, and accept of my solemn, free, and, I trust, unreserved, full, surrender of my soul—all I own and have—into thy hands! How unworthy of thy acceptance!"

There is something very impressive in this and kindred entries in his journal. They serve to reveal the man, not as he was seen by the great men of the world, or by the poor outcasts from society, but as he was in the sight of God: not as a theme for the orator, or a model for the artist, but as a subject for the pulpit—an example of the spirit and power of Christianity.

To this—his experimental acquaintance with religion, we refer that trustfulness in Divine Providence which carried him calmly through various scenes of danger; that truthfulness which would not permit him to do even customary homage to usurped authority in Church, or to withhold the fearless expression of his sentiments; that conscientiousness which would not allow him to misimprove a talent committed to his trust by spending it "for mere curiosity, at the loss of many Sabbaths, and thus for his own pleasure, suspending many donations;" that readiness "to endure any hardships and encounter any dangers to be an honor to his Christian profession," and that steadiness of resolution through the many solitary hours of his journeyings, for the continuance of which he often blessed God. Hence too, his contrition for sin, his aspirations after greater devotedness, his love to all who bore the impress of Christ, his desire to be remembered in the prayers of his Christian friends, his earnest desire that his afflictions might be sanctified to his spiritual benefit, and that he might return from his travels, "a wiser, better man — with a cheerful humility, a more general love and bevevolence to his fellow creatures; watchful of his thoughts, his words, his actions — resigned to the will of God, and enabled to walk with God and to lead a more useful and honorable life in this world." Hence, also, that marked reverence for the Sabbath, which led him to rest in whatsoever place the occurrences of the journey might have conducted him; his especial love of devotion, and the value he attached to the enjoyment of God's presence. "The presence of God," said he, "makes the happiness of every place. Wherever I pitch my tent, there God shall have an altar."

Howard's career reveals to us in a light that cannot be mistaken the spirit of a martyr. It is ennobling to thought to contemplate in him a courage that knew no fear, a purpose that nothing could shake, and a devotedness which privations and sacrifices only rendered the more intense. It is not surprising that some did not appreciate his motives, and that to others his course was a mystery. The vain and pompous Countess of the Governor of Upper Austria might have represented a large class of minds in that day; and the member of the House of Commons who "begged to be informed at whose expense Howard travelled," probably represented a larger class: yet the forsaken, the forgotten, the wretched — like the poor inmates of *Dela Stinche* would fain have worshipped him — knowing no other way of accounting for his goodness than by referring it to a supernatural cause. Nor were they under a delusion: that spirit which he evinced is not natural to man — the motives which prompted and swayed his actions had no alliance with self and earth: and hence it is that all other traits in his character fail in comparison with his simple faith, his serene trust, his single-eyed devotedness, his Christian

3

humility. Howard, though he seemed to the prisoners to be a superior being, took pains to convince them that "he was a poor mortal like themselves, whose only object was to do them good." Howard, though kings and nobles tendered invitations to him which most men would have been proud to accept, had but one reply: "Can I do any good by going? for I will not accept the invitation unless it can be made to answer some useful purpose." When thwarted in his beneficent efforts, so far from betraying any of that acrimony which is so characteristic of a false zeal in a good cause, he could only say of his opposers — "They seem not duly sensible of the favor of Providence which distinguishes them from the sufferers: they do not consider that we are required to imitate our Heavenly Father who is kind to the unthankful and the evil; they forget the vicissitudes of human affairs, that it is even possible for a man who has often shuddered at hearing the account of a murder, on a sudden temptation, to commit that very crime." And when at last his services were appreciated, and his admiring countrymen were about to erect a statue in honor of his deeds, — what did Howard, though when he heard of the project he was immured in the Lazaretto of Venice — but write at once to his friends "to put a stop to the progress of the Howardian Fund;" and on his return, he ceased not in his efforts until the money which had been subscribed was in part refunded, in part invested in a charitable fund, and the balance expended in the liberation from gaol of fifty-five poor debtors!

Were it consistent with our limits, we might avail ourselves of the incidents with which our author's work abounds, in illustrating several thoughts which have occurred to us while contemplating Howard's life: such as the obligation of the world to Christianity — how much good may be accomplished even by one man who unites in himself and in due proportions the qualities of faith and energy! — The necessary and unavoidable condition of a benevolent life, so much personal toil and self denial, for whatever good may be done. Active benificence, a security against morbid feelings, and a source of consolation for the afflicted. The greatness of goodness — the best men of not exempted from trials. How affecting to think of Howard's sorrows! to see the strong man bowing himself in the dust, yet committing himself with his poor son to the disposal of unerring Wisdom! Candidly and meekly does he acknowledge that his domestic afflictions did more to depress his spirits and shake his resolution than any danger he had encountered, or horrors witnessed.

Yet in drawing our notice to a close, we cannot refrain from glancing at the life and labors of Howard, as contradistinguished from some of his contemporaries. It is singular, and affords matter worthy of philosophic reflection — that the frightful catastrophe of 1755, which so deeply awakened Howard's sympathies for the survivors, and determined him to hasten with all possible speed to their assistance, should have disturbed the mental peace and occasioned the early skepticism of Goethe. But we may not enlarge.

While Goldsmith was fostering his muse amid classsic scenes, and Gray penning the incidents of his travels to gratify his literary friends, Howard journeyed to relieve misery and succor want and lessen crime. While Sterne — hard-hearted and selfish as he was in his conduct — had tears for all animated and inanimate nature ; and Mackenzie — all sensibility — was portraying his "Man of Feeling," Howard was acting out the promptings of humanity at the expense of ease and self. In an age, too, when Fielding and Smollet were depicting scenes of misery and crime — writing fictitious history or narrating fictitious adventures to stimulate curiosity and exalt themselves, Howard was wending his way through dungeons and hospitals, grappling with dire evils and gathering dark facts, that he might bring to light, — and remedy, if possible — the hidden works of darkness.

We read such literary productions as then attracted notice and still repay perusal : we are not insensible to the beauty of the "Seasons," the charms of "Rasselas," or to the merits of the "Vicar ;" but so far as the great ends of life are concerned, what did the literary men of that age, in comparison with Howard? But what a contrast does he present to not a few of his contemporaries! How much more rational and dignified his way of life at Cardington than that of the skeptical and self-sufficient historian in his residence at Lausanne! What a severe reflection was his course on the selfish moralists of his day! What a practical refutation of their theories! What a withering rebuke to the sensualism of Rousseau and the malignity of Voltaire. Be it so, that they, and others not less prominent, attacked Christianity with the weapons of sarcasm and sophistry, Howard defended it by arguments more potent than the logic of Campbell or the demonstrations of Leland — by a life of self-denying goodness! The spirit that breathed through his daily actions, was akin to the spirit of Him who came into our world "to seek and to save that which was lost;" who "went about doing good;" who "pleased not himself;" who had "a baptism to be baptized with." His faith was the faith of the Gospel — that same gospel which Whitefield preached "in demonstration of the Spirit and with power;" which Scott illustrated in his "Force of Truth;" which Wilberforce, shortly after, explained and enforced in his remarkable "Treatise" — *the Gospel*, which fired the zeal and directed the self-denying efforts of a Vanderkemp and a Martyn.

Under other circumstances — had his attention in early life been called to the condition of the heathen world, as it was, in the Providence of God, to the condition of prisoners in countries regarded as civilized — we can readily conceive that John Howard would have been a missionary to the heathen. His character unites those elements which are imperiously essential in every man who goes forth to labor for Christ in the dark realms of Paganism; and in all that betokens disinterested and unreserved devotedness in a good cause. Howard will compare not unworthily with even the first missionary to the Kafir-land, or the Martyr of Erromanga.

R. W. DICKINSON.

NEW YORK, December 1st, 1849.

PREFACE.

SEVERAL reasons combined to induce the writer to undertake the work of making out for the reading world a new biography of HOWARD; the chief of them fall under two heads:—

It lay in his path.—Years ago now, circumstances which do not require to be explained in this place called his attention to the vast subject of the prison-world. A few inspections served to interest his mind no less than his feelings in this novel field of inquiry. Desiring an exact acquaintance with its history, he naturally took the labors of Howard as his starting-point, and his invaluable works on English and Foreign Prisons as his guide. He studied the words of the philanthropist. He systematized his facts. He went over much of the ground in his very traces. He compared the opinions which he had taken up; and tested, so far as opportunities were afforded, the validity of the conclusions at which he had finally arrived in the closing lustre of his life. This process left the writer more deeply sensible than he had hitherto been of the great value of Howard's mature thoughts, on every matter connected with the treatment of criminals, even to the more advanced science of the present age, — and suggested the idea of their rehabilitation.

It needed to be done. — Few men — even of the well-read — know anything of the details of Howard's career. Beyond the vague notion that he was a very good man, who went about the world dispensing blessings, it is surprising how little is popularly known of a man whose name is so often found on good men's tongues. Yet his life is one not lacking in romance. Many of the elements of biographical attraction surround it. How then account for the general ignorance? Is it because the popular mind is indifferent to moral greatness? Or, is it not rather to be attributed to the want of a more worthy account of his life and labors than we yet possess? There are two works only of any mark or likelihood on the subject: the view of his Life and Character by Dr. Aikin, and the Memoirs by Baldwin Brown. The first is of undoubted value and authenticity; but it is a mere essay, written in haste, and issued to serve a temporary purpose. The second is voluminous enough and of good authority; but it is at the same time insufferably dull. Few have read it — and few can read it. Even the bright name of Howard will not suffice to lead men through such a mass of unredeemed darkness — over such a wilderness of words. Thirty years ago it was published.

The book is becoming scarce, and it is never likely to be reprinted. The brief notices which we have in Cyclopædias are miserably meagre and inexact.

This scantiness of information — or rather of works in which to spread it — is probably the real cause of so little being known about Howard. For the ignorance spoken of is not confined to the uneducated. It is far more profound. Men who would blush to be found at fault in their acquaintance with comparatively obscure characters, ask *naively* — if his life has ever been written! They have never seen it. At the great public discussion in the City on "Prison Discipline" — in which the writer took part — an hon. gentleman brought a copy of the "State of Prisons" forward as a discovery, and quoted from it as from a sybilline book. He — a man who has been an agitator on topics connected with prisons, police, and the administration of justice for years — admitted he had only just become aware of its existence! And this is but a common case. The increasing interest felt in prison reforms makes it, however, very desirable that Howard and his opinions — the lessons of wisdom and the example of virtue afforded in his life — should be better known. The prison world is now a popular topic. The press and parliament keep it constantly under attention. The State has set a vast machinery at work in connection with it, — for the maintenance of which considerable taxes are required. Governments are everywhere alive to its importance. Cabinet ministers think it necessary to visit the cell, — and one sceptred hand, at least, has written upon its mysteries. The growth of this intelligent interest in the subject to which Howard's energies were devoted, discovers to us one circumstance of importance — that although *he* was the father of prison-science, the story of his life has hitherto been made out without reference to that fact. His biographers were wanting in that knowledge of the subject which was necessary to enable them to assign him his position. Their studies disqualified them for their chosen tasks. Aikin was a physician — Brown a barrister: neither of them had any acquaintance with prisons, or with the workings of the gaol system. A person ignorant of fortifications would be as competent to write the life of Vauban — or one who never saw an army in the field, a history of Marlborough's military campaigns.

It has been the writer's study to render this biographical history of Howard as worthy of its subject and of the confidence of the reader as the nature of the materials at his disposal would allow. He has carefully collated every document already printed — made, and caused to be made, numerous researches — conversed with persons who have preserved traditions and other memorials of this subject — travelled in his traces over a great number of prisons — examined parliamentary and other records for such new facts as they might afford — and, in conclusion, has consulted these several sources of information, and interpreted their answers by such light as his personal experience of the prison-world suggested to be needful. The result of this labor is, that some new matter, of curious interest, has turned up — amongst other things a manuscript, throwing light on the early history of prison reforms in this country, found in the archives of the Society for Promoting Christian Knowledge, and for which he is indebted to the courtesy of the Secretary, the Rev. T. B. Murray; — and the writer is assured that no other paper exists in any known quarter. The material for Howard's life is therefore now fully collected; whether it is herein finally used, will entirely depend upon the verdict of the reader.

The mental and moral portraiture of Howard attempted in this volume is new. As the writer's method of inquiry and of treatment was different to that ordinarily adopted, so his result is different. His study of the character was earnest, and he believes faithful. After making himself master of all the mere facts of the case which have come down to us, biographically and traditionally, his plan was to saturate himself with Howardian ideas, and then strive to reproduce them living, acting and suffering in the real world. The public — the ultimate judges of all literary and artistic merit — will decide upon the fairness of his interpretation.

The writer lays down his pen not without regret. Long accustomed to contemplate one of the most noble and beautiful characters in history, he has learnt to regard it with a human affection; and at parting with his theme — the mental companion of many hours and the object of his constant thoughts — he feels somewhat like a father who gives away his favorite daughter in marriage. He does not lose his interest in his child: — but she can be to him no longer what she has been. A touch of melancholy mingles with his joy. He still regards his offspring with a tender solicitude, — but his monopoly of love is ended.

JOHN HOWARD.

CHAPTER I.

THE PRISON-WORLD BEFORE THE DAYS OF HOWARD.

THE history of prison science begins with Howard. Before his time there were no data on which to base a rule of criminal treatment. A few humane individuals — roused by the strange reports of cruelties and sufferings endured in the dungeon, which sometimes found their way into the social circles — had at long intervals forced their way into the dark adyta of the prison-world, and brought their secrets to the light. But little or no good had resulted from the exposures made. The action of charity had only been spasmodic — and the evils were too deeply seated to be removed by anything less than an herculean resolution. So gigantic were the vices which tainted the entire administration of the criminal law — so hopelessly corrupt and inculpated were all ranks of prison-officers — so irredeemably indifferent were the convicts themselves to their debased condition — so filthy and fever-haunted were the buildings in which they were confined, — it is not at all surprising that, after a short but fruitless crusade against the festering mass of moral plague, even benevolence itself should have shrunk from the peril and the pollution. Two very notable instances of such momentary and ineffectual intrusions into the gaol region occurred in the eighteenth century, before Howard commenced his labors — the first by a committee of the Society for Promoting Christian Knowledge, about 1701–2; the second by a parliamentary Commission of Inquiry, which sat and reported in 1728–9. Hitherto, the second of these attempts has alone been known to the public. It is very doubtful whether Howard even ever became aware of the labors or the earlier volunteers in his own selected walk.

While rummaging the archives of the Society, the Secretary, the Rev. T. Boyle Murray, unexpectedly turned up some old MSS., which, on examination, proved to be minutes and other records of the Society in the time of William III. and Queen Anne. From these it would appear that the disorders of Newgate were so great at that time as to attract public attention, and induce the Society to try some means of removing the more open and radical abuses. With this design a committee was nominated on the 12th of January, 1701–2, to visit that and other gaols. In a few days, Dr. Bray, who was at the head of the inspection, reported that they had visited Newgate, talked with the poor wretches in their cells, and distributed certain moneys amongst them. The same committee afterwards visited the Marshalsea and other prisons — with regard to all of which they rendered the most deplorable accounts. The council of the venerable Society appears to have requested Dr. Bray to put the result of his observations and suggestions into a concise form, that philanthropy might be directed to the most useful reforms. With this request the doctor complied, and made a brief but lucid report. This curious and important historical document has also been found in the Society's archives. It has never been printed; and as it is the earliest document of any value connected with penology in England, which we possess — throwing light not only on the state of the gaols a hundred and fifty years ago, but also on the state of public knowledge on the subject, — it would be unpardonable not to give it in its own quaint terms. It bears no date, — but we know from other papers in the Society's possession that it was written in the year 1701–2. It runs as follows:

"*An* ESSAY *towards ye* REFORMATION *of* NEWGATE, *and the other Prisons in and about London.*

"The vices and immoralities of prisons appear to be these following: —

I. The personal lewdness of the keepers and under-officers themselves, who often make it their business to corrupt the prisoners, especially the women.

II. Their confederacy with prisoners in their vices, allowing the men to keep company with the women for money.

III. The unlimited use of wine, brandy, and other strong liquors, even by condemned malefactors.

IV. Swearing, cursing, blasphemy, and gaming.

V. Old criminals corrupting new comers.

VI. Neglect of all religious worships.

For reforming these abuses the following methods are proposed:

I. For the keepers and under-officers.

1. That endeavors be used to procure an Act of Parliament to displace and punish such as are vicious and immoral.

But till that can be done,

2. That application be made to the Lord Mayor and Sheriffs of London, to use their authority for reforming the prisons. And as any officer (who hath purchased his place) dies, or is removed, they may be desired to have a special regard to the virtue and morality of his successor.

3. That a committee of Aldermen, Common Council, or some members of the Society for reformation be appointed distinctly for this purpose, who shall have power.

(1.) To appoint Ministers, the approbation of the Bishop of London first had and obtained, and also officers to all prisons; and shall be obliged once a week to visit them, and take an account of ye state of each prison, and give orders accordingly.

(2.) This committee to have power to license all ale-houses and taverns adjoyning to each prison, and they to be in the power of this committee and visitors, and other power as shall be thought convenient.

(3.) The disposal of all benefactions to prisons (without a particular designation of the donor) to be made by this committee.

4. That the officers be so ordered as to be made checks upon each other, and the superior always made answerable for the neglects of the inferior.

5. That officers who are notoriously lewd and vicious, and have bought their places, may be obliged by ye committee to sell their places at such a value as the committee shall think reasonable, and to such persons as shall be approved of by the committee for their good conversation.

6. That a Table of Orders, containing the duty of officers and ministers, as well as prisoners, signed by my Lord Bishop of London and the committee, be hung up in every prison, showing the mulcts and punishments of the several offences, together with the names and abodes of the committee and visitors, directing where complaints may be made of neglects.

(1.) That these orders be read once a month by ye Minister in the presence of all the officers and as many of the prisoners as may.

(2.) That there be a short preface or postscript, setting forth the good designed to their souls by these orders; and passionately exhorting the better sort to joyn their endeavors for promoting this good work.

II. Another abuse is the confederacy of the officers with the prisoners in their vices, allowing the men to keep company with the women for money, &c.

To prevent this, it is proposed,

1. That if possible provision may be made to keep every prisoner in distinct cells, as is practised in Bethlem Hospital. But till that be done,

That the women be strickly kept in separate apartments by themselves, and a severe penalty be laid on any officer that shall permit a man to converse with a woman, except it be his own wife.

2. That the men be employed in such work as they have been bred to, and in case of idleness or refusal, to be obliged to beat hemp, or any other hard labor.

3. That some expedient be found out that those women whose execution is respited on account of their bellies may not thereby for ever escape the rigor of the law, for this emboldens them in the commission of crimes which they would not probably be guilty of were they left without hopes of escaping, &c.

4. That the officers be restrained from taking any money, beside their salary, in consideration of their good usage towards the prisoners, unless in case of such lodging, diet, or apartments, as are more for their convenience. But let not money to the officers

atone for any crime whatsoever committed in the prison.

III. There is an unlimited use of wine, brandy, and other strong liquors in all prisons, and sold there, to the extraordinary profit of the keepers. And neither prisoner nor such as come to visit him shall be civilly used except they call for great quantities of liquor. Nay, condemned criminals go often intoxicated to execution.

To prevent which, I conceive,

1. That no wine or strong liquors ought to be sold in any prison, nor fetched from abroad, unless in cases of necessity, and that with the leave of one or more of the committee.

2. That all customs which promote drinking, such as paying garnish by new comers, &c., be peremptorily forbidden, and severe penalties inflicted on the officers that permit the continuance of them.

3. That no kind of luxury or intemperance be permitted to any prisoner, and that abstinency and mortification be strictly enjoyned, to condemned criminals in particular, from the very moment after sentence passed.

IV. Swearing, cursing, blasphemy, gaming, &c., are y[e] daily practices both of officers and prisoners.

And here it is offered,

1. That a Register Book be kept of all the officers' and prisoners' names, with the time of the

prisoners' commitment, and an alphabetical direction to each name.

2. That to each name a mark be affixed, with the date of all their oaths, curses, intemperance, &c.; as also to the officers' names a note of any corruption or neglect of orders.

3. That some marks of commendation be set to their names who shall be of good behaviour during their confinement, in which degrees may be shown as they shall be more exemplary or useful towards reforming others.

4. That this register be always produced in court at the trial and also at the release of all prisoners, and consideration be had to these particulars. That an ill behaviour in prison be made an article at their trial and a punishment adjudged to it distinct from that to their main crime for which they are tried.

5. That the punishments be either corporal or pecuniary, mulcts both to prisoner and officer.

(1.) Corporal punishments may be ye stocks for ye under officers. To stubborn, profane criminals, a confinement to so many meals of bread and water, or perhaps more weight of chains, or turning over to the common side, as is usual with the gaoler to inflict where money is not given to buy them off, or in some cases, a public severe whipping before execution, which may be more frightful to some than death.

(2.) Pecuniary mulcts, such as the Act of Parliament requires for oaths, curses, drunkenness, &c., out of which the register and informers may be considered; and after them the poorer sort of prisoners (if they shall have the mark of commendation to their names), for discharging their fees or supplying their necessities.

V. Old and incorrigible prisoners corrupt the new comers.

To reform this it is necessary,

1. That such offenders be kept in separate apartments, singly, by themselves, and by no means suffered to converse with others.

2. That they be obliged to hard labour so many hours in a day.

3. That when such persons be released out of Newgate, they may be sent to public workhouses, and so distributed amongst others, that an eye shall be always had to them, and not to be released from thence but upon sufficient security given and evidence made that they are entering upon an honest employment. Nor after their release suffered to depart from their abodes without security for their good behaviour, and taking to some business that may maintain them.

4. For the encouragement of those who have lived regularly during their confinement, and give good hopes of their living honestly, that all good people may be advertised of their abodes and pro-

fessions by some public notice in the sessions paper, and exhorted to help them in getting a livelihood in their trades, that they not return to their old courses.

VI. Religious worship is miserably neglected in most prisons, and therefore it is proposed,

1. That the salary of the Ordinary of Newgate, and all ministers of prisons, be a sufficient maintenance and encouragement for their constant attendance.

2. That choice be made of sober, pious divines for this purpose, and by no means of the younger sort, or of loose livers, such as are sometimes in prisons, and y[t] their conscientious discharge of their duty in these places be an efficient recommendation of them to preferment in the City gift.

3. That other ministers as are willing, and are allowed of by the Bishop of London, may weekly visit the prison, and have free access to the prisoners.

4. That books of devotion be given to all prisoners: a Bible to every chamber, many Common Prayer Books, Whole Duty of Man, Christian Monitors, Dr. Isham's Office for the Sick, Mr. Kettlewell's Office for Prisoners, &c.

5. That all Prisons (for debt especially) be considered as parochial cures, and it is the Minister's neglect if they do not come near the practice of what is done in other parish churches.

6. That morning and evening prayer be read in all prisons every day in the week, suitable sermons preached twice every Lord's day, and the Holy Sacrament monthly administered. And here let the Minister be very careful to apply himself to each communicant in examination and instruction, after sufficient notice given of his inclination to receive. And to prevent scandal, and too great presumption, it may be a good way, (commonly, I think, taken by my Lord Bishop of Chichester and others,) to enjoyn the most notorious malefactors to sign a paper, importing a public acknowledgement and recantation before they receive. Upon which some great offenders in Newgate have been admitted by them to the Holy Sacrament before execution. This will be a good lesson of instruction to others, and by the blessing of God may have good effect upon such as shall be released, and make them lead better lives for the future.

It is very much hoped the Right Hon. the Lord Mayor and the Sheriffs of the City of London will take this whole matter into their special consideration; considering that the reformation of prisons may much contribute to the reformation of the public, for prisons are one great part of our correction for criminals, and if they are well managed may prove effectual to their amendment: whereas, for want of discipline it now generally happens that prisoners are made much worse by them, and if an innocent person be committed by misfortune or mistake, he is commonly corrupted and turns profligate.

And care in this affair is more particularly recommend to the City of London, both because prisoners are here in greater number than in other places, and because the example of this capital city is like to have an influence upon the whole kingdom."

How delighted Howard would have been to have known this document! Its facts and suggestions would have greatly facilitated some of his operations, and a knowledge of them would have considerably smoothed his earlier path in benevolence. After the glimpse thus obtained into the prison world, darkness again falls upon the scene. A quarter of a century elapses ere the curtain is withdrawn anew. During this period all that was bad went rapidly worse; prisons became perfect pandemonia. Criminals and their keepers alike gave way to the worst excesses — unrestrained by any sense of justice, or even by any fear of the law. The prison was gradually withdrawn from the pale of the constitution. Gaolers constantly and openly set the court of law at defiance. When the malice or cupidity of a governor or warder was excited, it was no uncommon thing for him, — illegally, and on his own responsibility, it is true, but, as the sequel usually proved, with perfect impunity, — to rob, torture or even murder his unfortunate victim. And this too in the age of Pope and Swift — in the so-called Augustan period of English letters!

The gross and notorious license at length forced itself again upon the consideration of a busy and apathetic public; and on the 25th of February, 1728, the Legislature appointed a Committee of the House of Commons to inquire into "The state of the Gaols of this kingdom," and report to it thereon. From the first hour, this work of inquiry was carried on slowly, and never was completed: the evil was in truth too great to grapple with. The earliest stage of the investigation brought to the knowledge of the Committee such a mass of corruption in the management of prisons, — such flagrant instances of tyrannous illegality on the part of their officers, — such a wholesale and organized system of plunder, peculation and deceit, — cases of such daring violations of rule and justice in the infliction of punishments, in some of which the thumb-screw and other instruments of torture, quite unknown to the genius and practice of English penal law, had been used, — that they hastened to lay the facts before the House, in order that the delinquents who had so notoriously abused their powers might be brought to justice without delay. When the first part of their report was made in Parliament, the feelings of surprise and disgust which the horrid disclosures excited were such that the House at once ordered the arrest of the warders, tipstaffs, and other officers of the gaols reported upon, and passed a strong resolution, praying his Majesty to cause his Attorney-general, without delay, and in the most effectual manner to prosecute them for the high crimes and misdemeanors with which they stood charged.

The Committee then continued its inquiries, and, from time to time, printed fresh reports. The public were at that time comparatively callous to such revelations — the preacher of the new social doctrine, that society has duties even in relation to the inmate of a debtor's or a felon's cell, lay as yet at Cardington in his unconscious cradle, — but they nevertheless produced a shock of pain and indignation in every generous mind, the effect of which did not easily wear away, and would not be entirely lost upon the infant philanthropist.

It soon became evident to the Committee of Inquiry that the state of the various gaols of the kingdom was fatally similar. Degrees of corruption and maladministration there undoubtedly were; but there was no difference in the quality of the evil. Every one of them, from Marshalsea or Newgate down to the pettiest and obscurest provincial House of Detention, was a disgrace to an age and country pretending to civilization. Only that we have the sworn evidence on the trials, and the statements in the reports of the Committee, it would have been difficult to have believed that in the so loudly-vaunted Georgian era of England such things were, as a brief glance at the condition, discipline, and practices of one or two of the metropolitan gaols will reveal to us. As they cannot all be described, the Fleet and the Marshalsea are selected; for these gaols being used for the confinement of debtors, — men unfortunate rather than guilty, and therefore naturally entitled to every indulgence not denied to them by the law, — they are the fairest specimens from which to get a general notion of the work requiring to be done when Howard came into the world. Besides, at that period, lengthened imprisonments for breaches of the criminal laws were rare; while for insolvent debtors it was only too common. Shorter work was made with felons in those days than would be found convenient now. Almost every offence in the calendar was capital. A Draconic spirit presided over the conceptions of the legislator and the decisions of the judge. It was found much easier to kill than to cure, and cheaper; or, at least, so it seemed to the spurious economy of an age which looked only to the present moment and the individual culprit. Not knowing what else to do with the poor wretch whose necessities had driven him to steal a pair of shoes or a skein of thread, those who were charged with the maintainance of the law — hanged him! But this was a method of ending a difficulty hardly applicable to debtors: imprisonment was therefore necessary for them; and in these debtor-prisons we have consequently the best examples of the gaol-system as it flourished in England before the labors of Howard introduced a change therein for the better.

In the Marshalsea, debtors and pirates were confined; the former generally of the poorer classes, — many of them common sailors. The gaol was under the charge of the Deputy-marshal of the Marshalsea of the King's household — an officer, who, in defiance of the express prohibition of the deed constituting him governor, farmed out the fees, victualling, and lodgings of his prisoners to various parties, from whom he received ample considerations. Thus the corruption began at the very source. The inferior officers were only too ready to follow the example set before them. When a person was sent in — and his commitment might be for a debt of a single shilling, increased to forty by legal expenses — he had first of all to pay garnish, in the shape of a bowl of punch for his companions. If, as was often the case, the new comer had no money wherewith to buy his freedom of the gaol, he was stripped, in a riotous and disgraceful manner, of the greater part of his scanty clothes, which were sold or pledged to pay for the bumper. Next, he had to make his selection of a side of the gaol — namely, the master's side, where he would have to pay exorbitant prices for his bedding, food, and drink; or the common side, where he would have to fare as he could, on the occasional and utterly inadequate supplies of such charity as the cupidity of the official, might suffer to be applied to their legitimate purposes. Out of the persons confined on the master's side the profits of the establishment were chiefly made: — but it is not to be supposed that they were well treated on that account. On the contrary, the fact of their being able to pay for accommodation, pointed them out to the wardens as the best subjects for the exercise of their peculiar arts. Means the most barbarous and illegal were used to extort money from them, or from their friends.

As for the miserable wretches who were unable to buy the mercy of their keepers, no words can paint the terrible condition to which they were reduced more forcibly than the simple and matter-of-course language of the parliamentry report:— "The common side," it explains, "is enclosed with a strong brick wall; in it are now confined upwards of 330 prisoners, most of them in the utmost necessity; they are divided into particular rooms called wards, and the prisoners belonging to each ward are locked up in their respective wards every night, most of which are excessively crowded, thirty, forty, nay, fifty persons, having been locked up in some of them, not sixteen feet square; and at the same time that these rooms have been so crowded, to the great endangering the health of the prisoners, the largest room on the common side hath been kept empty, and the room over *George's ward* was let out to a tailor to work in, and nobody allowed to lie in it, though all the last year there were sometimes forty, and never less than thirty-two persons locked up in *George's ward* every night, which is a room sixteen by fourteen feet, and about eight feet high; the surface of the room is not sufficient to contain that number when laid down, so that one-half are hung up in hammocks, while the other lie on the floor under them; the air is so wasted by the number of persons who breathe in that narrow compass, that it is not sufficient to keep them from stifling, several having in the heat of summer perished for want of air." The more offensive part of this account is omitted, but it may be seen entire in the State Papers. Truly the reformer was much needed here!

Next follows an example of the infliction of the *question*, which Blackstone says is utterly unknown to the laws of England: — "In the year 1726, Thomas Bliss, a carpenter, not having any friends to support him, was almost starved to death in the prison, upon which he attempted to get over the prison by a rope lent to him by another prisoner. In the attempt, he was taken by the keepers, dragged by the heels into the lodge, barbarously beaten and put into irons, in which he was kept several weeks. One afternoon, as he was standing quietly in the yard with his irons on, some of the said Acton's men [Acton was a butcher and lessee of the prison] called him into the lodge, where Acton was then drinking and merry with company. In about half-an-hour Bliss came out again, crying, and gave an account, — That when he was in the lodge, they, for their diversion, (as they called it,) fixed on his head an iron engine or instrument, (which appears to be an iron skull-cap,) which was screwed so close, that it forced the blood out of his ears and nose. And he further declared, — That his thumbs were at the same time put into a pair of thumb-screws, which were screwed so tight that the blood started out of them; and from that time he continued disordered until the day of his death. He was let out of prison without paying his debt, and at his going out, Acton desired,—That all that was past might be forgot, and that he would not bear him any ill-will. This miserable wretch was put into St. Thomas's Hospital for help—but died very soon." What succeeds is still more horrible:—"The various tortures and cruelties before mentioned not contenting these wicked keepers, in their pretended magistracy over the prisoners, they found a way of making within this prison a confinement more dreadful than the strong-room itself, by coupling the living with the dead; and have made a practice of locking up debtors who displeased them in the yard with human carcases. One particular instance of this sort of inhumanity was of a person whom the keepers confined in that part of the lower yard which was then separated from the rest, whilst there were there two dead bodies which had lain there for days; yet was he kept there with them six days longer, in which time the vermin devoured the flesh from their faces, eat the eyes out of the heads of the carcases, which were bloated, putrified, and turned green during the poor debtor's dismal confinement with them!"

Let a glance be now directed upon the Fleet. It is not necessary to enter into the detailed history of this celebrated gaol: it will be enough to remark, in passing, that it is of considerable antiquity, and was probably used for the confinement of debtors as early as the reign of Richard I. During the ascendency of the Star-chamber, it was used by that iniquitous court, and often made the scene of punishments unknown to English law. On the fall of the tribunal it reverted to its original purpose. The general picture of the Marshalsea — that is, so far as concerns the crowding of prisoners in close rooms, the scanty and irregular diet, the dirty and costly lodging — applies also to the Fleet; but the latter had features of its own — for, containing a higher class of detenues, the chances of extortion were greater, and the abuses were consequently even yet more palpable and gross.

The custody or wardenship of the Fleet was private property. In fact, the establishment was a large business speculation, and the most flagitious malversation, iniquity, cruelty, and treachery were resorted to in order to make it pay a large per-centage. At the time of the Parliamentary Inquiry, one Bambridge was warden; he, in connection with a person named Cuthbert, having purchased the office from Huggins, a former warden, for 5,000*l.* In his own person, and by his subordinates, this man carried on various branches of trade, including — victualling, tavern-keeping, lodging, and so forth. To ensure large profits, his charges were fixed exorbitantly high, and in all cases were rigorously exacted, even if the consequence was the starvation and death of his victim — many instances of which are upon the records. One of the most fertile sources of wealth to the warden, was the sponging-house attached to the gaol. When a person was committed to prison, Bambridge would refuse him immediate admission, and send him instead to the sponging-house, kept by one of his agents, where in a few days, he would be thoroughly fleeced. After speaking at some length of the case of an unfortunate gentleman named Castell, whose affairs had fallen into confusion, the report thus continues:—"The said Bambridge having thus unlawfully extorted large sums of money from him in a very short time, Castell grew weary of being made such a wretched property, and resolving not to injure further his family or creditors for the sake of so small a liberty, he refused to submit to further exactions; upon which the said Bambridge ordered him to be recommitted to Corbett's [the sponging-house: by enormous presents Castell had obtained the liberty of the Fleet,] where the small-pox then raged, though Castell acquainted him with his not having had that distemper; that he dreaded it so much, that the putting him into a house where it was would occasion his death, which, if it happened before he could settle his affairs, would be a great prejudice to his creditors, and would expose his family to destruction; and therefore he earnestly desired that he might be sent into another house, or even into the gaol itself, as a favor. The melancholy case of this poor gentleman moved the very agents of the said Bambridge to compassion, so that they used their utmost endeavors to dissuade him from sending this unhappy person to the infected house; but Bambridge forced him thither, where he (as he feared he should) caught the small-pox, and in a few days died thereof, justly charging the said Bambridge with his death; and unhappily leaving all his affairs in the greatest confusion, and a numerous family of small children in the utmost distress." It is needless to add a word of comment to this painful recital.

As money was the sole object of Bambridge, so money was all powerful with him. No indulgence was denied of those who could and would pay the price demanded for it; and the custodian had everything to sell, from the simplest convenience up to the highest luxury — permission to break prison and escape. Each article in his scale had its price, and with golden keys every door in the gaol could be opened. These cases of escape were so numerous and so notoriously connived at, that when the keepers were questioned by the Committee on the point they confessed their inability to make any correct statement as to the escapes; the cases were so many as to defy the power of memory, and no account of them had ever been taken in writing.

They, however, who had not the means or not the inclination to bribe high enough, had no resource but to submit in silence; and very often, in spite of the just decision of the law, to fret away their lives in hopeless captivity. After every legal impediment to the release of a prisoner had been removed, his case was nearly as desperate as before, — unless he could contrive to command a handsome present for the warden; and even then, if the officer had conceived any grudge against him, or could expect by further detension to wring from him or from his friends a still larger sum. These latter cases were far from uncommon. The law availed no man unless the gaoler felt it to be his interest to obey its mandate. Dark days were those for the unfortunate; and a sad commentary are these facts on the reputed wisdom of our ancestors! When the Committee commenced their inquiries, they found in the Fleet alone not less than fifty-two persons who were illegally detained after their discharges had been ordered by the proper tribunals — and some of these miserable beings had been so illegally detained, nine, ten, and eleven years!

How little effect the fear of the law had upon the conduct of the governor — even when he was directly brought to its bar and threatened with its power — the following case will exhibit: — "Captain John Mackpheadris was a considerable merchant, and in a very flourishing condition until the year 1720, when, being bound for large sums to the Crown, for a person afterwards ruined by the misfortunes of that year, he was undone. In June, 1727, he was a prisoner in the Fleet, and although he had paid his commitment fee, the like was extorted from him a second time; and he having furnished a room, Bambridge demanded an extravagant price for it, which he refused to pay, and urged — that it was unlawful for the warden to demand extravagant rents, and offered to pay what was legally due; notwithstanding which, the said Bambridge, assisted by James Barnes and other accomplices, broke open his room, and took away several things of great value, amongst others, the King's Extent in aid of the prisoner, (which was to have been returned in a few days, in order to procure the debt to the Crown and the prisoner's enlargement,) which Bambridge still retains. Not content with this, Bambridge locked the prisoner out of his room, and forced him to lie in the open yard, called the Base. He sat quietly under his wrongs; and getting some poor materials, built a little hut, to protect himself as well as he could from the injuries of the weather. The said Bambridge, seeing his nnconcernedness, ordered Barnes to pull down his little hut, which was done accordingly. The poor prisoner, being in an ill state of health, and the night rainy, was put to great distress. Some time after this, he was (about twelve o'clock at night) assaulted by Bambridge, with several other persons, his accomplices, in a violent manner; and Bambridge, though the prisoner was unarmed, attacked him with his sword, but by good fortune was prevented from killing him; and several other persons coming out upon the noise, they carried Mackpheadris for safety into another gentleman's room; soon after which, Bambridge coming with one Savage and several others, broke open the door, and Bambridge strove with his sword to kill the prisoner; but he again got away, and hid himself in another room. Next morning, the said Bambridge entered the prison with a detachment of soldiers, and ordered the prisoner to be dragged to the lodge, and ironed with great irons; on which he, desiring to know for what cause, and by what authority he was to be so cruelly used, Bambridge replied, it was by his own authority, and that he would have his life. The prisoner desired he might be carried before a magistrate, that he might know his crime before he was punished; but Bambridge refused, and put irons upon his legs which were too little, so that in forcing them on, his legs were like to have been broken, and the torture was impossible to be endured. Upon which, the prisoner complaining of the grievous pain and straitness of the irons, Bambridge answered, that he did it on purpose to torture him; on which the prisoner replying, that, by the law of England, no man ought to be tortured, Bambridge declared that he would do it first, and answer for it afterwards, and caused him to be dragged away to the dungeon, where he lay without a bed, loaded with irons so close riveted, that they kept him in continual torture, and mortified his legs. After long application, these irons were changed, and a surgeon directed to dress his legs, but his lameness is not, nor ever can be, cured. He was kept in this miserable condition for three weeks, by which his sight is greatly prejudiced, and in danger of being lost. The prisoner, upon this usage, petitioned the judges, and after several meetings and a full hearing, the judges reprimanded Mr. Huggins and Bambridge, and declared, that *a gaoler could not answer the ironing of a man before he was found guilty of a crime*, — but it being out of term, they could not give the prisoner any relief or satisfaction!

" Notwithstanding this opinion of the judges, the said Bambridge continued to keep the prisoner in irons till he had paid him six guineas; and to prevent the prisoner's recovering damages for the cruel treatment of him, Bambridge indicted him and his principal witnesses at the Old Bailey, before they knew anything of the matter; and to support that indictment, he had recourse to subornation, and turned two of his servants out of places which they had bought, because they would not swear falsely that the prisoner had struck the said Bambridge, which words he had inserted in affidavits ready prepared for signing, and which they knew to be false... The prisoners being no longer able to bear the charges of prosecution, which had already cost 100*l.*, and being softened by promises, and terrified by threats, submitted to plead guilty, on a solemn assurance and agreement made with Bambridge, before witnesses, of having but one shilling fine laid upon them; but so soon as they had pleaded guilty, Bambridge took advantage of it, and has continued harassing them and their securities ever since."

Lust of gold was not, however, the only base passion which raged in the Fleet. If it were the most frequent, it was by no means the most active, or the most fatal. Captain David Sinclair, a gallant but unfortunate officer, had in some way excited the murderous malice of his keeper — the rest of the story is told in the language of the report: —

"At the latter end of June, or the beginning of July last, the said Bambridge declared to the said James Barnes, one of the agents of his cruelties, that he would have Sinclair's blood; and he took the opportunity of the first festival day, which was on the first of August following, when he thought Captain Sinclair might, by celebrating the memory of the late King, be warmed with liquor so far, as to give him some excuse for the cruelties which he intended to inflict upon him. But in some measure he was disappointed, for Captain Sinclair was perfectly sober when the said Bambridge rushed into his room, with a dark lantern in his hand, assisted by his accomplices, James Barnes and William Pindar, and supported by his usual guard, armed with muskets and bayonets, and without any provocation given, ran his lantern in Captain Sinclair's face, seized him by the collar, and told him he must come along with him. Captain Sinclair, though surprised, asked for what, and by what authority he was treated so? Upon which Barnes and the rest seized upon Càptain Sinclair, who still desiring to know by what authority they so abused him, Bambridge grossly insulted him, and struck him with his cane on the head and shoulders, whilst he was held fast by Pindar and Barnes. Such base and scandalous usage of this gentleman, who had in the late wars always signalized himself with the greatest courage, gallantry, and honor, in the service of his country, upon many the most brave and desperate occasions, must be most shocking and intolerable; yet Captain Sinclair bore it with patience, refusing only to go out of his room unless he were forced; whereupon the said Bambridge threatened to run his cane down his throat, and ordered his guards to stab him with their bayonets, or drag him down to the said dungeon, called the strong-room — the latter of which they did; and Bambridge kept him confined in that damp and loathsome place, till he had lost the use of his limbs and his memory, neither of which he has recovered to this day. Many aggravating cruelties were used to make his confinement more terrible; and when Bambridge found he was in danger of immediate death, he removed him, for fear of his dying in duresse, and caused him to be carried, in a dying condition, from that dungeon to a room where there was no bed or furniture; and so unmercifully prevented his friends from having any access to him, that he was four days without the least sustenance."

Sinclair seems to have had an iron frame: he recovered his liberty — but not his health. It is impossible to read these horrible disclosures without shame and indignation. How many more such cases must have been consigned to inevitable oblivion by the deaths of the victims! This picture of the state of prisons in England — not in any obscure and unnoted corner of the island, but in the very heart of the capital, under the eyes of the Legislature and the public press — might be easily darkened by mere multiplication of the sombre colors plentifully supplied by the parliamentary reports. It is, however, needless. The scenes here painted and the incidents described, afford a faithful and unexaggerated representation of the state of affairs in that great field in which the infant Howard was destined to carry out his work of charity and love.

CHAPTER II.

YOUTH. — EDUCATION. — SUFFERING.

A MYSTERY hangs over the birth of Howard. No particular day is marked off in the calendar of the year — no romantic Stratford-upon-Avon is made sacred to all time by his nativity. Guesses, it is true, have been made at time and site, and dogmatism has done its best to render all uncertain as to both. The noble monument erected by public subscription in St. Paul's Cathedral, asserts that —

"HE WAS BORN AT HACKNEY, IN THE COUNTY OF MIDDLESEX, SEPTEMBER 2D, MDCCXXVI."

But criticism is sceptical; it asks for proofs, and there are none to give. In this inscription, it is just possible that the year given may be the right one; but even that is doubtful — and the rest of the date is purely conjectural. Thus much is alone certain: he was born in the decade 1720–30. Each of the four years, 1724, 1725, 1726, and 1727, has been named as his birth-year, by personal friends of the philanthropist — men who would have been presumed likely to have known the exact truth — but the balance of evidence is in favor of 1725 or 1726. As even this fact, however, cannot be fixed with certainty, it would be idle to attempt to seek to refer it to a particular day or month. Similar doubts prevail as to the locality. Dr. Aikin, one of Howard's most intimate friends, believes he was born at Enfield; the Rev. Mr. Palmer, another of his most valued friends, says he was born at Clapton. There was at one time a general impression that Cardington, his favorite residence in later life, was also the place of his birth; and, after all, it is not unlikely that he was born at his father's usual residence in Smithfield: — thus we have four years and four localities in competition. In the absence of the original baptismal register, one would vainly endeavor to reconcile, or to arbitrate between, these conflicting accounts. Nor is it needful. Less, perhaps, than any other English Worthy, does Howard need to be localized. He belonged to no sect exclusively — to no district. His glories, like his exertions, are circumscribed by no cantonal bounds; the power of his name and the light of his example are the common heirlooms of mankind.

John Howard, the father, was a merchant of the city of London, — and seems to have been the architect of his own fortunes. More than one writer has labored to establish a real as well as a nominal relationship between the family of the philanthropist and the princely house of Norfolk; but the evidence adduced in support of such a theory will not bear a moment's investigation. Whether, in case it could be established, the subject of this history would receive any accession of dignity from the connection, each individual reader will determine for himself, but there is little temerity in his biographer venturing the opinion, that Howard owes nothing — can owe nothing — to his ancestry; that no pride of lineage, no family renown, however extensive, could add materially to a reputation which already fills the world, and must increase as the world learns more and more to reverence moral greatness. As soon as the elder Howard had amassed a moderate competency, he retired from business. This retirement happened about the time of his son's birth, — a circumstance which, however, throws no light on the uncertainty which hangs about the place and time of his birth. On his relinquishment of trade, it is probable that Enfield was, for a time at least, the principal place of his abode. But he had also a residence at Hackney, a larger and more commodious dwelling than that at Enfield, and a farm at the little village of Cardington, near Bedford, apparently a small patrimonial property. Tradition asserts that the philanthropist was born on that hereditary farm. It is certain that he passed his infancy there, and if not actually born on the spot, he was sent thither to nurse at a very early age. Of his mother, little is known beyond the fact that her maiden name was Cholmley. But a mother's gentle love and patient teaching were denied him; and as his mind was not of a precocious order, this loss was very serious to him indeed. Little is remembered of his childhood. None of those startling stories to which the early years of extraordinary men usually gave rise, are told of his. No one read the signs of genius in his sickly, silent face; and no one ventured to predict an eminent career for him in after life. But every one who knew him loved him. His gentle manners, his modesty, his self-sacrificing spirit, endeared him to every heart: but this was a sort of love nearly allied to pity—no one feared, no one admired him. As a child, he passed unnoticed, except when some Quixotic piece of benevolence marked him out for observation.

Howard's first master was a Rev. John Worsley. At what age he commenced his education under this worthy man is not known; but there is no concealing the fact, that he made no great progress in his scholastic studies for a long time. Whether this arose from torpidity in the pupil, or from want of tact and knowledge in the master, has been much disputed. "I left that school," Howard remarked to his friend, Dr. Aikin, in long after years, when speaking of his early life, "not fully taught in any one thing." Seven years were consumed under the direction of Mr. John Worsley—and the boy departed from beneath his roof nearly as great a dunce as the child had come. But let justice be done. However incompetent he may have been to teach, seeing that he translated the New Testament from Greek into English, and wrote a Latin Grammar, which had a sort of reputation in its day and generation, it would be hard to say that the Rev. John Worsley was without classical knowledge; yet this was precisely the branch of education in which his pupil was always most remarkably deficient. Let us blame no man lightly. The time has come when the admirers of Howard can afford to be just.

From the school of this gentleman, Howard was removed to an academy of much higher pretensions in London, then under the management of Mr. John Eames, a Fellow of the Royal Society, a friend of Sir Isaac Newton, and a man of most extensive attainments and exemplary character. This individual, now little known, was one of the not least notable men of a notable period. Originally intended for the ministry, he went through an extensive course of theological studies, and in pursuance of his plan, actually preached a sermon; but his inveterate modesty and bashfulness so overpowered him on the occasion of his first public effort, that he completely despaired of ever attaining success in his selected walk of life, notwithstanding his consciousness of the possession of great abilities, — and he resolved to abandon it. Losing no time in useless regret over the signal failure of all his long-cherished plans, he set himself resolutely to the work of tuition, and his connection with the Protestant Dissenters of London soon procured for him the appointment of Professor of Divinity to their seminary. In the lore of this subject he was profoundly versed, while his acquirements in languages, mathematics, classics, natural theology, and moral philosophy, were also far above respectability. With physical science, he was intimately acquainted; indeed, it was his vast and accurate scientific learning which procured for him the notice and friendship of Sir Isaac Newton, by whose influence he became a member of the Royal Society, and to whom he had the merit of rendering most important assistance. Several celebrated men were educated at the seminary under his care, and were formed by him for the stations which they afterwards occupied with dignity to themselves and usefulness to their fellows. Among the more distinguished of these, the names of Howard, Price, Furneaux, and Savage, stand prominent.

Here, then, at last, a teacher is found whose competency cannot be denied. The author of the Latin Grammar may be treated with contumely, but the friend of Newton and the master of Price is not to be dealt with in the same contemptuous fashion. In substance, Dr. Aikin says of his friend, — "Of the classic writers of Greece and Italy, his knowledge was next to nothing; of languages, ancient or modern, — excepting, perhaps, French, — ditto; in the literature of his own country, he was very imperfectly versed; and to his dying hour, he was never able to write his native tongue with either elegance of diction or grammatical correctness." These are hard words, and could they be accepted as literally true, it would be difficult to defend the subject of them from the obvious inference to which they point. Fortunately, another friend of the illustrious martyr, Dr. Stennet, who knew him at least as well as Dr. Aikin did, and was quite as competent a judge of his attainments, has also left behind him a description, which in common fairness should be collated with that just given. In substance, Dr. Stennet says,—"He was a man of great learning, deeply read in polite literature, and conversant with most of the modern languages." Here is a different story! Both these doctors knew him intimately, and in his maturer manhood. Each professes to speak from personal knowledge; yet how widely their statements differ! The truth, no doubt, lies between the two extremes. Stennet writes with the indulgence of a friend, Aikin in the exacting spirit of a critic.

Howard had little scholastic learning—that is perfectly certain; probably he knew little more than the names of the Greek letters and the Lord's Prayer in Latin. So far Aikin is right:—but he had, at the same time, a fair acquaintance with English literature, and he knew something of nearly all the languages of Europe. French, indeed, he spoke like a native, so as to be able to pass for a Frenchman when it suited his purpose,—as will be seen on more than one notable occasion hereafter. With science he had a general acquaintance, particularly with meteorology and medicine; and his knowledge of policy, of geography, of history, of the condition, social and commercial, of foreign countries, was various and exact. Indeed, there is every reason to believe that, although not a scholar, Howard was a remarkably well-informed man for his generation.

Two circumstances are to be considered in explanation of his inattention to classical studies. 1. *He felt no vocation to them.* The current of his thoughts took a different direction. His role in the historic drama was not an intellectual one. This is the personal circumstance. 2. *He was destined to the desk and the exchange.* His father had been a merchant, and wished him to adopt the same profession. Classics would therefore seem of little value to his future career. This is the worldly circumstance.

Like almost every other date connected with Howard's early history, the time when he quitted the academy presided over by Mr. Eames can only be conjectured. Partly on account of his delicate health, and partly, perhaps, because of his inaptitude to the ordinary studies of English youth, he does not appear to have distinguished himself at school. But even there, his original character must have shown itself, — for we find him contracting a warm friendship with the intellectual sovereign of the institution — young Price, afterwards so celebrated for his vigorous politics and polemics, the friend of Washington, the antagonist of Burke. With that instinctive faculty by which great minds attract each other, these two youths soon found each other out. They became intimate: their knowledge of each other soon ripened into a friendship, sincere and full of mutual admiration, which came to a period only with their lives. In itself, young Price's story was interesting, and would have warmed and won a colder heart than Howard's to the orphaned adventurer.

The elder Howard, though retired from business now for several years, still retained his old commercial tastes; and it was his settled purpose that his son should follow in the track which he himself had trod to fortune. The boy, therefore, was taken from his studies under Mr. Eames, and bound as an apprentice to Messrs. Newnham and Shipley, wholesale grocers, of Watling-street, City; seven hundred pounds being paid down with him — a premium sufficiently large to prove the seriousness of his father's design of making him a merchant. In the warehouse in Watling-street, Howard's external education was carried on and completed; and, under the circumstances, this selection of an *Alma Mater* was not so unfortunate as may be hastily imagined. The counting-house and the exchange have valuable lessons even for the gentleman and the scholar; while for such a career as that of the philanthropist, they are inestimable. While other youths of his station and prospects were engaged in storing their minds with the words of languages no longer living, and with the ideas of a world irrevocably lost — a storing very necessary and useful, if too much time be not devoted to it — Howard was furnishing his mind with a thorough knowledge of the living world, — with what Dr. Aiken, in the tone of a true pedagogue, styles "common affairs," — that is, with the relations of men and countries, their resources and habits, their buying and selling, their dependence and connections. This course of study pursued in the mart may seem very absurd to men like Dr. Aikin. But the statesman and the political philosopher know better: rulers have long ceased to look upon traders with the contempt which arises only from ignorance. Formerly, when a knotty point of polity had to be untied, recourse was had to the schools; but ministers of state have now begun to refer their difficulties to the counting-house. This fact is very significant of the change which is passing over our life-dream.

However, according to orthodox notions, apprenticeship to a grocer *is* a very strange way of bringing up a young man of fortune; but it must be recollected, that the elder Howard possessed little of the mental flexibility which induces ordinary men to assume with readiness the current opinions of their time; and he would not, therefore, be expected to take a common-place view of his duty. He had been himself a merchant, and he entertained a merchant's ideas of the honor and importance of his calling. He was a little imperious and patriarchal, too, in his way — was a firm stickler for unconditional compliance with his wishes — governed his family with paternal severity — and was altogether remarkable for the lofty way in which he kept his household in order. *He* also was a character. Not a little of the eccentricity of thought, the directness of purpose, the devotion to a sense of duty, which his illustrious son exhibited in the course of his subsequent career, were also displayed by him on that narrower stage on which he had been called to play his part. Stern, methodical, industrious, himself, — having a natural or habitual love of commerce, — and conscious of the value of a full and absorbing occupation, as an antidote to the rash impulses of youthful passions, as well as of the knowledge and experience which only actual dealings with men can bestow, there is little to cause surprise in the decision of the good old Puritan. Nor did the young man himself offer any objection to the path marked out for him by his father, though it but ill assorted with his personal views and predilections.

The scheme may have had a yet profounder meaning. Of all men, the true Puritan was the least disposed to trust to fortune. To hope for the best and be prepared for the worst, is every wise man's maxim. The circle to which the Howards belonged, was peculiarly alive to its importance, especially at the time of which we write. Troublous times were not far out of the range of memory of men still living, and were not unlikely to return,—

times in which property had been insecure, and some of the proudest sons and daughters of luxury had been thrown upon their personal resources for the means of life. Such a change is always possible. In more modern days, we have witnessed many such crises come and go; we have seen half the feudal aristocracy of Europe pining in exile; and we are therefore better able to judge of the forethought and wisdom of the custom which obtains in many patrician families in Germany — in that of the Imperial House of Hapsburg-Lorraine, for example — of having all the sons instructed in some trade or handicraft, so that should everything else fail, the common labor market of the world would still be open to them. No man can foresee, even for an hour, the turns of Fortune's wheel. It is the part of wisdom to be always armed and prepared for what may befall. Knowledge of a profession is no burden. A gentleman is not the less a gentleman because he is conversant with law, with trade, with medicine; nay, he is then more of a gentleman, for he is more entirely independent. He alone is perfect master of his actions who has a personal means of living — some art or craft, knowledge or skill, of which chance and change cannot divest him; wanting this, his present interests or his fears for the future must often modify and warp his conscience.

If there be one lesson more distinctly taught by history than any other, it is this — entire dependence upon property is more demoralizing than entire dependence upon labor. A man without the personal power of producing the value of what he is compelled by nature to consume, must be a frequent slave to his fears. In times of real danger and difficulty — in the throes, for instance, of a revolution — how few there are who dare to be true to themselves! And why? Because their parchments are their only possessions. As the education of the higher orders in this country is now conducted, the virtues which arise from a confidence in powers of self-sustaiment have no room for growth. All are taught to rely on something alien — on property. How many find it only a broken reed! How much of the suffering of noble exiles in this and other countries in modern times, springs only from their inability to do anything, except brood over their wrongs, repine at their misfortunes, and wait for the hand of charity to succor them! A false and foolish notion — the last shred of a barbarian code of honor — lies at the root of this evil. Labor is thought beneath the dignity of noble fingers. Vulgar and fatal mistake! Nobler doer — noble deed. The world needs very much to come to some sounder thinking on this point. The elder Howard happened to be before his age in this respect — and so his son was formally bound as an apprentice to the grocers of Watling-street.

The memorials of his life in the shop are not very ample. He appears to have entered upon this service entirely from a sentiment of duty. From first to last, his heart was not in his work; and it is evident that he failed to contract any of those sordid habits which are vulgarly attributed to trade and traders. He certainly never learned to love money; nor to respect those who possessed it — on the mere score of its possession. No evil, so far as appears, flowed from this choice of a profession; or from his mixing in the curious scenes to which it must necessarily have introduced him. On the contrary, he thus learned to like employment for its *own* sake; and in the Watling-street warehouse, contracted that valuable habit of devotion to the matter in hand, which, directed into a new path, and exercised under more congenial circumstances, afterwards enabled him to perform such prodigies of labor. It is pleasant to dwell upon the idea of this youth — born, as he was, to the inheritance of a large estate, and destined to leave behind him one of the loftiest names in the pantheon of history — toiling and thinking through his routine tasks; moulding and pruning-out his own great character; gaining a thorough mastery over himself; obtaining a plain, practical acquaintance with men and affairs; and laying, deeply and permanently, the foundation of those hardy qualities of mind and body which enabled him to prove so useful to mankind, when he had once found out his natural sphere of action, and the work which had to be done therein!

Before the period of apprenticeship had run out, that is, on the 9th of September, 1742, Howard, the elder, died. The property which he left was very considerable — the division of it being thus made:— To his son, he bequeathed seven thousand pounds in money; the whole of his landed property; his plate, furniture, pictures, and a moiety of his library; to his daughter — the only other child — on coming to age, he left eight thousand pounds as her portion of the personal estate; the other moiety of his library; almost all the family jewels, and the female wardrobe. Towards the son, he testified the high confidence which he felt in his discretion and in his knowledge of the administration and management of property, by naming him sole residuary legatee — as soon as he should attain his majority. The executors of the will were, Lawrence Channing, the husband of the testator's sister — Ive Whitbread, of Cardington, a relation of deceased — and Lewin Cholmley, one of his most intimate friends and a distant connection of his first wife — the mother of the joint inheritors. These gentlemen, moreover, displayed the same confidence in the heir that his father had done, for they did not scruple to allow him, even at his comparatively very early age, — he was not more than seventeen — a considerable power over the management of his property.

The condition of the family house at Clapton was amongst the foremost objects which engaged young Howard's attention. Through the negligence and parsimony of his parent, it had been suffered to fall into a state of almost ruin. Personally, he undertook to superintend its restoration; and in order to expedite the work, went over to Clapton daily — to give directions and forward the repairs by his presence and counsels. This house was a favorite with the philanthropist always; for though he did not, could not, live in it himself, he strenuously refused to let it on lease, or in any way allow it to pass from under his immediate control. Sixty years ago — Howard's name had then become one of the best known and most cherished household words in Europe — a venerable old man, of ninety summers, who had for many years been gardner to the elder Howard, and who occupied that post at the period of which we now write, used to take delight in recalling — as he was often requested to do — for the edification of visitors from far and near, anecdotes and reminiscences of his young master. The favorite story of the old man, told how, during this restoration of the dilapidated mansion, Howard used to arrive every morning — never missing a single day — under the buttress of the garden wall, just as the bread cart was passing at its punctual hour: when he would purchase a loaf, throw it into the garden, — and then entering at the gate, would cry out, laughing — "Harry! see if there is not something for you there among the cabbages." Even this simple anecdote has the true Howardian mark upon it, and foreshadows somewhat of that punctuality and charity which afterwards made so much of his character.

Having, as has been said, entered into business pursuits rather to please his father than because they harmonized with his own tastes and predilections, Howard no sooner found himself his own master, than he sought to terminate his apprenticeship. Under the circumstances of the case this was not difficult. A contract was soon made out of the purchase of his remaining period of service, and a sum of money having changed hands, the affair was settled, and he was a free man. This preliminary step secured, he determined to inform his mind and restore his health — which had never been very good, and had recently, from close confinement and laborious occupation, entirely given way — by foreign travel. The interest of the ready money which had descended to him was found to be amply sufficient to cover the expenses of his proposed journey, without drawing upon the trustees ; and, having made a few necessary arrangements, he set out. France and Italy were the countries which he now visited. Few persons from the northern latitudes ever sojourn in these vine-laden lands, without finding, in their sunny gardens, and under their benignant skies, new life and health. The benefits of the change of scenery, of atmosphere, and employment, were soon visible in

Howard's renovated frame. Debility, almost amounting to physical prostration, had nearly weighed him down to the grave. A change had become absolutely imperative — and this consideration would strengthen, if it did not originate, his determination to quit the merchant career so soon after his father's death. Mind and body alike benefitted by the step he had now taken. While his health was gradually being restored, his intellect was occupied, enlightened, and enlarged. At this period of his life, the embryo philanthropist was somewhat of a connoiseur — loving art, and all that pertained to it, fervently, and for their own sakes. His unclassical education, and subsequent commerce with the supposed vulgarities of trade, had not prevented him from acquiring some knowledge and taste in higher things; and in the old and glorious cities of republican Italy, he had now the opportunity of enlarging and gratifying these to the fullest extent. He did not fail to use his advantages as became a lover and a student; — every gallery and exhibition of note he visited, so far as he was able. Nor did the mere contemplation of the many marvels of skill and beauty with which that gifted land abounded — far more abounded then than now, for as yet the wholesale spoiler had not been among her treasures — content him; but, so far as his means permitted, he became a purchaser of them also. In this and other of his early journeyings upon the continent of Europe, — in his later movements he had far more serious and engrossing occupations, — he made a fair collection of paintings, which in after years adorned his favorite residence in Cardington.

How far he travelled in this his first tour — where he stayed — the particulars of his individual experience — and even how long he remained away — are all matter of inference and conjecture now. A trip to France and Italy, at that day, could hardly be performed in much less than one year, and there is good reason for believing that he was not absent more than two. On his return, it does not appear that his health, though improved, was re-established, — as we find him immediately afterwards compelled to leave London for a more salubrious residence. His new tent was pitched at Stoke Newington, where he took a lodging and proposed to reside for some time.

Howard was now grown up to man's estate, and had assumed all the responsibilities of self-government. Here, too, we begin to have better, more complete, data for his history. Thus far, a few dates and incidents have been our only positive guides. Now, we arrive at a point whence facts will conduct us onward; here we begin to get larger glimpses of his real characteristics, — to trace in his acts the workings of a most original mind, evolving itself spontaneously and independently from within, little regardful of the frowns, and utterly fearless of the opinions of that great tribunal which men call the world, — though it arrogated to itself then, as it arrogates to itself now, the right to sit in judgment, and pronounce heavy sentences upon social heresies.

He went to live at Stoke Newington, — quietly, — as an invalid. Neither the state of his constitution, the bent of his disposition, nor the inspirations of his passions, inclined him to enter into that fascinating round of pleasures and vices, into which the young and wealthy, who are suddenly let loose from the restraining hand of authority, commonly plunge. Howard was too much master of himself, even at this early age, to fall into the customary errors of youth — errors towards which society is so indulgent. Surrounded by his books — attending to his religious exercises — engaged with the studies most congenial to his tastes — at peace with himself, and with all the world — he seems to have passed at least a portion of the time which he remained at this pleasant village, in a manner highly delightful to think of. Among the subjects of study which at this time engrossed his attention, some of the less abstruse branches of natural philosophy, and the theory of medicine, were the most prominent. In these departments of science he made a not inconsiderable progress: of medicine, especially, he acquired sufficient knowledge to render it of the most essential service in carrying out the benevolent objects of his later life, as we shall see in the sequel of this narrative. His adopted mode of life was of a very simple kind, and the lodgings which he occupied were anything but ostentatious. Owing, in the first instance, to a constitutional tendency to consumption, his diet had been regulated on a perfectly ascetic scale. The particular malady from which he was suffering, while at Stoke Newington, was nervous fever, and a general breaking up of the whole physical system. At this epoch of his life, his final recovery was very doubtful; for he was not merely in a state of tempory debility — his constitution was unsound, and he was organically predisposed to be affected by disease; but owing to his great abstemiousness, and the primitive simplicity of the little food which he did take, his constitution at length rallied. Providence reserved, nay, through these very trials and sufferings, prepared and strengthened him for his great task. A part of each day he regularly passed on horseback, riding in the lanes about the village. It is said, in a contemporary biographical notice, that he would frequently ride out a mile or two into the country, fasten his nag to a tree, or turn him loose to browse upon the wayside ; and then, throwing himself upon the grass, under a friendly shade, would read and cogitate for hours. This statement, if true, would indicate more of a romantic and poetical temperament in Howard, than the generally calm and Christian stoicism of his manner would have led one to expect.

We now arrive at one of the most curious and characteristic incidents of his life. In the early part of his sojourn at Stoke Newington, he appears to have been much dissatisfied with the conduct of his landlady; and not thinking that he received that considerate care and attention at her hands which his sickly condition entitled him to expect, he removed his lodgings, going to reside at the house of a Mrs. Sarah Loidore, (or Lardeau: the *alia dicta* is given by Dr. Aikin), from whom he expected to receive better treatment. He was then five-and-twenty, in the very blossom of his strange youth. Mrs. Loidore was an ordinary-looking woman of fifty-two, — the widow of a man who, while living, had been clerk in a neighboring white-lead manufactory. She had no wealth to tempt, no beauty to attract admirers; and moreover, she was so confirmed an invalid, that for more than twenty years she had not known the blessing of a single day's uninterrupted health. She appears, however, notwithstanding her own sufferings, to have been a very kind, attentive, and cheerful woman; a good housekeeper, and an admirable nurse. She was possessed of a small property, the savings of her deceased husband, upon which, together with the profits arising from the letting out of her apartments, she contrived, by dint of much frugality, to live in humble respectability.

While residing in this good lady's apartments, Howard experienced a very severe attack of illness. For various short periods before this attack came on, he had rambled into different parts of the kingdom in search of renovation, — but without success; still, however, keeping his home quarters fixed at

Stoke Newington, to which he finally returned as he went out — weak, low-spirited, restless. For several weeks he was confined to his bed, in the most critical condition, his life almost despaired of; still, in the end, he rallied once again. The consumptive tendency was overcome by a prudent regimen, and his health gradually restored.

During the whole period of this trying sickness, the invalid received from his kind and gentle nurse every attention and care which a true woman's instinct could suggest. Her constant and considerate devotion to him, — a stranger in her house, — contrasting as it did so strikingly with the treatment he had experienced from others upon whom he had equal claims, under similar circumstances, made a profound impression upon his mind, and his ingenuity was taxed not a little to devise by what means he might adequately express his gratitude for services to which he felt convinced he was in a great measure indebted for his recovery. As he became convalescent his plan ripened into form. When the danger had entirely passed away, and his health was restored to its accustomed state, he offered her as the only fitting reward of her services — a toy? an ornament? a purse? a house? an estate? or any of those munificent gifts with which wealthy and generous convalescents reward their favorite attendants? No. He offered her his hand, his name, his fortune! Of course the good lady was astonished at the portentous shape of her patient's gratitude. She started objections, being older, and having more worldly prudence than her lover. It is even said that she seriously refused her consent to the match, urging the various arguments which might fairly be alleged against it, — the inequality in the years, fortune, social position of the parties, and so forth — but all to no purpose. Howard's mind was made up. During his slow recovery he had weighed the matter carefully — had come to the conclusion that it was his duty to marry her, and nothing could now change his determination. The struggle between the two must have been extremely curious: the sense of duty on both sides, — founded upon honest convictions, no doubt, — the mutual respect, without the consuming fire, — the cool and logical weighing of arguments, in place of the rapid pleadings of triumphant passion; the young man, without the ordinary inspirations of youth, on the one hand; the widow, past her prime, yet simple, undesigning, unambitious, earnestly struggling to reject and put aside youth — wealth — protection — honor — social rank — the very things for which women are taught to dress, to pose, to intrigue, almost to circumvent heaven, on the other, — form together a picture which has its romantic interest, in spite of the incongruity of the main idea. One of the contemporary biographers has thrown an air of romance over the scene of this domestic struggle, which, if the lady had been young and beautiful, — that is, if the element of passion could be admitted into the arena

— would have been truly charming. As it is, the reader may receive it with such modifications as he or she may deem necessary. "On the very first opportunity," says this grave, but imaginative chronicler, "Mr. Howard expressed his sentiments to her in the strongest terms of affection; assuring her, that if she rejected his proposal he would become an exile forever to his family and friends. The lady was upwards of forty, (true enough! she was also upwards of fifty, good master historian,) and therefore urged the disagreement of their years as well as their circumstances; but after allowing her four-and-twenty hours for a final reply, his eloquence surmounted all her objections, and she consented to a union wherein gratitude was to supply the deficiencies of passion." Criticism would only spoil this pretty picture — so let it stand.

They were married. And, contrary to the general experience of such strange mis-alliances, neither party to the contract had ever occasion to regret it. As at the commencement, so throughout — it is impossible to believe in the existence of any of the consuming passions of youth between them. Howard's mind was not demonstrative — his temperament not excitable; and his bride was at that calm period of life when the blood is cool and waits upon the judgment. The depths of tenderness which existed in his soul, were not now fathomed as they were to be hereafter; still, there is every reason to believe that he was greatly attached to his grave and gentle spouse. Once his conscience had dictated a course of conduct as a matter of duty, he was not a man *to shrink from any* of the consequences which might follow in its train; and so long as she remained to bless his hearth, or test the constancy of his heart, he never wavered in his affection and respect. But the time was short. Never thoroughly well, her marriage for a time exercised a beneficial influence over her health, but the improvement was only temporary. Her old debility returned after a few months with greater force than before, and through manifold sufferings, which her husband did his utmost to alleviate, she gradually wore away, expiring in the third year of her marriage, sincerely lamented by her lord. With every mark of respect which affection could suggest, her remains were deposited in a vault in the church-yard of St. Mary's, Whitechapel, where a nearly obliterated tombstone still testifies to her whereabouts, and to the simple piety of the heart which once beat in response to her own. For the rest, there is every reason to believe that she was a person of most exemplary character, gentle and affectionate in her disposition, beyond the generality of her sex; of good, though not great, natural endowments; sincere and humble in her religious sentiments; patient and pure both in her thoughts and actions; — in a word, a woman not unworthy of the love of the great and good man with whose fate she had become connected in so singular a manner.

Her demise was one of the great epochs — or turning points — in Howard's life. It left a chasm in his existence, a desert in his daily life. The scenes which had been the witnesses of his calm felicity soon became distasteful to him. Though he had now resided several years at Stoke Newington — had made many valued friends there — and had become much attached to the neighborhood, when she was gone he resolved to quit it forever. It was too full of recollections, in which the bitter preponderated, to be endurable to a mind so sensitive ; and he needed a change, both of air and of objects, to restore the customary calmness to his spirit. On marrying Mrs. Loidore, Howard had settled her little property upon her sister ; and a similar act of generosity marked the final breaking up of his establishment at Stoke Newington. Such portions of his furniture — in fact, the great bulk of it — as he had no need for in the temporary lodging which he now took in St. Paul's Churchyard, he distributed amongst the poorer inhabitants of the village.

With the dissolution of his domestic ties, and the cessation of those daily occupations to which they had given rise, the desire for action again grew upon him and consumed him like a passion. Howard was born to be a worker in the great hive; he could not dream away his energies. His early life had been devoted to daily toil — severe, regular, absorbing toil ; something to do had therefore become to him a necessity of nature. Labor was his habit ; idleness, either of body or of mind, of the intellect or of the affections, was quite intolerable to him. As yet, he had not found his office in the world; but his restless instincts urged him unceasingly towards the arena wherein it was most likely to be found. Wearied of quiescence, he determined to go abroad; but with no distinct and definite object before him, beyond a change of scene, and a desire to see and study mankind under new aspects. The country which he proposed to visit, in the first instance, was Portugal, the capital of which at that time lay buried in ruins. The terrible earthquake of 1755, had shaken Lisbon to its foundations; a vast number of dwellings and thousands of the poor inhabitants, had been overwhelmed in the wreck; and the consequences of this frightful catastrophe engaged the attention of all Europe. Howard, attracted by reports of the unexampled sufferings of the survivors, no sooner found himself at his own disposal, than he determined to hasten with all possible speed to their assistance. He took a passage for the scene of the calamity by the packet *Hanover*,— but, man proposes, God disposes. Providence had willed otherwise, and the missionary of mercy was not permitted to reach his destination. France and England were then at variance; the Seven Years' War was raging with its worst fury. The western coasts of Europe were swept by innumerable privateers, and by one of these the *Hanover* was captured, and the crew and passengers carried into the port of Brest, where, according to the custom of that period, they were treated with the utmost barbarity. Howard refers to this incident in one of his subsequent publications. Before the captured vessel was carried into the harbor, he says he was kept without food, and even water, for forty hours — to most men an intolerable punishment; but his abstemious habits had well prepared him to bear such a trial — the commencement of a long series — without serious detriment to his health. When they were at length landed, he was confined, with many other prisoners, in the castle of the town, in a dungeon, dark, damp, and filthy beyond description, where they were kept for several additional hours without nourishment! At last a leg of mutton was brought and thrown into the cell — as horseflesh is thrown into the dens of wild beasts — for the starving captives to scramble for, tear with their teeth, and devour as best they could. In this horrible dungeon, thus fed, they were detained for a week. Six nights were they compelled to sleep — if sleep they could, under such circumstances — upon the cold floor, with nothing but a handful of straw to protect them from the noxious damps and noisome fever of their over-crowded room. Thence our countryman was removed to Morlaix, and subsequently to Carpaix, where he resided for two months on parole. At both these places he had further opportunities of witnessing the treatment which prisoners of war received at the hands of their enemies, — such as soon made him sensible that his own case had been one of comparative leniency. Whilst living at Carpaix, he tells us in a few terribly graphic lines, that he had corresponded with the various English captives at Brest, Morlaix, and Dinan, and had thereby gained "ample evidence of their being treated with such barbarity that many hundreds had perished, and that thirty-six were buried in a hole in Dinan in one day." This was only at a single point of that extensive coast, which stretched along, hundreds of miles, from the Netherlands to the Pyrenees; and on the opposite shores of England the same species of barbarities were also being perpetrated.

It has been preferred as a charge against Howard, that he behaved towards his keepers—or at least towards his captors—much *a l' Anglais;* that is, with somewhat of contemptuous *hauteur* (how singular that the English language should have no word to express that mixture of icy politeness and imperial reserve, which, all over continental Europe, has become the recognized characteristic and distinction of Englishmen); and this, though not stated on the best authority, is not unlikely in itself. Howard had a very high sense and sentiment of honor, and an unconquerable disdain for the man who could be prevented from doing what was strictly right in itself, by any fear of political or conventional consequences. It is more than probable, that a person of his mental and moral constitution would be apt to consider a privateer as nothing more than a tolerated ruffian, and deal with him accordingly. But once on shore, and placed in legal custody, he seems to have inspired every one who came into contact with him, respect and confidence in his uprightness. More than one occasion saw this exhibited in a remarkable manner. While at Carpaix, although not an officer, and therefore not entitled to claim any indulgence according to the law of nations and the usages of war between the two countries, he was yet permitted by his gaoler to reside in the town, upon his mere word being given that he would not attempt to escape. A similar kind of confidence was exhibited by the person at whose house he lodged. Though penniless, and a perfect stranger to his host, this man took him in on the strength of his unsupported representations — housed, fed, clothed, supplied him with money, and finally saw him depart, with no other gurantee for re-payment than his bare promise. Even official persons were not impervious to the charm of this great character — for, after some negotiation with these, he was permitted by them to return to England, in order that he might with greater chance of success endeavor to induce the Government to make a suitable exchange for him on simply pledging his honor that if unsuccessful in his attempts he would instantly return to his captivity.

When he arrived in London, the friends who had heard of his misadventure poured in their congratulations upon his recovery of his freedom; but he at once desired that all such congratulations might be reserved, until the conditions on which he had accepted his liberty were complied with — an event which was at least uncertain, for, being only a private individual, with no means of powerfully interesting those in authority in his case, it was no improbable supposition that the Government might find itself too much engrossed to spare time to listen to his application, or too deeply concerned for those persons — servants of its own — for whose safety it was more directly responsible, to care about the recovery of a too adventurous civilian. Happily, however, the point was gained; the necessary exchange was affected; and all his obligations being honorably discharged, he had no need to return to France.

Once assured of his liberty, and made capable of acting on his own responsibility, Howard instantly set about to relieve the more pressing necessities of the other captives, while at the same time he endeavored by every means in his power, to procure their liberation. His attention was naturally enough addressed in the first instance to the inmates of the prisons in which he had himself been confined, respecting the condition of which he could report from personal knowledge. In an application made to the Commissioners of Sick and Wounded Seamen, he portrayed, in striking terms, the miseries and privations to which the gallant but unfortunate fellows were exposed — made a pathetic appeal on their behalf, and prayed that their case might be examined and their wrongs redressed. This measure had an instant effect. The Commissioners bestirred themselves in the matter. The Friend of the Captive had the satisfaction of receiving their thanks for his timely information, and such definite proceedings were adopted that he soon after had pleasure of knowing that his efforts had caused the restoration of his fellow-prisoners to their liberty and country, as well as mitigated the miseries of many others.

CHAPTER III.

HOME LIFE AT CARDINGTON.

WHEN complete success had crowned these efforts in the cause of human suffering, the young philanthropist, still shrinking timidly from a public vocation, and, as yet, unconscious of the great ministry which Providence had assigned to him in the history of the world, retired quietly to his small patrimonial estate at Cardington, near Bedford. Here he had been nursed — perhaps born; here he had received his first impressions of life — his earliest lessons of love and charity; and the locality was endeared to him by all those sweet associations which a thoughtful childhood never fails to create and spread like a charmed atmosphere over the scenes of its earliest joys and sorrows. Cardington is the place most intimately connected with the name of Howard. To him it had at least the interest of a natal place. He remembered no other. When first awakening to a consciousness of the world around, his infant eyes had opened on its sylvan scenes. In the neighboring meadows he had gathered his first chaplet of flowers; in the green lanes thereabout he had caught his first butterfly; in the little church of the village he had first listened to the hymn of praise — and so it had become the object of his infant love. This fact — and the sad circumstances of his domestic history — about to be related — caused him to cling with fond and enduring affection to the spot: — henceforth it was his resting-place — the centre of all his most solemn, tender, and mournful memories; and even in long-after years, though other worlds of action had opened up to him, drawing him for long and frequent intervals from its coveted seclusion — though his feelings and his heart in time grew larger and more cosmopolitan in their mould — though scenes of suffering and of horror, whether they had to be sought for in Stockholm or in Constantinople, in Cadiz or in St. Petersburg, became the spheres of his labors and his thoughts; and though he became early conscious that the pilgrim's staff which he had assumed was never to be laid aside until he should find his final resting-place in a far distant land — his heart still turned to that simple rustic village, it continued to be the sacred pole and centre of his thoughts; in a word, endeared to him by every childish thought and aspiration, by the recollection of all his sweetest, saddest hours — the living happiness and the buried love, — sanctified to his soul by the memory of both the morning-light and night-solemnity of life, — Cardington was henceforth, absent or present, evermore his HOME.

At Cardington, then, he settled. The property which his father had owned and bequeathed to him in the neighborhood, consisted of a single farm of no very large dimensions. To render the estate a befitting residence, and in order to obtain that personal influence in the place which he considered necessary for the proper carrying out of a plan which he had conceived for the amelioration of the condition of the surrounding peasantry, he found it necessary to greatly enlarge it,—which was done by the purchase and addition of another property. The superintendence of various alterations and improvements, which he at once began to carry into operation, fully employed his time. Never was he for a moment unoccupied. The spirit of order, the attention to details in the management of his property, the systematic regularity in his way of life—he had learned in his father's house: and the habits of patient industry which he exhibited in his own person, and infused into his tenantry, had no doubt been contracted in the Watling-street establishment.—Engaged in these simple and honorable occupations, time flew rapidly on. It was somewhere in the early part of 1756 that he went to reside at Cardington, and many years wore away, ere he was again called upon to appear prominently before the world in a public character. The memorials of these years, though they contain some of the finest mental passages in his history, afford but little of that exciting material which is so dear to the general reader, and so valuable to the biographer. They have no connection with great and stirring events; they are not charged with more than the ordinary tragedy of human life; there are no plots and counter-plots to detail, no deep intrigues to incite curiosity, no sudden surprises to startle it into morbid activity; nothing in fact of the melo-drama of private history. Yet it is the progress and history of a true, earnest life, which they relate to; and as such should be read, as much for its own sake as for the light it throws upon its subject's after career. There is the due amount of wooing, wedding, love, and misery. Death, too, has his share in the little drama; and when it appears, the scene acquires a solemn, almost a tragic interest; but let us not anticipate our tale.

To appear great in action is comparatively easy. The grandeur of an important deed communicates itself in part to the agent which performs it. To seem great in repose is far more difficult. No man, it is said, is a hero to his valet; moral grandeur is not readily exhibited in an easy chair. Few men are at once striking in rest and in action. Howard was, however, one of the few. He was equally, because unconsciously, great in all spheres and in all attitudes. His public achievements have commanded the fullest meed of honor ever accorded, perhaps, to a human being; still the world can only reward that of which it can take broad and tangible account; and it may be doubted, whether the picture of the philanthropist, going forth, armed with no talisman but his trust in God, and inspired only by his own apostolic heart, to' encounter, without fear, the horrors of death-infected dungeons, sublime as it undoubtedly is, sublime alike in its means and its object, in its beginning and its end, uncommissioned by thrones or governments, yet gradually requiring in his sacred character of missionary, a voice and power, whose admonitions and warnings even kings and cabinets did not always dare to disregard, it may we think, be doubted, whether this picture suggests an idea to the mind more noble, colossal, and divine, than that of the undistinguished citizen of Cardington, quietly laboring in that little vineyard of the Lord. Let the judicious reader judge.

When Howard settled down at Cardington, it may be surmised that his mind had regained its habitual composure. The incidents which, for a while, frustrated his intended visit to Lisbon, and the active exertion in which they unexpectedly gave rise, distracted his thoughts from the recent cause of grief, and gradually restored him to his natural equanimity of mind.

In this subdued and reconciled disposition, he seems to have gone down to Cardington; and after two or three years spent there in study, and in carrying out his plans of practical benevolence, the thought of taking to himself another bride appears to have come upon him with the bland and insinuating witchery of a virgin passion, and such undoubtedly it was. The object on whom his affections were now really showered, was in every way worthy of them. She was about his own age, and of his own social rank. Although her features were not cast in the choicest mould of Grecian beauty, she was very fair,—had large impressive eyes, an ample brow, a mouth exquisitely cut, a soft and gentle style of physiognomy — and overspreading all, there was that chaste and fascinating light with which a well-cultivated mind will illumine and inspire the most ordinary face, covering it with a radiant and enchaining loveliness. Her portrait stands before the writer of these lines. It has about it a look of home — a quiet suggestion of domestic love and peace. In a ball-room, or at the opera, that gentle countenance would certainly not arrest the gaze of rude and curious eyes; but few thoughtful and discriminating men would look upon it for a moment, without feeling that it was the index to a heart which needed only to be known in order to be highly valued.

Henrietta Leeds was the eldest daughter of Edward Leeds, of Croxton, in Cambridgeshire, Sergeant at Law, — a sincere and generous woman, in every way a proper partner for the future philanthropist. Mild, amiable, pious, tolerant; she was well prepared to act on all occasions in the spirit of her husband's views. The marriage was solemnized on the 25th of April, 1758. We must not, however, omit an incident that occurred before the ceremony, which is very significant of Howard's frankness and firmness at this epoch. On observing that many unpleasantnesses arise in families, from circumstances trifling in themselves, in consequence of each individual wishing to have his way in all things, he determined to avoid all these sources of domestic discord, by establishing his own paramount authority in the first instance. It is just conceivable that his former experience of the wedded life may have led him to insist upon this condition. At all events, he stipulated with Henrietta, that in all matters in which there should be a difference of opinion between them, *his* voice should rule. This may sound very ungallant in terms — but it was found exceedingly useful in practice. Few men would have the moral honesty to suggest such an arrangement to their lady-loves, at such a season; though, at the same time, few would hesitate to make the largest mental reservations in their own behalf. It may also be that few young belles would be disposed to treat such a proposition otherwise than with ridicule or anger: however conscious *they* might be, that, as soon as the hymeneal pageantries were passed, their surest means of happiness would lie in the prompt adoption of the principle so laid down.

A few days after their marriage, the sedate and happy lovers went down to Cardington, and immediately set about building, planting, altering, and improving, their dwelling and neighborhood. Their minds were nicely fitted to each other; they worked together harmoniously, and the union was perfectly happy; henceforth their lives were not two, but one. Before proceeding to describe their labors for the good of their tenantry, it may be desirable to present a brief account of the interior and spiritual building up of the great character whose lines we are endeavoring to trace. He is now married — settled — thirty; his character is formed: — let us look more closely at the process of its formation.

The intellectual education of Howard, as has been already admitted, was not of the best or most comprehensive kind. At the time, and in the particular sphere in which he was brought up, the study of ancient literature was not cordially recognized as necessary to the training of good and useful citizens. His father and his connections were stern religionists; of that famous puritanical school, which, in the previous century, — by its thorough earnestness and the genius of its leaders making up for paucity of numbers — had been able to wrench the government of the country from the feeble hands which had so long desecrated the majesty of power, by wielding it for selfish and tyrannical ends, — and from the centre of their revolution shake the despotic thrones of Europe to their foundations. The father of the elder Howard might have seen some of these glorious events: he might have stood in presence of the power of Cromwell, the genius of Milton, the virtue of Marvel — or, at least, he might have remembered and conversed with men who had. Great traditions of the days when puritan ideas had been in the political ascendant, were religiously conserved in the family, as they still are in many households — their most valued heirlooms ; and the sterner shades of the proscribed opinions would only be clung to the more earnestly for the fact of their being politically overthrown. With the exception of a few brilliant and extraordinary men — men who would have been exceptions to the rule of any age or country — the Protestant dissenters of England had never, up that time, been remarkable for their cultivation of polite letters ;—they were too rigidly scriptural to devote themselves to studies which were deemed of a profane or merely ornamental nature. The old war of the primitive fathers against the seductions of pagan literature arose again ; but the idea underlying this struggle of a too rigid Christianity against the intellectual means of a loose, and in some respects impure, polytheism — well and honestly intentioned as it was —proved fruitful of not a little loss to the champions and their cause ; for it was, in fact, a voluntary surrendering of the finest weapons with which the great battle of truth against error can be maintained. As a body, the living representatives of the heroes of the seventeenth century, have fully redeemed themselves from this mistake. A wider induction has happily shown them, that that wondrous Greek and Roman lore — though it was inspired by other than the Christian gods, and enshrines many thoughts which the progressive spirit of the present age cannot but regret to find embalmed in such immortal beauty—still forms the world's grand repository of eloquence, philosophy, and logic,—the armory whence truth's best human weapons must be drawn. But this conviction — as a general rule — is of recent growth: a hundred years ago, the puritan mind deemed differently; and there is every reason to believe, that the elder Howard would have no desire to see his son devoted to any of this so-thought vain and heathenish learning. The philanthropist himself was in this respect far above the prejudices of his order. As he came to years of maturity, he became painfully conscious of the vastness of his deficiencies; — and not only determined to pursue a different plan with *his* son, but seriously set about to repair his own losses. At his leisure, while at Stoke Newington, and now at Cardington, he made incessant efforts to recover his ground — devoting himself to the study of natural philosophy, and particularly to such departments of science as require but little fundamental preparation, or such as have a direct relation to natural theology. The religious element was that always uppermost in his mind. In every pursuit in which he was engaged, he sought for fresh proofs of the wisdom and goodness of the Almighty. Religion was, in fact, his vital principle. God was present to him always. The grand and solemn image of a guiding and controlling

Providence — a Spirit bounteous in its mercies, but exacting in proportion to its bounty — was never absent from his mind. In everything he said, or did, or thought, the end in view was always lofty, the aspiration ever up towards heaven.

In the course of Howard's frequent visits to the metropolis, he became acquainted with several persons of eminence in the learned world, whose society naturally strengthened his love of science, — and soon after one of these visits he was made a Fellow of the Royal Society — his election taking place on the 20th of May, 1756. This honorable distinction was not sought for by Howard from any vain-glorious motive, but from a real love of scientific pursuits and a laudable desire to associate with men of learning. On the other hand, the fact of his election into such a body is in itself no proof of his scientific proficiency; — as it has always been the policy of that Society to choose its members from amongst men of property and worldly station, as well as from amongst scholars and great writers. Yet Howard was not altogether an idle associate; at least he took an intelligent interest in the transactions of the Society; and if his personal contributions to science were of no great value, the fault did not arise from apathy, or from any disinclination to learned labors. At intervals, he sent into the Society three short papers, which were communicated to the members at their regular periods of meeting, and deemed of sufficient interest to be printed in the yearly Transactions.

The first of these contributions, as it was sent in about the time now treated of, may be inserted here: especially as it will give an idea of the kind of investigations to which he devoted his leisure, and also furnish, once for all, a specimen of his imperfect mastery over his native language. Thus it stands in the Philosophical Transactions, vol. 54, page 118:—

"An account of the degree of cold observed in Bedfordshire, by John Howard, Esq. F.R.S., in a letter to John Canton, M.A., F.R.S. Read April 12th, 1764.—Sir, I would beg leave to acquaint you of a degree of cold that I observed at Cardington, in Bedfordshire, the 22d of November last, just before sunrise, Fahrenheit's scale, by one of Bird's thermometers, being so low as ten and a half. If it will throw any light upon the locality of cold, or think it worth the Society's observation, would leave to your better judgment, and remain with great esteem, Sir, your obedient servant, John Howard."

During the whole of his stay at Cardington, astronomy engaged a large share of his attention; but his favorite science — next to medicine — was meteorology. All his communications to the Royal Society have reference to this subject. The second was on the heat of the springs at Bath — which he often visited for the purposes of health. The third contained some observations on the heat of the crater of Vesuvius. There can be no doubt but that Howard was a curious, if not a careful, observer of nature;

and although his direct additions to physical science were not of much value — Bacon's were not — it must nevertheless be owned, that he set a laudable example of diligence in prosecuting his chosen studies. A note-worthy instance of his devotion to the business in hand, whatsoever that might be — the quality which, more than any other, was the source of his great after-reputation — is related in connection with these meteorological observations. At the bottom of his garden at Cardington, he had placed a thermometer; and as soon as the frosty weather had set in, he used to leave his warm bed at two o'clock every morning, walk in the bitter morning air to his thermometer, examine it by his lamp, and write down its register, — which done to his satisfaction, he would coolly betake himself again to bed.

All these quasi-learned pursuits, however, did not and could not make Howard a man of letters. His intellectual life, though adorned perhaps by such studies, was not built upon them. Science is not a thing on which, or out of which, character can be formed. Life must be modelled on life — not on inductions; on creative thoughts and heroic acts — not on physical, or even on philosophical principles. Science, of itself, can do little to make men — though it may make students, — and for Howard it did nothing. Neither from the science of England, nor from the literature of Greece and Rome, did he levy those contributions on which character can be erected; nor do we find that he ever proposed to himself, as models, any of the heroes or sages which the classic lands produced. His antitypes lay in another country — in a different history; and with all their splendid virtues and antique ideas — he formed himself upon them. These were, the apostles, prophets, and patriarchs of old. There was one literature — and only one — with which he was thoroughly acquainted, — that of the Holy Scriptures. There was but one system of life developed in the history of the past, which commended itself completely and unreservedly to his conscience and his heart — that of the early Hebrew times. This was the source of his weakness as of his strength. He almost rejected modern life and the morals of a civilization, which is at once more advanced and more corrupt. In all this, we trace the paramount influence of puritan ideas. Education had directed Howard to study the Book of Life. In its pages, he found the principle of all science — the foundation of all wisdom. He had conned it early and late; had taken it to his soul, until it became to him a Living Law. To its righteous spirit he sought to assimilate all his being. To him, the Word of God was in the place of all other literatures and lores. On its doctrines, its moralities, its social sentiments, his life was built up on system. More completely, perhaps, than any other individual in modern times, by dint of incessant contemplation of this history, had Howard re-created and realized the ideal of a devout and dignified

Hebrew patriarch. This fact is the key to his whole character: — whatever was special, unmodern, in the life and conversation of the philanthropist, was — next to the natural impulse of his own genius — the result of meditation on the writings of the prophets and apostles; and whatever estimate may be formed of the character which he has left behind him in the world, it is certain that it received its distinctive sign and impress from this admiration of the ancient kings and heroes of Israel.

It is of great importance to mark this fact — for on it turns his entire history; and only through it can that history be intelligibly studied. The consequences of this intellectual and moral building up show themselves in his sublimest as in his most trifling acts. Everything which Howard did, meant something — involved or expressed a principle. No man ever lived who was less a creature of impulse. In every word or deed of his, there was a latent sense. His genius was the reverse of wild, boundless, and creative. But calm, watchful, self-possessed, when he moved it was always with effect. His decision was great, because he was convinced in what he did. When he entered the path of duty — of action — the road lay mapped out broadly, distinctly before him. To the comprehending mind there was no mystery in his motives, no misapprehension about his position; hence his footsteps never needed to be retraced, nor his work to be undone. Having deliberately fashioned his character on the patriarchal, that is, on the highest model of a primitive and selected race, every incident of his life was tested by the accepted standard. He kept himself always struggling up to the height of his great argument. Once convinced that the scriptural ideal which he had learned to venerate was the noblest that man can propose to himself for imitation, he adopted without hesitation — because without fear and without haste — its austere and lofty forms of thought — the striking mixture of affection and authority in its domestic life. All Howard's social and family arrangements reveal the presence of Hebrew ideas — his assumption of supreme government in his household, not less distinctly than the large, though paternal power, which he claimed to exercise over his tenantry — a claim to which all his benevolence failed to reconcile his sturdy Saxon neighbors, who liked not despotism, even though it were both paternal and enlightened.

As has been said before, Howard and his wife retired from the great world to their quiet home at Cardington within a few days of the celebration of their nuptials. Many alterations were necessary in order to make their abode commodious and agreeable, both house and grounds being small and inconvenient. Harriet, who seems to have possessed an exquisite taste in all things, suggested the improvements which she deemed desirable, and her husband superintended their execution. The house was partly rebuilt and enlarged; the gardens and grounds were laid out afresh, and on a more extended scale. Nor was their attention confined to the comfort of their own establishment. Before his marriage, Howard had devoted a considerable portion both of his leisure and his fortune to a plan for improving the dwellings of the poor on his estate; and that, not from a feeling of personal pride and generosity, but from a sense of duty. He entertained what may be thought very strange notions about property — notions which would find little favor with some of the economical philosophers of these days — and, which is more germain to the matter, he acted upon them. In the first place, he did not believe that the wealth which he inherited from his parent was entirely his own, or that it could be altogether made use of as his personal caprice might suggest. He rather looked upon it as a deposit which society had entrusted into his keeping for the common benefit of mankind. He no more believed that he was at liberty to waste it upon his individual gratifications, than a banker would have been. It must be allowed that these were very extraordinary heresies for a man who had received his commercial training in Watling-street, to broach — heresies, some will think, subversive of the very principles of political economy — but they arose from studying the Bible instead of the Wealth of Nations, and may be classed with the other deplorable results of an imperfect education. However ridiculous and contrary to all sound science, these notions may be deemed, they were held by the philanthropist. His biographer is not responsible for his weaknesses. Instances, not a few, are still on record which illustrate this ignorance; nay, it even seems that he was able to endoctrinate his wife Harriet with his views on this subject — perhaps a yet greater marvel than that he should have surrendered himself to such revolutionary opinions. A not incurious example of her willing cooperation in carrying out the principles here involved, may be related. In the middle of the eighteenth century — as the fair reader will not fail to be aware — it was *costume* to wear quantities of jewels; and, of course, no lady in fashionable life and courtly style was considered dressed without a goodly display of brilliants upon her person. Now the rank and social position of Henrietta Leeds, required her to deck her beauties out as women of her class were wont to do; but somehow, Henrietta Howard very soon learned to disregard such meretricious ornaments, and within a short period of her marriage she is reported to have sold the greater part of her jewels, and applied the money to the formation of a fund for the purpose of relieving the sick and the destitute.

Howard and his partner had not been settled long at Cardington before the rather delicate state of the latter's health induced them to try a change of air. Watcombe, near Lymington, in the New Forest, Hampshire, was recommended for this purpose; and a suitable residence having been found, they removed to that locality. Howard bought the house and a small estate for seven thousand pounds, purposing a settled residence, if the change proved beneficial to Harriet's health. But the course of existence never will run smooth; and the state of trial was a necessary education for the future mission of mercy. The habitation thus coming into his possession happened to be in bad odor at the time with the good folks of the neighborhood. Its former proprietor, a gentleman of the name of Blake, had been a captain in the service of the East India Company; and his military education in Hindostan had given him certain dogmatic and domineering habits which rendered him by no means popular. He was disposed, moreover, to carry matters with a very high hand. He had been accustomed to make short work with the ryots of the east, and was disposed to carry the same tactics into operation in England; so, entrenching himself behind a variety of offensive and defensive weapons, he invited and defied hostilities, as became a landlord and a soldier. Between the gallant captain on the one side and the non-content Watcombers on the other, a sort of rural war was perpetually raging, and a good deal of ill blood was made, if but little was actually shed. The atmosphere was still warm with the effects of this feud, when the new comers arrived. The mansion still lay under the ban of the village, and its occupant was watched with suspicion and distrust; but the state of siege and suspicion did not last long under the new *regime*. In a short time Howard's kindness and urbanity overcame the general feeling of hostility, and even gained him, from contrast, great popularity. As Dr. Aikin observes, Howard had none of those propensities which so frequently embroil country gentlemen with their neighbors, great and small. He was no lover of sport, and no encroacher upon the rights and privileges of others. Above all — and this trait of character will probably sink him in the opinion of another class besides the economists — he was no executor of the Game Laws. For the three or four years that he resided at Watcombe, he got on remarkably well; and when he finally quitted the locality to return to his beloved Cardington, he left an impression of his goodness behind him, and a regret at his removal, which survived even his life.

The principal cause of this return to old scenes, was a conviction that, on the whole, the air of Hampshire was not so favorable to Harriet's health as that of Bedfordshire. Henceforth the Howards determined to make Cardington their home. The various improvements which had been projected — if not actually commenced — during their previous residence there, were now carried into effect. The house had formerly been a farm; it was, however, pleasantly situated, and had the advantage — to the Howards, and to minds like theirs, an indescribable charm — of overlooking the rustic churchyard of the village. The improvements were tastefully adapted to the nature of the site. The back part of the house was taken down and rebuilt on an enlarged and more picturesque plan. A new suite of rooms were made to abut on the pleasure grounds, into which an elegant entrance was formed. The old-fashioned casements were taken from the front, and replaced, by a series of chaste and simple cottage windows; while the walls were covered with a light lattice work, about which were trailed and twined the most fragrant garden plants and flowers. The pleasure grounds were formed out of a field of about three acres extent, formerly attached to the farm; it is said that they were laid out in the best possible taste, having a kitchen garden in the centre, so completely shut in with shrubs and flowers, that a stranger might have strolled about for hours without being made aware of its existence, unless he chanced to come upon a slight and narrow opening, overarched with the interlacing branches of trees, through which it might be entered, no gate or artificial barrier stopping the way. Between the shrubbery and the cottage there was a beautiful lawn surrounded by a broad gravel walk, which being thickly bordered by evergreens and fine well-grown trees, was sheltered from the heat of the summer sun, and afforded a delightful promenade. In one part of the grounds this path was skirted by a row of magnificent firs, which are said to have been brought by the philanthropist from the continent, in one of his early rambles, and planted there with his own hands. This shady walk was his favorite re sort when the society of his friends, or his own brooding thoughts, suggested a pleasant saunter in the open air :—his more studious hours being spent in a rustic building, half summer-house, half library, situated at the bottom of the garden. This oratory was chastely and simply fitted up with statues, books, — including most of the great puritan authors — and a few philosophical instruments.

Such, in a few words, was the charming home which the Howards made unto themselves at Cardington. In connection with the idea of such a home, think of the illustrious and gentle individuals who occupied it, their interlacing love and perfect correspondence of sentiment and thought, and the reader of taste and poetic imagination will be able to realize one of those breathing pictures of rural and patriarchal life, which it nerves the mind and educates the heart to comtemplate. But not for himself alone did Howard devise, and alter, and amend. Others had claims upon him, the validity of which he could not and would not contest. More than once we have intimated that his benevolence — founded on a sacred sense of duty and responsibility — extended to all who came within the sphere of his influence. His assistance was always available to those in pain or want. His heart, too, was as open as his hand; his sympathy was as warm as his munificence was wide; but, in every case, improvement, not charity, was his object. His scheme aimed at effecting permanent results; consequently, his work began at the foundation. When Howard first went to reside at Cardington, he found it one of the most miserable villages which could have been pointed out on the map of England. Its peasant-inhabitants were wretchedly poor, ignorant, vicious, turbulent, dirty; its gentry idle, frivolous, fashionable; and though possessing some collegiate and academical learning, so ignorant of its obligations to society, as not to know that property has its duties as well as its rights;—in fact, it was in that normal condition of an agricultural hamlet which is yet so greatly admired by certain noble and right honorable writers. The county possessed no manufacturers to draw off and exhaust the surplus population. The lace trade of Bedford barely afforded to a few persons an uncertain pittance, and offered no resource to the masses of the unemployed. These facts, taken in connection with the ignorance and consequent improvidence of the peasant population, give an ample reason for their low condition.

With his characteristic energy and earnestness, Howard set himself, within the sphere of his own competence and influence, to ameliorate their state, both in a worldly and spiritual sense. Beginning with his own estate, he saw that the huts in which his tenantry, like all others of their class, were huddled together, were dirty, ill built, ill drained, imperfectly lighted and watered, and, altogether, so badly conditioned and unhealthy, as to be totally unfit for the residence of human beings. With the true instinct of a philosopher, he perceived that while the people were thus miserably cabined, compelled to be uncleanly on their domestic hearths, uncomfortable in their homes, any attempt to improve their minds, to induce them to become more sober, industrious, home-loving, must be only so much good effort thrown away; and resolved to begin his work at the true starting-point, by first aiming to improve their physical condition, to supply them with the means of comfort, attaching them thus to their own fire-side, the great centre of all pure feeling and sound morals, to foster and develop in them a relish for simple domestic enjoyments, and thus open for them a way to the attainments of such moderate intellectual pleasures as their lot in life did not forbid. But, more than all, it was his desire to establish in their minds the foundations of moral and religious convictions.

The first step which he took in furtherance of these objects was obviously a wise one, that of rendering the *homes* of the poor, dwellings fit for self-respecting men. This must, indeed, be the starting-point of every true social and industrial reformation. In carrying his plan into effect, Howard does not seem to have troubled himself much about that paramount question, the percentage. Though an arithmetician and a man of business, he considered that his wealth was merely held in trust for the benefit of mankind, and consequently he had no hesitation in investing it with a view to returns rather in the shape of order, virtue, intelligence and happiness, than in money.

Having decided that the miserable mud huts in which he found his cottagers living when he returned to Cardington should be taken down, he carefully selected some good and convenient plots of ground, on which he caused a number of very superior cottages to be built; and as soon as these were ready, he transferred into them such persons as he most strongly approved of for tenants. As he had a great many applications for the hire of his new homesteads, — which, it may at once be stated, he let out on the same terms as the hovels which they were built to supersede, he was usually able to make a judicious choice; his absolute requirements being — habits of industry, temperance, and observance of the Sabbath. The doctrinal opinions of his tenants he did not interfere with. Himself a firm and consistent discipline of Anglican dissent, the sacramental idea of which is the right of individual opinion, he could not do otherwise than tolerate where he could not convince; in this respect, as in so many others, setting an example which might be profitably followed by parties within the pale of almost every communion of the Christian church. In this wise and noble scheme of private duty Howard was fully seconded and supported by his wife. Long after her demise, and when her memory had become to the patriarchal old man almost a part of his religion, he told his friend, Dr. Aikin, a simple anecdote, which places her virtues in the most amiable light. It must be noted that one of her husband's strange ideas with regard to property, was that he had no right to hoard up his superfluous wealth. He thought the bounties of Providence should be annually distributed — that the hungry should be fed, the naked clothed, the houseless sheltered — without the owner taking care for the morrow; hence, when his accounts were made up at the end of each year, if there was a balance of income over expenditure — instead of heaping up riches, he deemed it to be his duty either to lay the surplus out in some useful work, or else to carry it in a lump to the charitable fund founded on the proceeds of Harriet's sale of ornaments. He looked upon that superfluity — like the gleaning of the corn-field, which his Bible told him belonged of right to the poor — as a sacred portion, over which he had no control beyond the power to determine upon the way in which it should be laid out. This too was an ancient Hebrew idea. A short time after their marriage, on striking the balance at Christmas, they found a small surplus — and as they had been toiling and building for a considerable time, to indulge his wife, Howard proposed that this money should be spent in a trip to London. The dear Harriet generously relinquishing her own pleasures, suggested that the money would just be enough to build another of their delightful cottages for a poor and deserving family! Her desire, of course, decided the question — the homestead was erected. Despite the letter of their curious domestic compact, it would not be difficult for such a woman, from the altitude of her own great heart, to govern the affections and the will even of a Howard.

When he had thus with a wise aim and forethought laid—as far as his time and means would permit — the foundations of a permanent improvement in the condition and circumstances of his tenants, he proceeded to the next stage of his plan — the cultivation of their minds and morals. To accomplish these most desirable objects, he established a number of schools in the vicinity — not only for the children of his own cottagers, but for all who chose to avail themselves of their advantages. Unfortunately, it was one of the maxims of that age, that adults could not be taught — that persons who had grown up without learning to read or write could never afterwards acquire either of these useful arts. Bowing to this mistaken assumption, Howard devoted the whole of his educational energies to the young, leaving their parents to such instruction as could be conveyed to them from the pulpit, and to the oral advice given by the ministers of religion on their visits. But he considered that with the rising generation the process of schooling was a far more safe and certain work, and to this object he was warmly and entirely devoted. The discipline adopted in his schools is described as of a very superior order: competent and skilful persons being engaged and paid by Howard to conduct them. As in the case of his cottiers, he retained a sort of patriarchal authority over the scholars, and imposed strict conditions upon them as to diligence, cleanliness and order; in addition, it was also indispensable that they should attend Divine service twice every Sunday, either at church or chapel. This parental control — in Howard's case always exercised for good — he considered as a part of the system of duties and responsibilities which the possession of property had devolved upon him. The exercise of this power does not appear, however, to have gratified his ambition or flattered his sense of self-importance; he regarded its possession rather as a trial than as a privilege. To him it was no assumption. He had no small passions to indulge, no cliques to gratify, no petty interests to serve. He exercised authority only to do good. Convinced that social influence had been given to him for grave and solemn ends, he wielded it with fear and trembling — with anxiety and self-distrust, rather than with egotism and pleasure.

In the exercise of this high discretion, it will not be expected that Howard should always have come up to the mark of more modern and advanced ideas. He was only human, and liable to error. He belonged to his age too — now a century past in years, and five centuries past in thought. In a few nooks and corners of England, remnants of old opinions on the philosophy of education may still be found; but on the great theatre of life — in the open face of day

— learning has ceased to be a thing proscribed. Howard, however, was a man of the eighteenth century — and he suffered the notions of that epoch in some sort to mould his programme of education. The girls in his schools were taught reading and plain sewing — nothing more. What could more strongly mark the difference between society in 1749 and 1849, than the fact, that then *that* was thought enough of education for women to acquire, and that even a Howard was haunted by the fear of giving them — daughters of the soil, and inheritors of a laborious life — the dangerous desire to elevate themselves in the world! The boys were treated in the same spirit: they were all taught to read; but an acquaintance with the subversive arts of writing and accounting was bestowed only upon a carefully selected few! Still, while regretting the short-coming of the time, it would be very unwise to ignore the vast importance of the movement which was then commenced in the right direction. The teaching given — though limited — was useful: it was not adapted to develop the latent genius of any gloriously endowed Cardington Milton or Cromwell, but it was nevertheless well calculated to foster habits of order and regularity in the poor; and it may be added here, that the village of Cardington is still distinguished for the presence of these very qualities. Howard's schools, and others of the same character, have been the pioneers of national education. They paved the way for the advance of larger truths in social politics. They proved that the peasant might be entrusted with knowledge without danger to the institutions of the country. By scattering some of the elements of popular education, they have made national instruction possible; and if they have not done all the good which might have been effected by the machinery employed, had it been more wisely and liberally directed, it should still be remembered to their honor, that their experience has finally abrogated that dread of an educated laboring class which was once next to universal in this country.

In all Howard's relations with his domestics and tenants, we see the very form and pressure of ancient oriental manners. His habits recall a thousand exquisite pictures of primitive life — Boaz going forth amongst the reapers where he first encountered Ruth — Miltiades sitting at the portico of his dwelling, calling to the strangers from the Chersonese, as they were passing by tired and soiled by travel, and offering them the hospitalities of his house — and other charming images rise up to memory as fitting counterparts to the frequent glimpses which we get of the patriarch of Cardington. Howard regularly visited all the cottagers on his estate — entered their habitations in the most familiar manner — conversed with them about their humble affairs — listened to their representations, and administered to their wants. Nor were the Howards long alone in their work of improvement. The example produced its effect upon their neighbors; one of whom, Samuel

Whitbread, Esq., father of the distinguished politician of that name, and himself Member for Bedford during several years, was a distant relative of the reformer. This Mr. Whitbread was the principal of the well-known brewery firm, whose Entire is still a favorite beverage with the gentle denizens of Cocaigne. He was immensely wealthy; his vast possessions introduced him into high society, and enabled him to make an aristocratic alliance. He married Mary, third daughter of the first Earl of Cornwallis, and in 1758, his son Samuel, afterwards celebrated in political circles, was born. Young Whitbread was born to the inheritance of the brewery. A clause in his father's will compelled him to retain in his own hands a majority of the shares; but he did not find that his connection with trade was any bar to his success in society, for he afterwards married the Lady Elizabeth, eldest daughter of Earl Grey, and in this way the family of Howard became distantly connected with that of Grey, upon a member of which — the present C. Whitbread, Esq., of Cardington, second son of Mr. and Lady Elizabeth Whitbread — his property has subsequently devolved.

The efforts of two such men as Howard and the elder Whitbread, wisely contrived and unceasingly directed, could not fail to be highly productive of good. In the course of a very few years, from being one of the worst, Cardington became one of the most orderly and prosperous localities in the kingdom — the cottages of the poor were rendered neat, clean, and comfortable; the poor themselves, honest, sober, industrious, well-informed and religious. And all this was the work of one benevolent man — earnestly impressed with a true sense of his duty to his fellows—and the gentle lady whose high privilege it was to second his humane endeavors, as well as to discharge in person all those offices of grace, which, in the ministry of charity and love, can only be safely confided to a woman's delicate tact and taste.

And here, in this little Eden of his own creation, — in the society of his darling wife, and a selected circle of attached and faithful friends, — surrounded by a prosperous and contented tenantry, looking up to him as to a father and protector, — happy in himself, and given up to his contracted but important spheres of duty, — apart from the great world, and beyond the influence of its seductive snares, whether winged to the soul in the alluring shapes of interest and pleasure, or presented in the grander forms of fame and power, — anxious only to consecrate his talents to the good of mankind, and to render himself less unworthy of the crown of everlasting life: in this sweet retreat, the life of this excellent man might have passed noiselessly away — unknown to the world — leaving no trace behind it in the past, to incite the great and to direct the good — had it not pleased heaven, in its inscrutable wisdom, again to wound him in his tenderest affections, and thus send him forth once more with a torn and bleeding heart, in quest of peace, into that great arena wherein humanity is doomed for evermore to struggle and aspire.

On Sunday, the 31st of March, 1765, Harriet Howard suddenly and unexpectedly died. On the foregoing Wednesday, she had been delivered of her first and only child — a son. For several years they had been issueless: how fervently they had prayed for such a blessing as had now come to them, was not unknown to some of their more intimate friends. At length heaven had heard their supplication: a man-child was vouchsafed to them. The circumstances attending Harriet's delivery were not suggestive of more than ordinary danger. On the Sunday morning she was thought beyond all risk. Howard went to church as usual. Soon after his return, however, she was seized with a sudden illness; and in a very short time expired in his arms. No tongue can tell, no pen describe the awful misery of the bereaved husband. The unforeseen blow struck out at one fell swoop his bright, illusive future. His soul was pierced with the burning rod; deeply and immedicably it went home. His affections thus rudely cut away, grew never more again. He had loved as men love only once. Henceforth his sunniest side of life was blank and dark. All his religion — and to Howard religion was everything that fortitude, philosophy, resignation are to other men — was needed to support the crushing dispensation; but he bowed his head to the chastening rod of the Almighty, with the meekness of a Christian and the resignation of an oriental patriarch.

His wife's remains were interred, quietly and without pomp, in the churchyard of Cardington, where a tablet still bears the following inscription to her memory:

IN HOPE OF A RESURRECTION TO ETERNAL LIFE,
THROUGH THE MERCY OF GOD BY JESUS CHRIST,
RESTS THE MORTAL PART OF
HENRIETTA HOWARD,
DAUGHTER OF EDWARD LEEDS, ESQ.
OF CROXTON, IN CAMBRIDGESHIRE,
WHO DIED THE 31ST OF MARCH, 1765, AGED 39.
"SHE OPENED HER MOUTH WITH
WISDOM;
AND IN HER TONGUE WAS THE LAW OF KINDNESS."
PROV. XXXI. 26.

By temperament, Howard was calm and undemonstrative; but there were depths in his nature not easily fathomed. His love for his wife had been an illimitable passion. The day of her death was held sacred in his calendar,—kept for evermore as a day of fasting and meditation. Everything connected with her memory, how distantly soever, was hallowed in his mind by the association. Many years after her demise, on the eve of his departure on one of his long and perilous journeys across the continent of Europe, he was walking in the gardens with the son whose birth had cost the precious life, examining some plantations which they had recently been making, and arranging a plan for future improvements. On coming to the planted walk, he stood still; there was a pause in the conversation; the old man's thoughts were busy with the past: at length he broke silence: — "Jack," said he, in a tender and solemn tone, "in case I should not come back, you will pursue this work, or not, as you may think proper; but remember, this walk was planted by your mother; and, if you ever touch a twig of it, may my blessing never rest upon you!"

CHAPTER IV.

DISCIPLINE OF A WOUNDED SPIRIT.

Howard's domestic arrangements were not broken up at once. For a time, the good man strove to find, in the care of his infant son — all that now remained to him of his buried love — in the exercise of his devotions, in the management of his estate, in attending to his schools, and the general welfare of his people, antidotes and soothers of his affliction; and that he succeeded, to some extent at least, in this design, may be inferred from the calmness and regularity of his outward life. The struggle within, against the sense of heart-loneliness, vacuity and desolation — the contrast between the dreary silence which now reigned in the deserted chambers of his soul, and their recent state, when the full swell of an affluent love filled them with music, joyousness, and life, none can ever know, ever can conceive, unless he be himself called upon to pass the dark and trying ordeal. That he should love the child so dearly purchased, with even more than a father's fondness, every reader of sensibility must feel from the inspirations of our common nature. Yet, this fact has been denied. The only blot which envy and malignity have ever attempted to affix upon the stainless, the almost immaculate character of Howard — is a denial of his natural affection for his only child!

The youthful irregularities and misfortunes of that son in after life, lent a certain air of possibility to this charge. Unhappily he became insane. That he became so from perfectly natural causes, there is now no manner of doubt. Baldwin Brown has been at considerable pains to collect together every fact and circumstance connected with this point; and, after an impartial survey of the whole case, every man capable of weighing evidence must admit that the philanthropist stands triumphantly vindicated from the charge. That he entertained a very exalted notion of the paternal office, the portion of his history already before the reader will have shown; but in all his relations with others, he was as gentle as he was firm, as calm and mild as he was convinced and resolute. That he held a peculiar theory with respect to the best way of educating children — and, being a conscientious man, applied his theory in practice — is also certain; but the assumption that his mode of treatment disordered the intellect of his child, or even that it could strengthen a constitutional tendency to mental derangement, is not only gratuitous in itself, but contradicted by the facts of the case, and by the inferences of mental and physiological science. The discipline which he adopted in reference to his son, is thus described by Dr. Aikin, from personal knowledge :—

"Regarding children as creatures possessed of strong passions and desires, without reason and experience to control them, he thought that nature seemed, as it were, to mark them out as the subjects of absolute authority; and that the first and fundamental principle to be inculcated upon them, was implicit and unlimited obedience. This cannot be effected by any process of *reasoning*, before reason has its commencement; and therefore must be the result of *coercion*. Now, as no man ever more effectually combined the *leniter in modo* with the *fortiter in re* — the coercion he practised was calm and gentle, but at the same time steady and resolute. I shall give an instance of it which I had from himself. His child one day wanting something which he was not to have, fell into a fit of crying which the nurse could not pacify. Mr. Howard took him from her and laid him quietly in his lap, till, fatigued with crying, he became still. This process, a few times repeated, had such an effect, that the child, if crying ever so violently, was rendered quiet the instant that his father took him. In a similar manner, without harsh words or threats, much less blows, he gained every other point which he thought necessary to gain, and brought the child to such a habit of obedience, that I have heard him say, he believed his son would have put his finger into the fire if he had commanded him. Certain it is, that many fathers could not—if they approved it—execute a plan of this kind; but Mr. Howard, in this case, only pursued the general method which he took to effect anything which a thorough conviction of its propriety induced him to undertake. It is absurd, therefore, to represent him as wanting that milk of human kindness for his only son, with which he abounded for the rest of his fellow-creatures; for he aimed at what he thought the good of both, by the very same means; and, if he carried the point farther with his son, it was only because he was more interested in his welfare. But this course of discipline, whatever he thought it, could not have been long practised, since the child was early sent to school, and the father lived very little at home afterwards.

The atrocious slander to which reference is made, was promulgated in the Gentleman's Magazine, in an obituary notice of the philanthropist. The charge was made on the strength of one asserted fact—namely, that Howard had once locked up his son for several hours in a solitary place, put the key into his pocket, and gone off to Bedford, leaving him there till he returned at night. On the appearance of this article, the friends of the illustrious dead came forth publicly to dispute the fact and to deny the inferences deduced from it. Meridith Townsend, one of Howard's most intimate friends, sifted the story to the bottom — and gave the following account of its origin:

"It was Mr. Howard's constant practice to walk out with his child in the garden, while the servants were at dinner. In one of these little excursions, with Master Howard in his hand, (who was then about three years old,) the father being much entertained with the innocent prattle of his son, they went on till they came to the root-house, or hermitage, in a retired part of the garden, with which the young gentleman was familiarly acquainted; and were there for some time, diverting one another. During this, the servant came in great haste to inform his master that a gentleman on horseback was at the door, and desired to speak with Mr. Howard immediately, upon business of some importance; and as he wished to be with him as soon as possible, he said to his son, 'Jack, be a good boy, and keep quiet, and I shall come very soon to you again;' and so locking the door to prevent the child from going out and prowling about the garden by himself, to the hazard of getting into some mischief, he put the key in his pocket, and ran to the person in waiting as fast as he could. The conversation between them lasted much longer than he had expected, and put the thought of the child out of his mind. Upon the gentleman's departure, he asked the servant where Jack was, and received for answer, that he supposed him to be in the root-house where he had been left. And then instantly recollecting the incident, he flew to set him at liberty, and found him quietly asleep on the matting; and when he was waked, could not perceive that the confinement had made any disagreeable impressions upon his mind."

Upon such a trival incident has malice founded this preposterous charge! The libel was advanced anonymously; and no one has ever had the courage to come forward and own it — although often challenged to do so. "Some men," says Burke, "are at once contemptible and content." The unknown traducer of Howard may be one of them.

When Jack was about four years old, his father sought to make up in some sort to *him* for his maternal loss, by placing him under the care of a discreet and worthy woman, who kept a school for young ladies at Cheshunt, in Hertfordshire; — a judicious proceeding, which he never had any reason to regret. Thence he was removed in proper season to an academy for boys — after which he was successively placed under the ablest tutors at Daventry, Nottingham, Edinburgh, and Cambridge. The unfortunate issue of all this care and cost, to which allusion has been made, was a source of inexpressible grief to his devoted parent; but that parent never had the slightest occasion to arraign his own conduct as having contributed to the painful result.

For eighteen months, the widowed heart lay buried in the seclusion of Cardington — shrouded in a grief too sacred and too great for the eyes of the common world to rest on. But this sorrow, too long indulged, threatened to sap the very foundations of life. Towards the close of 1766, the health of the bereaved had become such, that a change of air and scene was considered by his medical attendants indispensable to his recovery. Bath and its immediate neighborhood were recommended; — and while there, he diverted his attention from his consuming sorrows, by entering into a series of investigations respecting the heat of the mineral springs of the locality — the results of which were communicated to the Royal Society, and published in the Philosophical Transactions, as already mentioned. From Bath he probably went up to London — spending some considerable time there in the society of his learned and distinguished friends. During the ensuing spring, he made a short tour into Holland. Foreign travel, by the excitement which the sight of novel and ever-changing objects causes to the mind, was an unfailing remedy for Howard's ailments; and on his return thence, he seems to have been calmer and more resigned to his deprivation. The active superintendence of his estate — the thousand cares and calls upon his attention growing out of the schools and cottages which he had erected — and the society of his little boy, appear to have now engrossed the whole of his time. The engaging prattle of his child was the solace dearest to his heart; but the time soon came when it was necessary, for Jack's own good, that his education, properly so called, should begin; and the fond father was obliged to give him up to the charge of those who were chosen to undertake it. When this arrangement was carried into effect, and the house was denuded of the last living suggestion of its former mistress, Cardington quickly became an intolerable residence to its master. Howard again resolved to travel — this time into Italy. That sunny land has ever been the hope of the invalid in heart — the coveted home of the bereaved and widowed mind.

His route lay through Calais to the South of France;—thence he passed to Geneva, where he spent a few weeks in serious retirement, such as the prophets of old are said to have at times indulged in — a grand and sacred purpose forming in his mind — and then coming out into the world again, he proceeded into Italy. We have seen that in his first journey into that country, he was a devoted worshipper at the shrine of art; it is not to be supposed that he now omitted any fair opportunity of contemplating the same master-works of genius — but this was no longer his only — not by any means his chief — purpose. A change was now passing over the spirit of his dream. In all the vicissitudes of his career, his mind had been ever noble, elevated, religious; but his recent sorrows had sublimed and purified his heart into something saint like and angelic, — and he now sought to take more intimately and permanently than he had yet done the great initiation of the cross, — to dedicate in a more formal and solemn manner his soul to God — to devote his active services to his fellow-creatures. The history of this Italian tour is, in truth, the history of a great sacrament and covenant. It is a fair and worthy object of ambition, to wish to acquire a correct and cultivated taste; Howard was well aware how much it is capable of adding to the charm of intellectual pleasures; but, at the same time, he felt how immeasurably more important it is to have a calm and self-approving conscience — a soul, spiritually without fear and without reproach; and this consummation he sought to compass for himself by severe self-discipline and by earnest aspiration after all that is most holy in human life. From his youth, his piety had been always fervent; chastened by much affliction, it now burnt up with a new and brighter flame, and his entire being, under these influences, assumed a loftier and serener aspect.

Some of the private memoranda which he made at this period — as well as many of his private letters — have heen preserved; and although mere fragments, these invaluable documents throw a complete, and, for those who love to trace a great mind through all its phases, a most interesting light upon his mental condition. The notes, it should be said, were not intended for publication; they were his secret thoughts put into form solely for his own use. By no means remarkable for literary excellence — and especially deficient in the rhetorical graces of style — neverthelsss, as mental revelations of one of the purest of human beings, they possess an interest, in spite of their homeliness, which but few fragments can justly boast. Like their author, they are simple, earnest, sincere, — consciously and unconsciously indicating real humility, trustfulness, and truthfulness of heart. Upon these resources it is impossible not to draw largely for the remainder of this period of his mental history — the essential prelude of his future work — without which it can, in fact, hardly be understood. It may be stated here that these fragments have been edited. Howard's style was elliptical even to obscurity. Verbal inaccuracies have been corrected so far as they could be without changing the structure of his sentences; but in no case has the sense been tampered with in the slightest degree.

When Howard quitted England in search of health, his idea was to pass the winter in southern Italy; but the change of air acted upon his debilitated frame with such immediate and revivifying power, as to render that journey no longer an absolute necessity. When he arrived at Turin he abandoned his original design of proceeding towards the south and wintering at Naples — for the reasons stated in the following memorandum:

"Turin, Nov. 30, 1769. — My return without seeing the southern part of Italy, was on much deliberation, — as I feared a mis-improvement of a talent spent for mere curiosity, at the loss of many Sabbaths, and as *many donations must be suspended for my pleasure* — which would have been, as I hope, contrary to the general conduct of my life; — and which, on a retrospective view on a death-bed, would cause pain, as unbecoming a disciple of Christ — whose mind should be formed in my soul. These thoughts, with distance from my dear boy, determines me to check my curiosity and be on the return. Oh! why should vanity and folly — pictures and baubles — or even the stupendous mountains, beautiful hills, or rich valleys, which ere long will all be consumed, *engross* the thoughts of a candidate for an everlasting kingdom! . . . Look forward, my soul! How low, how mean, how little, is everything but what has a view to that glorious world of light, and life, and love!"

What a beautiful nature is unconsciously drawn in these few lines! Such words need little comment: — but it is impossible not to remark how those strange notions of his about property affected all his arrangements. The absolute injuctions of his health so far complied with as seemed inexorably necessary, he would indulge in no further outlay on his personal account; well knowing that it would curtail the resources of his Charitable Fund — still supplied and dispensed, though Harriet was no more; and leaving behind him, unvisited, the gorgeous plains and luxurious cities of the south, he retraced his steps northward, lest the poor of Cardington should be suffering want while he was far away and could not minister to them. Here was duty, to the strictest letter of the social law.

His route backward was by way of Geneva and Paris. In the latter city he mixed in the best society for about ten days, but without descending to any of its frivolities and follies. Thence he went into Holland — on the road to which he wrote the following letter to the Rev. Joshua Symonds, Minister of the congregation at Bedford; "Abbeville, Jan. 4, 1770. — Dear Sir: having an opportunity, by an Italian gentleman with whom I have travelled, I thought a few lines would not be unacceptable. After landing in France, my first object was Geneva, where I spent some time before I went into Italy. The luxury and wickedness of the inhabitants — amidst the richest country — abounding with the noblest productions of human skill and power — would ever give a thinking mind pain. I was seven days re-crossing the Alps. The weather was very cold; the thermometer eleven degrees below the freezing point. The quick descent by sledges on the snow, and other particulars, may perhaps afford a little entertainment some winter evening. I returned to Geneva. There, are some exemplary persons; yet the principles of one of the vilest of men, with the corruptions of the French, who are within one mile of the city — have greatly debased its ancient purity and splendor. I spent about ten days at the dirty city of

Paris. The streets are so narrow — with no footpaths — that there is no stirring out but in a coach; and as to their hackney-coaches, they are abominable. There were but few English at Paris. I dined with about twenty at our embassador's. I am now on my route to Holland, a favorite country of mine; the only one, except our own, where propriety and elegance are combined. Above all, I esteem it for religious liberty. Thus, dear sir, I am travelling from one country to another; and I trust, with some good hope, through abundant grace, to a yet better. My knowledge of human nature should be enlarged by seeing more of the tempers, tastes, and dispositions of different people. . . . . I bless God I am well. I have a calm and easy flow of spirits. I am preserved and supported through not a little fatigue. My thoughts are often with you on the Sabbath-day. I always loved my Cardington and Bedford friends; but I think distance makes me love them more. But I must conclude with my affectionate remembrance of them, and my ardent wish, desire, and prayer for your success in promoting the honor of God and the love of our Divine Redeemer."

From Abbeville he proceeded to the Hague — where we find him making the following reflections. They mark the commencement of a new development of the religious elements in his character.

"Hague, Sunday evening, Feb. 11, 1770. — I would record the goodness of God to the unworthiest of his creatures. For some days past I have been in an habitual serious frame — relenting for my sin and folly — solemnly surrendering myself and babe to Him — and begging the conduct of his Holy Spirit. I hope for a more tender conscience, by greater fear of offending God — a temper more abstracted from this world — more resigned, to death or life — a thirsting for union and communion with God. O the wonders of redeeming love! Some faint hope have even I — through redeeming mercy — that the full atoning sacrifice shall ere long be made. O shout! my soul — grace, grace! free, sovereign, rich and unbounded grace! Not I, not I, an ill-deserving, hell-deserving creature — but where sin abounds I trust grace superabounds — even I have still some hope — what joy in that hope! — that nothing shall separate my soul from the love of God in Jesus Christ. My soul! as such a frame is thy delight, pray frequently and fervently to the Father of Spirits to bless his Word and thy retired moments to thy serious conduct in life. My soul! let not the interests of a moment engross thy thoughts, or be preferred to thine eternal interests. Look forward to that glory which will be revealed to those who are faithful unto death."

In a man of poetic and imaginative temperament, such an outburst — and it occurs again frequently — would be ascribed to the inspiration of fanaticism; but in the case before us, this ascription would be absurd. Howard's nature was too deep and still,—

his self-command too thorough, to admit of the idea of his being possessed by a mere raving enthusiasm. We may rest assured, therefore, that whatever Howard says, or writes, is a sincerity — to him a truth — and that his words have a pregnant meaning, whether our wisdom may be able to fathom it or not. These facts cannot fail to suggest to men of the world — men to whom religion is nothing but an idea — that expressions such as these constitute a part of the natural, faithful language of the soul in one of its mysterious phases, and that they may co-exist with perfect moral health and intellectual vigor.

As the wanderer drew nearer home, his state of health again declined. When he arrived in Holland, his debility had become so great, and his spirits had fallen so low, that a return to Cardington was declared by his medical adviser eminently perilous to his life! He was, therefore, reluctantly compelled to resume the original plan of the journey, and by slow marches to retrace his steps towards Italy. Taking Paris again in his route, he passed through that city, and continued his course by way of Champagne and Burgundy to Lyons—in which town he probably remained some few days for repose, as we find the following reflections there written down among his papers:

"Lyons, April 4, 1770.—Repeated instances of the unwearied mercy and goodness of God! preserved hitherto in health and safety! Blessed be

the name of the Lord! Endeavor, O my soul, to cultivate and maintain a thankful, serious, humble and resigned frame and temper of mind. May it be thy chief desire that the honor of God — the spread of the Redeemer's name and Gospel — may be promoted. O! consider the everlasting worth of spiritual and Divine enjoyments; then wilt thou see the vanity and nothingness of worldly pleasures. Remember St. Paul, who was determined to know nothing in comparison of Jesus Christ and him crucified. A tenderness of conscience I would ever cultivate: no step would I take without acknowledging God. I hope my present journey — though again into Italy — is no way wrong; rejoicing if in any respect I could bring back the least improvement that might be of use to my own country. O my soul! stand in awe, and sin not. Daily pray fervently for restraining grace. Remember, that if thou desirest the *death* of the righteous, and thy latter end like his, thy *life* must be so also. In a little while thy course will be run — thy sands finished. . . . . A parting farewell with my ever-dear boy, and then, oh my soul, be weighed in the balance! In the most solemn manner I commit my spirit into Thy hands."

The touching reference to his "ever-dear boy," in these solemn passages, would be an ample reply to all that malice had invented on the subject — even if it admitted of no other. From Lyons to Rome the route which he travelled is thus given in his own words: "Quitting Lyons, I then descended the Soane to Avignon — the great beauty of which are its walks. From thence I proceeded to Aix; thence to Marseilles — whose course is elegant and its harbor commodious. The road to Toulon is romantic and pleasant; I saw many of our flowering shrubs in the hedges, and in most gardens oranges and lemons. From Toulon, I travelled to Antibes — from whence I sailed in a felucca to Nice and Manaca. I then travelled over the mountains to Genoa, the stateliness of which city is not exceeded by any I have seen. From Genoa I went to Pisa, remarkable for its elegant church — the gates of which were brought from Jerusalem. From thence I went to Leghorn and Florence; from Florence the road is pleasant, though depopulated, through Sienna to Rome, — where there are many monuments to humble the pride of man, and show how luxury and wickedness will sink a nation."

The following letter contains all that is necessary to state in connection with his present stay in the Eternal City, and is in other respects of great interest. It is addressed to the same reverend gentleman as the last: "Rome, May 22, 1770. — Dear Sir: With pleasure I received your obliging letter as I passed through Flanders. The esteem which you and some of my friends have for me humbles me to think what I ought to be. But, how mean and defective! Yet, amidst all, I have, I hope, a sincere love to all who bear the impress of our Divine Master. Since I left Holland, and through all the southern part of France, and over the Appenine mountains into Italy, I have not travelled a mile with any of our countrymen. These mountains are three or four days in passing; for many, many miles, there is hardly a three-feet road, with precipices into the sea, I should guess, three times the height of St. Paul's; but the mules are so sure-footed there is nothing to fear, though the road is also very bad. Through the mercy and goodness of God, I travel pleasantly on. I have an easy, calm flow of spirits. A little tea equipage I carry with me, with which I regale, — and little regard if I have nothing else. Florence being the seat of the arts, I visited the famous gallery many days, from which I travelled to this renowed city. The amazing ruins of temples, palaces, aqueducts, &c., give one some faint idea of its ancient grandeur; but comparatively all is now a desert. The description of them, as also of St. Peter's church and the Vatican, I must defer till I have the pleasure of seeing you. The Pope passsd very close to me yesterday; he waved his hand to bless me: I bowed, but not kneeling, some of the cardinals were displeased. But I never can nor will prostrate myself to any human creature or invention, as I should tremble at the thought of the adoration I have seen paid to him and the wafer. My temper is too open for this country; — yet I am in possession of an important piece of news of this court [the expulsion of the Society of Jesus] that I now know I durst not commit to writing. That cruellest of inventions — the Inquisition — stops all mouths. I set out to-morrow for Naples. As I return to see the great procession on the 15th of June, I intend staying there about a fortnight. Afterwards I am bound for Loretto, Ancona, Bologna, and Venice, at which last place it will be a great pleasure to receive a line from you. My thoughts are often with my Bedford friends. I beg to be remembered to Mrs. Symmonds, Messrs. Seguses, Mr. Palmer, Mr. Odell, Mr. Wiltshire; and as they know it is the Divine presence and favor that makes every place happy and comfortable — my most grateful acknowledgments for any interest I have had in their sacred moments. Thus, my dear friend, am I travelling over desolate places of ancient grandeur, and feel the influence of the past overpower that selfish and vain principle that is rooted in my constitution. When, at other times, we view in statues, painting, architecture, &c., the utmost stretch of human skill, how should one's thoughts be raised to that glorious world, that heavenly city, the city of the living God, — where sin, sorrow, and every imperfection will be done away!"

Whilst at Naples, Howard's mind was occupied with the most serious thoughts. On one of the Sabbath days which he passed in that seducing city, he employed himself in preparing and signing a solemn covenant — a practice once common among the more earnest class of the Protestant Dissenters of England, and even now not altogether unknown to that body. This document, fortunately preserved among his papers, is one of the most important which we possess for his mental history. It is as follows:

"Naples, May 27, 1770.—When I left Italy last year, it then appeared most prudent and proper. My return I also hope is under the best direction—not presumptuously being left to the folly of a foolish heart. Not having the strongest spirits or constitution, my continuing long in Holland—or any other fixed place—lowers my spirits; so that I thought, on the review, returning to Italy would be no uneasiness, as sinful and vain diversions are not my object—but my highest ambition, the honor and glory of God. Did I now see it wrong—by being the cause of pride—I would go back; being deeply sensible that it is the presence of God which makes the happiness of every place. So, O my soul, keep close to him in the amiable light of redeeming love! And, amidst the snares thou art particularly exposed to in a country of such wickedness and folly, stand thou in awe and sin not. Commune with thine own heart. See what progress thou makest in thy religious journey. Art thou nearer the heavenly Canaan—the vital flame burning clearer and clearer?—or are the concerns of a moment engrossing thy foolish heart? Stop; remember thou art a candidate for eternity. Daily, fervently, pray for wisdom. Lift up thine heart and eyes unto the Rock of Ages,—and then look down upon the glory of this world! A little while longer, and thy journey will be ended. Be thou faithful unto death. Duty is thine, though the power is God's. Pray to him to give thee a heart to hate sin more — uniting thy heart in His fear. O, magnify the Lord, my soul, and my spirit rejoice in God my Saviour! When I consider and look into my heart, I doubt, I tremble. So vile a creature! Sin, folly and imperfection in every action! Oh dreadful thought! I carry about with me a body of sin and death, ever ready to depart from God. And with all the dreadful catalogue of sins committed, my heart faints within me, and almost despairs; but yet my soul, why art thou cast down — why art thou disquieted? Hope in God and His free grace in Jesus Christ; Lord, I believe, help my unbelief! Shall I limit the grace of God? Can I fathom His goodness? Here, on His sacred day, I once more, in the dust before the eternal God, acknowledge my sins, heinous and aggravated in His sight. I would have the deepest sorrow and contrition of heart, and cast my guilty and polluted soul on His sovereign mercy in the Redeemer. O, compassionate and divine Redeemer! save me from the dreadful guilt and power of sin; and accept of my solemn, free, and, I trust, unreserved, full surrender of my soul — my spirit —my dear child — all I own and have — into Thy hands! How unworthy of Thy acceptance! Yet, Lord of mercy, spurn me not from Thy presence. Accept of me: I hope —

vile as I am—a repenting, returning prodigal. I glory in this my choice—acknowledge my *obligations* as a servant of the most High. And now may the Eternal be my refuge,—and thou, my soul, be faithful to that God that will never forsake thee. Thus, O Lord God, even a worm is humbly bold to covenant with Thee. Do thou ratify and confirm it, and make me the everlasting monument of Thy mercy. Amen, amen, amen. Glory to God the Father, God the Son, and God the Holy Ghost, forever and ever. Amen. Hoping my heart deceives me not, and trusting in His mercy for restraining and preventing grace—though rejoicing in returning what I have received from Him into His hands—yet, with fear and trembling, I sign my unworthy name. JOHN HOWARD."

This solemn and affecting covenant was renewed at Moscow, on the 27th of September, 1789, within a very short period of his death. From Naples, the pilgrim returned to Rome, in time to witness the ceremony of the 15th of June, as he had annonnced his intention of doing; but it does not seem to have affected him much. Two days later we find him making the following memorandum:

"Hoping I shall be carried safely to my native country and friends, and see the face of my dear boy in peace, remember, oh my soul, to cultivate a more serious, humble, thankful and resigned temper of mind. As thou hast seen more of the world by travelling than others—more of the happiness of being born in a Protestant country — and the dreadful abuse of holy Sabbaths — so may thy walk — thy Sabbaths, thy conversation, be more becoming the Holy Gospel. Let not pride and vanity fill up so much of thy thoughts; learn here [in Rome] the vanity and folly of all earthly grandeur — endeavor to be a wiser and better man when thou returnest. Remember, many eyes will be upon thee; and above all, the eye of that God before whom thou wilt shortly have to appear."

The pilgrim did not remain long in Rome. From Italy he passed into Germany. As will have been gathered from the foregoing, Sunday was with Howard a sacred day, — a section of time not belonging to this life or to this world. He never travelled, nor did any manner of work on it. When *en route*, he rested the Sabbath over in whatsoever place the accidents of the journey might have conducted him to. If no opportunities offered for attending public worship, he retired for the whole day into his secret chamber, and passed it in pious services and spiritual self-examinations. Upon these occasions it was his custom to think in writing — obeying in this a very early habit which he had contracted — common to many clear thinkers — of reducing his ideas into words, thereby to test their value more severely. A day thus spent at Heidelberg left the following memorial of itself in these papers:

"Heidelberg, Sunday evening, July 29, 1770. — Through the goodness of my unwearied Father and

God, I am still a monument of his unbounded mercy. Thou, my soul, record His goodness! What are thy returns for all this mercy? How it should have led thee to a life of exemplary piety and holiness! But, alas, how low thou art! My God, I take shame to myself, lie low before thee, and cry earnestly for pardon and mercy for Christ's sake. Would to God I had wisdom given me to redeem the time lost — to live a life more suitable to the mercies I am receiving! . . . . If thou art spared to return, acknowledge the goodness of God, both in public and private; look into thine own heart, and beg of God to show the evil of it. If thou bringest home a better temper, and art a wiser man, then wilt thou have cause to rejoice that the great end of travelling is answered." Weeks passed on, as the traveller — thus solemnly devoting himself to the service of God and humanity — wended his way towards home; where he was destined to find the great work for which the strange course of discipline he was now passing through was so necessary a preparation.

The eminently practical nature of Howard's piety cannot have escaped the observation of the reader: duty and work were its two normal ideas. Religious fervor, which so often overthrows — paralyzes, more poetic and impulsive minds, was to him an element of health and strength. The curious passage in his history developed in this chapter may be concluded in his own words. The reflections explain themselves: "Rotterdam, Sunday Evening, September

2, 1770. — This morning, on the review of the temper of my mind, how humbled I ought to be before God! An evil and wicked heart, being ever ready to depart from him — starting aside like a deceitful bow. Mourning, yet trusting in the Lord — in my calm, retired thoughts, I would hope I am one step forward in my Christian journey; — yet, alas, in company, how many steps backward! With such a heart, how watchful, how earnest, should be thy supplications at the throne of grace; that, as Jesus died for such as thou, thou mightest have an interest in the glorious salvation he has wrought out. The review of the temper of my mind, on probably the last Sabbath before I return to my happy native country, — I desire with profound veneration to bless and praise God for his merciful preservation of me in my long journey. No danger — no accident has befallen me. I am amongst the living; I trust ever to praise God; and, as to my soul, amongst all its weakness and folly, yet I have some hope it has not lost ground this year of travelling. Very desirous am I of returning with a right spirit, not only wiser, but better; with a cheerful humility — a more general love and benevolence to my fellow-creatures — watchful of my thoughts, my words, my actions — resigned to the will of God, that I may walk with God, and lead a more useful and honorable life in this world."

Such was the serene and lofty frame of mind in which the pilgrim returned to England!

CHAPTER V.

THE CRUSADE COMMENCED.

ON Howard's return to England his health again declined. Nor was his mind yet thoroughly healed. Some remnants of the old sorrows burnt up afresh on his arrival in Bedfordshire. Old friends and familiar scenes recalled too vividly the past, and for sometime longer, Cardington was not to be endured as a residence. But in process of time he grew more and more reconciled to it; and, as he became convalescent, he busied himself more than ever with those plans of cottage building and schooling, which had formerly engaged so large a share of his and his wife's attention. Soon, however, he was called away from this labor of love to a larger and more important sphere of duty. In 1773 he was nominated to fill the office of Sheriff of Bedford. By what means and through whose influence he arrived at such a distinction, is not known. His property in the county was not so great as to offer, of itself, a sufficing recommendation to the ministry of the day; and his religious opinions were of a kind rather to prevent than to induce his selection. At that period, it was the policy of the Government to exclude Dissenters from all offices of trust and honor in the State; while the state of the law was such as to render it perilous for a person not following the established ritual to accept an appointment even when offered. The Test Act was then in force. Howard — being an Independent — could not, of course, receive the Anglican Sacrament, and go through the other formalities required on investiture with the magisterial office; and he had no choice between a refusal of the proffered trust, on conscientious grounds, or its acceptance without complying with the ordinary forms — thus braving a bad law, and taking the consequences at his personal peril. He adopted the latter course. It was a bold proceeding, for the penalties to which he rendered himself liable were monstrously severe. He placed it in the power of any bigoted or mercenary individual who might choose to bring the case before the courts, to amerce him in a heavy fine, and inflict upon him a sort of civil and political degradation. The informer too — and it will be readily felt how much this circumstance added to his peril — could sue for damages in his own person, and for his own emolument. The fine to which he was liable for the non-observance of these preliminary formalities, was five hundred pounds — in itself a powerful temptation, to the envious, the venal, and the fanatic. In addition to this penalty, he might have been disqualified, forever, from holding any, even the most insignificant, office in Church or State — from suing a person who inflicted upon him the most grievous bodily injury — from prosecuting any one who might withhold from him his acknowledged rights — from being guardian to any child, or executor or administrator to any person whatsoever! Such were the clear, positive, unmistakable terrors of the law, through which Howard had to break on his personal responsibility before he could enter upon his holy mission; and, be it remembered, there was no power in the county — neither residing in judge, minister, nor monarch — which could save him from these penalties, should any one choose to cite him before the tribunal. It is well for the world that Howard was not a man to shrink from personal peril where a principle was at stake. Great public good was almost certain to result, and did result, from the course he adopted. Thus, he reasoned with himself: — If this breach of a bad law should be challenged, and the pains and penalties imposed, the probability is that public indignation will be so aroused thereby, as to force the Legislature to interfere and amend it. If it is not challenged, my example will establish a precedent against the law itself, and so help to render it a dead letter. The former was most likely to be the result of his bold determination, and for that event he was prepared.

Thus he entered upon his office in the spirit of a martyr: he would not disobey the voice of his country, when it called him to its councils, on account of a scruple as to a point of form; yet, as that point of form involved a question of conscience, he could not, and would not, submit to violate it. The only way, then, in which he could reconcile two such obvious, and yet conflicting, duties, was to sacrifice the legal form to the substantive thing — to obey at once his conscience and his country, and to take the consequences, whatever they might be. The expected evil did not follow. No one was found base enough to stand forth as the prosecutor of Howard — even though the law of the land sanctioned and tempted to the act. This result is to be attributed to the ascendancy of his pure and manly character, and to the more liberal ideas which at that time began to pervade society generally. At all risks, he did *his* duty.

Howard had no sooner accepted his high function, than he set about the discharge of its serious and most responsible duties. At that period, it was too much the fashion for High Sheriffs of counties to consider their offices merely as posts of honor and dignity — to which no work was attached but such as might be safely left to the care of the Under-Sheriff; while that functionary thought that his only business was, to make as much money as possible out of his situation. To marshal his javelin men — to parade in his carriage at the head of the gentry of the county — to go forth, surrounded by a petty pomp, to meet the judges in their half-yearly visits to the locality — to escort them to their lodgings amid the joyous pealing of bells — to do the honors of the assize ball — and such like easy and gentlemanly duties, were all that custom required from High Sheriffs; the rest, if there were such, was left as a matter of course to the underlings.

Such, however, was not Howards's reading of the part. He had long had a curious and scrutinizing way of viewing these things, — and the events of the last few years had only tended to increase his lofty and serious manner of regarding life and its many duties. He revolutionized the Bedford shrievalty. For his own part, he rarely went in search of precedents. Provided with a living law in his own conscience, he could dispense with much routine teaching. Without surrounding himself with the insignia of his office, he prepared to personally superintend the administration of justice. The criminal world was new to him. There was no science of prison treatment then — hardly any literature on the subject; and probably none at all that he was acquainted with. But it was a thing likely to attract his attention deeply. Laying aside all pomp, he sat in the court during the trials; and in the intervals visited and inspected, with the utmost care and minuteness, every portion of the prison. Not a single cell was suffered to escape his notice. Every abuse was brought to light. Every inmate of the gaol received the benefits of his visits. This was in reality the beginning of his life-work.

In other respects, and apart from the accidents of the case, the prison at Bedford, was a fitting scene for the inauguration of his philanthropic career. Its walls were already glorified by the long captivity of Bunyan. Seldom does such a combination occur. From that obscure and petty prison proceeded, but at a long interval of time, two of the noblest and most precious works of man — Bunyan's Pilgrim's Progress, and Howard's labors of charity and love. Here that famous Puritan — a man whom Milton and Cromwell would have loved and honored — was confined, for twelve long years, after the restoration of the Stuart dynasty — 1660–72 — for the high crime and misdemeanor of denying the right divine of kings and hierarchs to govern wrong; and here, he not only conceived, but also wrote, his famous allegory, that true and genuine book — which has perhaps done more for the spread of real piety and religious sentiment in this country, than any other uninspired production; — supporting himself the while, by his industry in the art of making tags and purses; which he, in common with his fellow-captives, was permitted to sell to visitors. Himself a Puritan of the grand and genuine Miltonic stamp, Howard would certainly feel a deep respect and veneration for this prison on Bunyan's account; and here his own efforts and investigations were to begin. In the introductory remarks to his great work on The State of Prisons, he observes: — "The distress of prisoners, of which there are few who have not some imperfect idea, came more immediately under my notice when I was Sheriff of the County of Bedford; and the circumstance which excited me to activity in their behalf, was the seeing some, who, by the verdict of juries, were declared *not guilty* — some on whom the grand jury did not find such an appearance of guilt as subjected them to a trial — and some whose prosecutors did not appear against them — after having been confined for months, dragged back to gaol, and locked up again until they should pay *sundry fees*, to the gaoler, the clerk of assize, &c. In order to redress this hardship, I applied to the justices of the county for a salary to the *gaoler*, in lieu of his fees. The bench were properly affected with the grievance, and willing to grant the relief desired; but they wanted a precedent for charging the county with the expense. I therefore rode into several neighboring counties in search of a precedent; but I soon learned that the same injustice was practised in them; and looking into the prisons, I beheld scenes of calamity, which I grew daily more and more anxious to alleviate."

He had not been long engaged in these preliminary inquiries, before he became convinced that the general style of prison building in this county, at that time, was radically bad. In the gaol over which he was invested with a nominal charge, the two dungeons for felons were both eleven feet below the surface of the ground; one of the consequences was, that they were always damp, and sometimes the walls and floors — upon the latter, the inmates had also to sleep — were quite *wet*. There was but one court-yard for both sexes — a fault, which monstrous and revolting as it appears, he afterwards found to obtain in almost every gaol in the kingdom. In addition to these fundamental misprovisions, there were the common errors of administration — some of which are so pithily set forth in the extract just quoted. A person who had been incarcerated for debt, when he had arranged and settled with his creditor, could not obtain his liberty unless he had the wherewithal to fee the gaoler to the extent of 15*s*. 4*d*., and the turnkey 2*s*. In default of his ability to raise these sums — though the competent tribunals had pronounced him at liberty — he was thrust back into his dungeon, literally *to rot* — for in those days that common expression of the relentless creditor had the naked and terrible significance of truth. The same course was adopted with persons accused of crime — if declared *innocent*. For being innocent, a poor man might be imprisoned for life! The crying injustice of this last circumstance roused up all the energies of the Philanthropist's mind. It was indeed a wrong so manifest and flagrant, as to be almost difficult of belief. Our criminal code was then, in some respects quite diabolical: — a man might be left to die of starvation or fever in a gaol for *not* being guilty of any crime; and he might be hanged for breaking a hop-band in a garden in Kent, or stealing an old coat to the value of five shillings in Middlesex. And this was in the age of Pitt and Fox, of Burke and Sheridan, of Howard and Paley. Truly, it would seem that we have only just escaped from a state of semi-barbarism!

The sketch of the Fleet and Marshalsea, offered in the opening chapter of this history, will have made the reader acquainted with the mode of conducting prisons in the first half of the century. It may be here remarked, in brief, that no fundamental reforms had resulted from the parliamentary inquiry. Some few changes had taken place in the persons employed to administer the penal law — but the system, with all its defects, its folly and its crime, remained intact.

Howard's plan of dealing with these abuses, was by redeeming the fees, and at once changing them into a salary to the gaoler; — this was obviously the plain, practical way of meeting and mitigating the glaring wrong — as well as the shortest and cheapest. But if the Fee-system were abolished, how was the gaoler to be paid! At the present day one can hardly realize the strength of this obstacle. The new Sheriff proposed that the county should pay its own servants; but the magistrates must have precedents for such an innovation upon established custom. The right or wrong, the policy or impolicy of the thing was not to be considered: — only its traditions. And as the innovator could obtain no support from those who ought to have been his natural allies in the work of reform, until he could produce a warrant from prescription in its favor, he set forth in search of one. Towards the close of the year 1773, he began his tours of inspection — and was gradually led on to extend them into the nearer counties, — then into the neighboring kingdoms of the British empire, — then over the greater part of Europe, — and finally, to the other continents of the globe.

The first stage of his inquiries was Cambridge; the prison of which town he found very insecure and without a chaplain; here, in addition to the fee to the gaoler, the prisoner had to pay another to the sheriff, before he could obtain his liberty. He extended his journey to Huntingdon: the gaol of which he likewise inspected. He returned to Cardington, powerfully affected by the miseries which he had seen, but without having found the precedent of which he was in search. These glimpses, however, into the state of prisons, rather whetted his appetite for further investigation than allayed it; and he had not been many days at Cardington after his return, before he commenced a much wider range of inspection — taking in his route the large cluster of midland counties. His first point of observation, on this second journey, was Northampton, where he found that the gaoler, instead of receiving a salary for his services, actually paid forty pounds a year for his situation! This fact was not an unfair index to the material condition of the prison. The felons' court-yard was close and confined; and prisoners had no straw allowed them to sleep on. — Beds for prisoners were never thought of in those days. Leicester was next visited; the situation of the gaol received his explicit condemnation; it was pronounced incapable of being rendered either convenient or healthy. When debtors were unable to pay for accommodation — and it will be remembered that this would always be the case with honest insolvents, who had given everything up to their creditors — they were confined in a long dungeon, which was damp and dark, being under ground, and had only two small holes, the largest not more than 12 inches square, to let in light and air. The felons were kept in an under-ground dungeon — night and day; but they were provided with the luxury of coarse mats to sleep on. Altogether, the place was close and offensive; the court-yard was small; there was no chapel; and the governor had no salary, except what he could wring from his victims. At Nottingham, things were in much the same condition. The gaol was built on the declivity of a hill: down about five and twenty steps, were three rooms for such as could pay for them. The poorer and honester prisoners were compelled to descend twelve steps more into series of cells cut in the solid rock for their reception, — only one of which was in use at the time — a cavern, 21 feet long, 30 broad, and 7 feet high; in this horrible hole, human beings were sometimes immured for years!

Derby and Stafford presented, in some respects, a pleasing contrast to these pictures; in the former of these towns the prison was much cleaner than usual — in the latter, the prisoners were better fed. The state of the gaol at Lichfield is briefly portrayed: — "The rooms too small and close; no yard; no straw; no water." The privations expressed in these few words, assume a terrible form to those who can distinctly realize them. Howard next visited Warwick, Worcester, and Gloucester; the castle of the last-named city was in the most horrible condition. It had but one court for all prisoners — only one day-room for males and females. The debtor's ward had no windows, a part of the plaster wall being broken through to let in light. The night room (or main) for men felons, though up a number of steps, was found to be close and dark; and the floor so ruinous that it could not be washed. The whole prison was greatly out of repair, while it had not been whitewashed for years, Many persons had died in it the year preceding Howard's visit — a circumstance attributed to a fever engendered by a large dunghill which stood directly opposite to the stairs leading up to the sleeping-room. The keeper had no salary — the debtors no allowance of food! The first lived on extortion, the second on charity. Through Oxford and Aylesbury, the gaols of both of which places the self-appointed inspector examined, he returned to Cardington, to ponder on the strange scenes which he had witnessed, and to project schemes for their improvement.

The philanthropist may now be considered as fairly committed to his vocation. His unsleeping energies had at length found their fitting work; and he threw himself into it perfectly *con amore*. Ten days had hardly elapsed from the completion of his second journey, before he commenced a third. The more he saw of the gigantic evils of the gaol-system, the more he became convinced of the absolute necessity of a searching investigation into its practical details. This time, his plan included a series of visits to the prisons of the various counties of Herts, Wilts, Berks, Dorset, Hants, and Sussex — the general condition of which he found to be of a character with those already described. We can only notice here a few of the more salient points. The prison of Salisbury had only one yard, and no day-room at all, for either felons or debtors; each of these classes had, however, fires in their respective sleeping rooms, made on a brick hearth — but no chimneys! Just outside the gate of the prison was a large chain passed through a staple fixed in the wall, at either end of which a debtor, padlocked by the leg, stood selling to the public, nets, purses, laces, and other similar articles of gaol manufacture — as good old Bunyan had often done in the previous century. There was another still more singular custom practised and permitted here — which consisted in chaining prisoners together at Christmas time, and sending them thus secured into the city to beg; one carrying a basket to receive donations of provisions, another a box for money, and so forth. The gaoler had no salary; but made his living by farming out the diet of the detenues; how the latter would fare under such a dispensation, the reader may readily surmise. The other visits of this journey required no particular remark. Even the best gaols were bad — the worst were quite intolerable to men of ordinary human feeling.

Returning to spend the Christmas at Cardington, in company with his boy, Howard determined afterwards to extend his inspections into the northern counties of England; and as soon as his son's holidays were over, he started off — taking Okeham in Rutlandshire on his way. At York Castle, the difference of the accomodation for debtors and felons was very striking. The debtors' apartments were airy, spacious, healthy, and the provisions were sufficient and regularly doled out. Few English gaols, could boast so excellent a plan. But the criminal department fully redeemed the Riding from the charge of ultra-humanity. Its court-yard was small and without water — the pump being ingeniously placed just outside the palisades; water had consequently to be carried in by the servants of the establishment — a circumstance which sufficiently accounted for the filthiness of the place. Considering the very imperfect means of ventilation then known, the cells were horribly small — being only 7½ feet long, 6½ wide, and 8½ high; that is, each cell contained about 414 cubic feet of air, being less than thirty-six hours' consumption for a single individual; in addition to which they were close and dark — having only a hole of about 4 inches by 8 over the door, or half a dozen perforations of an inch or so in diameter, by which the scanty and poisoned air of the narrow passages serving to divide the cells might enter, if it could. Yet, in these dungeons, *three* human beings were commonly locked up for the night, which in winter lasted fourteen to sixteen hours! There could be no wonder that the destroyer was so busy in this gaol, — for into these loathsome holes the victims were nightly thrust, with only a damp floor, barely covered by a wretched pittance of straw, for their bed of rest; while a sewer, which ran through one of the passages, rendered them still more intolerably offensive. The infirmary for the sick consisted of but a single room, — so that when there was in it an inmate of one sex, the sick of the other — should there be any, as was frequently the case — had to remain in their noisome dens until death relieved them from their sufferings! A case of this kind came under Howard's immediate notice. At the time of his visit a woman was sick, and of course she occupied the infirmary; a man was afterwards seized with the distemper — always raging with greater or lesser virulence in the prisons of that period — but he was forced to remain, ill as he was, in his fever-infected cell. It is really difficult to realize a fact like this, and so near our own day too! "Sick and in prison" is a phrase which at all times and under all circumstances conveys to the heart and mind of man a strange sense of desolation and misery — the thought of being sick and in prison in York Castle, must have had far more of the flavor of hell than of earth in it. The city gaol of York was no better than that for the county.

Leaving these sickening sights behind, Howard turned again towards the south, visiting on his way the prisons of Lincoln, Huntingdon, and Ely. In the episcopal city of Ely, some reforms had recently been made, in consequence of a public exposure of the cruelties exercised in the old gaol. The building was ricketty and ruinous — totally unfit for the safe custody of criminals. Of this the wardens were well aware; but instead of strengthening the walls and doors — which would have cost money and affected the episcopal coffers — they adopted the cheaper plan of chaining the prisoners on their backs to the floor, passing over them several bars of iron, and fastening an iron collar, covered with spikes, round their necks, as well as placing a heavy bar of the same metal over their legs, to prevent attempts to escape! Prisoners were confined in this inhuman manner because the Bishop chose to allow his prison-house to fall into decay. A year or two before Howard's visit to Ely, a spirited magistrate named Collyer, brought the case of these atrocious cruelties under the notice of the King; the statement of the matter was so flagrant, that an inquiry was immediately ordered to be instituted; and in 1768, Bishop Mawson was compelled to rebuild, in part, and otherwise repair the gaol, so as to render such cruelties unnecessary for the future; but in spite of these improvements, considering that the prison was the property of a bishop, when Howard entered it, it was still in a sickly, filthy, miserable condition. The keeper received no salary — save what he could extort from the poor wretches under his charge; there was no chapel for public worship — no surgeon to attend upon the sick. Neither felons nor debtors had any fixed allowance of food; the former had a small court — in which however was a most offensive sewer — appropriated to their use, but no water; the latter had no free ward; no straw to lie on; no infirmary for the sick. Nor did the owner of this property think proper to adopt any one of the suggestions of the philanthropist for its improvement — as was almost ever the case with lay proprietors; for all these evils remained and accumulated, even when the whole kingdom was alive and ringing with the cry for reform in such matters. On Howard's last visit to this gaol — many years subsequent to this period, *i.e.* on the 6th of February, 1782 — instead of the better state of things which he had a right to expect, he found that — the march of improvement in this case going backward — debtors and felons had actually been placed together! One of the former was confined for a debt of 3*s.* 5½*d.*, and costs 8*s.* 3*d.* Another, a man who had a wife and five children depending on his care and labor, was detained for costs only — namely, for charges 4*s.* 9*d.*, and fees 3*s.* 6*d.* In cases like these, it was the custom of the philanthropist to discharge the obligation, and set the captive free; but his modesty has kept from the knowledge of the world the particular instances in which his generosity was so taxed. At such a time what a blessed thing is wealth!

From Ely he proceeded to Norwich, where he found the cells built under ground, and the keeper paying forty pounds a year to the Under-Sheriff for his situation. The gaol delivery was but once a year; and the allowance for straw for the whole prison was only a guinea per annum. In the castle of this city — used as the county gaol of Norfolk — there was an under-ground dungeon for male felons, into which the inmates descended by a ladder, the floor of which was often one or two feet deep in water! However, some parts of the establishment met with thc cordial approval of the inspector. From Norwich, Howard went to Ipswich — all the gaols of which he examined, and found in tolerable order; and thence to London, where he stayed about a fortnight, going through several of the chief prisons, visiting his friends, and arranging his future plan of operations. The crusade had now commenced in earnest.

At the end of a fortnight, he started upon a tour through the west of England — his first halting-place being Exeter, where he found that the felons' gaol for the great county of Devonshire, was the private property of an individual, John Denny Rolle, whose family had long held it as a grant from the Duchy of Cornwall, and who at this time received from it an income of twenty-two pounds a year paid by the keeper — who, in his turn, had no other means of recovering this sum, and of gaining a livelihood for himself and family, than out of the fees of the prisoners and the profits of the sale of small beer. These facts would naturally prepare the visitor to expect any amount of disorder, corruption, and petty tyranny in its government — and he was not disappointed. The night dungeons, though but a few steps under ground, were close, dark, and confined; the windows small, and the whole very unhealthy. An infirmary had been built, but the steps leading up to it were in a ruinous state; and the surgeon told his visitor that he — the surgeon — was excused by contract from attending any prisoner in the cells, who might be sick of the gaol fever!! As we have said, the keeper paid Mr. Rolle a yearly sum for his office — though the family possessed an estate granted for the purpose of enabling it to uphold this very prison in a state of security and conveniency: into such a state of corruption had the administration of such like trusts then fallen! At the period of Howard's first visit, two sailors were in the gaol, who for some petty fault had been fined by a magistrate 1*s.* each, detained because unable to discharge the large fees of the gaoler and the clerk of the peace — the first amounting to 14*s.* 4*d.*, the latter to 1*l.* 1*s.* 4*d.*; total 1*l.* 15*s.* 8*d.* Having no means of satisfying these claims, the honest blue-jackets were condemned "to rot in gaol." The other prisons of this city also received a number of careful inspections from the philanthropist — the report of which are of like character with the foregoing.

In the intervals of these various examinations, he made a short trip to Launceston in Cornwall, the prison of which he thus paints: — "The prison is a room, or passage, 23 feet by 7½, with only one small window, and three dungeons, or cages on the side opposite; these are about 6½ feet deep; one 9 feet long, one about 8; one not 5. This last for women. They were all very offensive; no chimney; no water; no sewers; damp earth floors; no infirmary. The court not secure, and prisoners seldom permitted to go out to it. Indeed the whole prison is out of repair, and yet the gaoler lives distant. I once found the prisoners chained two or three togother. Their provision was put down to them through a hole in the floor of the room above; and those who served them there, often caught the fatal fever. At my first visit, I found the keeper, his assistant, and all the prisoners but one, sick of it; and heard that a few years before many prisoners had died of it — and the keeper and his wife in one night." From Exeter, Howard went to Ilchester, Bristol, Hereford, Monmouth, and finally returned to London.

About this period, as will be more particularly related in the sequel, public attention began to be addressed to the subject of prisons and prisoners. The palpable injustice of incarcerating a man declared *not guilty* on a pretence of a claim upon him for fees, had presented itself to such enlightened minds as accident had directed to contemplate the condition of the pariahs of our society — and before the commencement of Howard's inquiries, that is, on the 18th of February, 1773, Mr. Popham, member for Taunton, brought a bill into the House of Commons abolishing gaolers' fees, and substituting for them fixed salaries, payable out of the county rates. This bill went through two readings, but was withdrawn on the third, with a view to its being again brought forward in an amended form. Between that and the following session of Parliament, the Recluse of Cardington had been called from his village life to the work whose commencement we have narrated: the two men most anxious for a reform in these matters soon came together; and before Howard set off on his tour to the west of England, it is probable that the plan of the campaign in the Legislature had been agreed upon between him, Mr. Popham, and their mutual friends. This western journey completed his first series of investigations, and prepared him to undergo that personal examination before the House of Commons, which he was most likely aware would take place on his return.

In the course of the inquiries, so rapidly passed over in this narrative, Howard had collected together a great mass of elementary material — of hard, dry, tangible facts, — the only real data on which reasoning could proceed or enactments be safely based. And of this, statesmen of all parties seem to have been conscious. On the conclusion of his rapid survey, the House of Commons resolved itself into a Committee of the whole House, to cite him to its bar, hear his report, and examine him thereupon. This examination, on a subject so novel, and at the same time so important, excited no small degree of public attention. Howard's answers to the various questions proposed to him were so clear, unreserved, and practical — his testimony against the manifold abuses of the penal system was so logical and conclusive — his evidence, amply supported by facts and illustrated from minute personal knowledge as to the unhealthiness of the majority of the prisons of this country, and his several suggestions for their improvement, were all so satisfactory to his auditors that, on the House resuming, the chairman, Sir Thomas Clavering, at the instance of the Committee, moved — "That John Howard, Esq., be called to the bar, and that Mr. Speaker do acquaint him that the House are very sensible of the humanity and zeal which have led him to visit the several gaols of this kingdom, and to communicate to the House the interesting observations which he has made upon that subject." He was accordingly called for, and in the name of the supreme Legislature of his country was thanked for his philanthropic exertions — an honor seldom accorded by that body to other than the minsters of war and conquest. A circumstance, however, occurred during this very examination, which shows how little his sublime patriotism and philanthropy were appreciated at first — even in the highest assembly in the land. One of the members, surprised at the extent and minuteness of his inspections, requested to be informed at whose expense he travelled! "A question to which," Dr. Aikin says, "he could hardly reply without expressing some indignant emotion."

CHAPTER VI.

THE PRISON-WORLD OF ENGLAND.

His public examination was no sooner over than Howard again continued his inquiries. Hastily passing from town to town, much of the information which he had collected required revision and confirmation — and, as yet, he had only seen a few of the principal houses of detention in a few of the chief cities of the empire. Ireland was untouched — perhaps as yet unthought of. Scotland lay equally far away. Even London, with its swarm of gaols, was almost unknown to him. His new labors began with these. On the 16th of March, 1774, he made his first call at the Marshalsea, in Southwark. Some improvements had been introduced into this establishment in consequence of the inquiries referred to in the opening chapter of this work, but they were only of a minor nature, and it was still the model of a bad gaol. The buildings were greatly out of repair; the charges were exorbitantly high; the promiscuous intercourse of persons of all grades, debtors and felons, young and old, male and female, still continued; the largest portion of the premises was let out to a man not a prisoner, who kept a shop in some of the rooms, lived with his family in others, and sub-let the remainder; there was still no infirmary for the sick, the fees were heavy, and garnish had not been abolished. In addition to all which facts, came the crowning one — the prisoners had no regular allowance of food! This is no doubt a tolerable list of grievances, but on this occasion we hear nothing of those extreme punishments which had formerly been inflicted at the caprice of the warden or his subordinates — cruelties which more readily suggested the idea of a Portuguese inquisition than that of an English gaol.

Four days after this visit to the Marshalsea in London, we find him inspecting the high gaol at Durham. The earnest spirit of enterprise which urged him on — contrasting the magnitude of the work with the brief space of time in which it must be done, if done by him — caused a rapidity in his movements which tends not a little to baffle the follower of his footsteps. His account of the condition of this gaol is terrible beyond the power of language to deepen: —"The debtors have no court; their free wards in the low gaol are two damp, unhealthy rooms, 10 feet 4 inches square. They are never suffered to go out of these, unless to chapel, and not always to that: for on a Sunday when I was there I missed them at chapel; they told me they were not permitted to go thither. No sewers. At more than one of my visits I learned that the dirt, ashes,

&c., had lain there many months. . . . . The felons have no court; but they have a day-room and two small rooms for an infirmary. The men are put at night into dungeons; one 7 feet square for three prisoners; another, the great hole, 16½ feet by 12, has only a little window. In this I saw six prisoners, most of them transports, chained to the floor. In that situation they had been many weeks, and were very sickly. Their straw on the stone floor almost worn to dust! Long confinement, and not having the king's allowance of 2*s*. 6*d*. a-week, had urged them to attempt an escape, after which the gaoler changed them as above. . . . Common-side debtors, in the low gaol, whom I saw eating boiled bread and water, told me that this was the only nourishment some had lived upon for nearly twelve months. . . . . At several of my visits there were boys between thirteen and fifteen years of age confined with the most profligate and abandoned." Yet this was an episcopal prison, the property of the bishop of Durham, and boasted a regular chaplaincy.

From this scene, Howard went to Newcastle-upon-Tyne, in which he found an honorable contrast to the above. The rooms of the prison were over ground, light and airy; the inmates had food, bedding and fuel provided; and the entire place had an aspect of cleanliness and order. At Morpeth, principles of administration of a very different kind prevailed. Here he found three transports chained to the floor of a dark, offensive dungeon — merely on *suspicion* of a desire to escape, because they had been illegally deprived of the convict's usual allowance! At Carlisle, again, he witnessed another specimen of the same injustice and indignity. A rapid excursion through the counties of Cumberland, Westmoreland and Lancaster, the chief prisons of which he inspected on the way, brought the philanthropist to Chester — on the prison of which he has the following notes: "This castle is the property of the king. The first room is a hall. There are two staircases leading up from it to four rooms for master's-side debtors. Down eighteen steps is a small court, which was once common to debtors and felons. It is lately divided; but the high, close pales which separate the two courts, now so very small, deprive both debtors and felons of the benefit of fresh air, and the keeper has no view of the felon's court or day-room, in which men and women are together. . . . . Under the pope's kitchen is a dark passage, twenty-four feet by nine; the descent to it is by twenty-one steps, from the court; no window; not a breath of fresh air; only two apertures lately made with grates in the ceiling into the room above. On one side of it are six cells (stalls), each about 7½ feet by 3, with a barrack bedstead, and an aperture over the door about 8 inches by 4. In each of these are locked up at night sometimes three or four felons. They pitch these dungeons two or three times a-year. When I was in one of them I ordered the door to be shut, and my situation brought to mind what I had heard of the Black Hole at Calcutta." The city gaol and the city bridewell were in much the same general condition; in the latter were seen a number of leaden weights marked respectively, 30, 40, 60 pounds, with a ring and chain attached to each. If any prisoner became refractory, one of these weights was fastened to his leg, so that he could not move without carrying the weight with him. The practice is still found in some parts of Switzerland. Howard's next point of observation was Wrexham. Although this was one of the largest towns in the principality of Wales, the county gaol only occupied a part of a house — the remainder being used as a parish workhouse; a circumstance which was thought to indicate a low average of crime in the neighborhood. But, if smaller, it was not better than other prisons. The two chambers set apart for prisoners were dark and dirty, being entirely without windows, and having a dead wall within six feet of their doors. The poor wretches confined in them often complained of being almost suffocated, and begged to be taken out for a little air! The whole place was out of repair — dirty — offensive — and without water. Passing through Shrewsbury — where some improvements were making — Stafford, Derby, Nottingham, Leicester, and Northampton, in all of which places Howard visited and revisted the various abodes of misery, he returned once more to Cardington.

He did not, however, remain long in seclusion. Time had now acquired a new value. Only seven days were given up to repose, to the classification and arrangement of the materials which he had got together, to private intercourse with his family and friends, to the superintendence of his own affairs — and way he went again on his great errand. The middle of April, 1774, he employed in inspecting the various prisons of Kent; the remainder of the month, and the commencement of May, was occupied in further researches amongst those of the metropolis. Several of these he had not before visited — the bridewell of Clerkenwell was one. This gaol he found to be much out of repair; it had not even been whitewashed for years. The night-rooms for the women were dark and unwholesome in the extreme — having beds for those only who could pay for such a luxury, — whilst the others were not even permitted to have a little straw to keep them from the cold, hard floor of the cell! One of the rooms for the men was so densely crowded, that there was absolutely not space enough for them all to sleep on the ground — and many were compelled to sleep in hammocks slung to the ceiling. There was no infirmary for the sick — and yet the gaol distemper raged with tremendous virulence amongst this mass of filth, disease, want, and licentiousness. The only allowance of food to the wretched captives was one penny loaf per day.

The bridewell of Tothill Fields, thanks to the humane efforts of the keeper, George Smith — of whom Howrad makes most honorable mention, — was in a much better condition. The Fleet retained its old character. If it did not actually present to its philanthropic visitor those darker aspects of guilt and cruelty which it offered to the parliamentary committee fifty years before, it still exhibited, on the whole, a picture of riot, dissipation, and extortion which it was most painful to contemplate in a prison. The various fees amounted to 1*l*. 8*s*. 8*d*. The garnish, though declared illegal, was still rigorously exacted. There was no surgeon. The prisoners had no regular allowance of food, and the charities, on which the poorer sort depended for the means of existence, were mis-managed in the most shameless manner. The idle and dissolute part of the public was admitted, as into any other public-house, and, along with the prisoners, passed the day in playing at billiards, skittles, mississippi, fines, and other games — in drinking, chanting lewd and bacchanalian songs, and in various other debaucheries. Convivial parties made another feature of the establishment. On Monday evenings there was a wine club; on Thursday evenings a beer club held its weekly saturnalia. The orgies usually lasted till two or three in the morning, and on these occasions — openly connived at, because to the benefit of the tap — the riot and excess were beyond all bounds. The Fleet was burnt down during the riots of 1780, and was afterwards rebuilt on an improved plan; but the fundamental faults in its administration remained, and were not finally done away with until the edifice itself was levelled with the ground in our own time.

During the whole of his stay in London, Howard was out daily — traversing the vast area of the metropolis, penetrating into all kinds of dark nooks and corners. Nothing was too obscure to escape his vigilance; no prison, compter, or spunging-house, was too paltry for his visitations. Besides those greater gaols already spoken of in detail, The King's Bench, The Poultry Compter, The New Ludgate, and a whole host of inferior places of detention, were searched out thoroughly, and their strange secrets brought to light. No fry was too small for him. Every hole into which unfortunate beings could be thrust — and misery made more miserable — was considered worthy of his attention. Petty prisons, belonging to courts, manors and liberties, of which very few even suspected the existence, until he found his way into them, were explored and reported upon. Many of these petty gaols were perfect hells in their small way. There was a petty prison in Whitechapel, used for the confinement of debtors in sums of more than two pounds, and less than five. For these trifling amounts, five-and-twenty persons were incarcerated in a gaol quite out of repair, and only possessing the most miserable accommodation for such as could pay the exorbitant demands of the keeper; who, on his part, had not merely no salary paid to him for his services, but had to share with the lady of the manor — whose property the prison was — the proceeds of his extortion, to the extent of twenty-four pounds a year. Although these wretches were confined for sums which only the very poor would be unable to pay, they were nevertheless forced to find 2*s.* 10½*d.* each for garnish, to be drank by their new comrades at the keeper's tap; besides which they were not permitted to share in the produce of the begging-box, miserable as it was, until they had paid the gaoler an additional fee of 2*s.* 6*d.*, and treated the community to half-a-gallon of beer. Howard found there ten or twelve noisy fellows playing at skittles, and noticing the fact, was told they were only visitors! A few days after his visit to this strange place, we find him pursuing his inquiries at a house of detention for Tower Hamlets; being a public-house in Weliclose-square, kept by an honest Swede — who was at once host and gaoler. French captives used to be confined in this place. When Howard first called, there was only one prisoner; and although, at intervals, he continued to look in for several years, he never saw more than one person here at a time. The house was almost in ruins. Similar to this was St. Catherine's Gaol — a small house, two stories high, and having but two rooms on a floor. At his first visit, it had no inmates;

but he did not therefore neglect it in his subsequent rounds. He never found any one, however, in its durance — and the last time he called, even the keeper had vanished, and it was uninhabited. The last prison which he examined during his present sojourn in the metropolis, was the Borough Compter, in Tooley-street, Southwark. Here, debtors and felons were huddled together in the most approved fashion of the times. "The prison is much out of repair, and ruinous; no infirmary; no bedding; no straw" — such is the laconic description given of it by the philanthropist. The debtors, however, enjoyed the advantage of a legacy from Nell Gwynn, consisting of sixty-five penny-loaves every eight weeks — but a scanty provision for such numbers as were here commonly crowded together. This building was pulled down by the rioters of 1780.

From the 4th of May to the 24th of June, we have no trace of Howard's whereabouts. It is probable that his health had suffered somewhat from his constant exertions, and the many perils to which they had exposed him — perils which even medical practitioners in some cases, and gaolers in many, refused to participate with him, — and that, on the completion of his laborious survey of the London prisons, he returned to Cardington for a few weeks of repose and quiet. While thus lying by, recruiting his strength for fresh trials, he had the gratification to see his efforts in the cause of prison reform begin to bear the most precious fruits. In consequence of the information which he had laid before the House of Commons, two bills had been brought forward — based on the original draft of Mr. Popham — for the better regulation of prisons, which in due course received the sanction of the legislature and the crown. The first of these enactments, passed on the 31st of March, 1774, declares that all prisoners against whom no bills of indictment shall be found by the grand jury, or who shall be discharged by proclamation for want of prosecution, shall be immediately set at large in open court, without payment of any fee or sum of money to the sheriff or gaoler, in respect of such discharge; and, abolishing all such fees for the future, it directs the payment, in lieu of them, of a sum not exceeding 13*s*. 4*d*. out of the county rate — or out of the public stock of cities, towns, and hamlets not contributing to such rate — for every prisoner discharged in either of the cases provided for by the statute. The other bill, which became law on the 2d of June,—*i. e.* while Howard was resting from his labors at Cardington — authorizes and requires the justices to see that the walls and ceilings of all prisons within their respective jurisdictions, be scraped and whitewashed once a year at least, — that the rooms be regularly washed and ventilated, — that infirmaries be provided for the sick, and proper care taken of the same, — to order clothes for the prisoners when they see occasion — to prevent their being kept in under-ground dungeons, whenever they can,—and, generally, to take such measures as shall tend to restore and preserve their health.

With what satisfaction Howard would receive these humane and necessary laws, may be readily imagined; but he did not content himself with merely seeing them placed among the statutes at large. His work did not end there,—for his experience had shown him how powerless were even good laws in the hands of ignorant or selfish functionaries; and how much uncertainty prevailed amongst them as to what was or was not strictly legal. In order, therefore, that no time might be lost in rendering the new laws operative, he caused them to be reprinted in a larger character—at his own expense—and sent a copy of them to every warden and gaoler in the kingdom.

Having dispatched this business, and put the new laws into a fair train for coming into speedy operation, Howard again set out upon his sacred mission—still further to complete and correct his gleanings, and personally to overlook the enforcement of the Acts. This time his visits lay to the principal gaols in the different counties of North Wales, and many of those in South Wales—in addition to revisitation of such English prisons as lay in his routes. During this tour of inspection a new subject of investigation forced itself upon his attention—The Bridewells. He thus refers to the origin of these new inquiries;—"Seeing in two or three of them [the county gaols] some poor creatures whose aspect was singularly deplorable, and asking the cause of it, the answer was, 'They were lately brought from the bridewells.' This started a fresh subject of inquiry. I resolved to inspect the bridewells; and for that purpose travelled again into the counties where I had been, and indeed into all the rest — examining houses of correction, city and town gaols. I beheld in many of them, as well as in the county gaols, a complicacation of distress; but my attention was chiefly fixed by the gaol-fever and the small-pox, which I saw prevailing to the destruction of multitudes, not only of felons in their dungeons, but of debtors also." Toward the end of July, 1774, we find the indefatigable tourist setting out on a new journey — not having been at Cardington for more than a few days. In this tour he travelled many hundreds of miles — traversed fifteen counties — and examined, with very minute attention, fifty prisons; but as the particular reports present only the same general features as those already produced, we shall pass them over very rapidly in this place, noting only a few points of especial interest, by the way. Re-calling at Reading and Ilchester, he moved on — inspecting, advising relieving, as he went — to Taunton, Shepton, Mallet, Devizes, Marlborough, Bath, Gloucester, Hereford, Monmouth, Brecon, Cardigan, Haverfordwest, Carmarthen, and Cardiff. At this last-named town, a new gaol was being built. A circumstance came to his knowledge here, which must have caused him not a little regret that his visit had not been somewhat earlier. A poor man had been confined in the gaol for an exchequer debt of seven pounds; for ten long years he had borne up against the hardships of his dungeon — but with small hope of ever regaining his liberty. At length his strength and patience were exhausted. He had given way, and died of that sickness of the heart — long baffled hope — only a short time before the Friend of the Captive entered his now deserted cell.

From Cardiff, Howard proceeded through Cowbridge into England, where he continued his journey by way of Usk, Berkley, Bristol, Taunton, Bridgewater, Exeter, Bodmin, and Lostwithiel, to Plymouth, the gaol of which had a room for felons called the Chink, 17 feet long, 8 wide, and only 5½ high — so that a person of ordinary stature could not stand erect in it! This diabolical dungeon was also dark and stifling — having neither air nor light, except such as could struggle through a wicket in the door, 5 inches by 7 in dimensions. Yet Howard learned with horror, that *three* men had been kept in this den, under a sentence of transportation, for nearly two months! They could neither see, nor breathe freely, nor could they stand upright. To keep alive at all, they were forced to crouch — each in his turn — at the wicket, to catch a few inspirations of air: otherwise they must have died of suffocation — for the door was rarely opened. When Howard saw it, the door had not been opened for five weeks — and yet it was inhabited! He caused the bolts to be shot and an entry made; but the indescribable stench which issued, would have driven back any less courageous visitor:—he, however, forced his way in, and found there a pallid, miserable wretch, who had languished in that living grave for seventy mortal days, awaiting transportation. The prisoner declared to his questioner that he would prefer being executed at once, to being buried any longer in his loathsome dungeon—and no wonder. The rest of the gaol was in keeping with this specimen. With his usual chariness of words, Howard thus describes it:—"The whole is dirty, and has not been whitewashed for many years; no court; no water; no straw."

From this scene of horror, we trace the footsteps of the philanthropist through Dorchester, Sherborne, Salisbury, Winchester, Gosport, Southampton, Portsmouth, Newport, in the isle of Wight, Petworth, Chichester, and Horsham, home again to Cardington, where fresh labors awaited him, and a new path opened before him, which for a time threatened to divert or at least divide his attention with the one great subject which had lately engrossed his thoughts.

All the world knows that Woburn Abbey, the princely residence of the ducal house of Russell, is situated in the vicinity of Bedford, from which town the family obtains its title—and that, as usually happens in the neighborhood of English aristocratical domains, the influence of the family is, and ever has been, almost paramount in the politics of the place. At that period it owned, however, a not undisputed supremacy. The corporation of the town was sometimes more than a little restive under the yoke — and then, particularly, quite a feud was raging between the rival influences. As is well known, the Duke of Bedford of that day was not a popular man — and in the year 1769 — forever rendered memorable by the appearance of the letters of Junius, in which the duke makes but a wretched figure — the corporation finally broke with him, and set up for independence. "Wilkes and Liberty!" was then the great cry of the country. The unrivalled irony of Junius — the clever diatribes of Horne Tooke (then simple parson Horne, son of honest John Horne, poulterer, of Newport-street, Westminster) — the city eloquence of Alderman Townshend and Sawbridge — and the turbulent energy of a whole host of minor antagonists, had considerably shaken the credit of the ministry with the nation, and raised up opposition to its members, even among their more immediate friends and dependants — as it was then the custom to call all parties having any political connection with the heads of great families. The public assaults upon the Lord of Woburn Abbey had been too frequent and decisive — the corruptions charged home to him too outrageous and well sustained, not to have aroused the vindictive feeling of those who had but too deeply felt his former power.

The corporation of Bedford, assuming a patriotic attitude, determined to free their town, if possible, from the yoke of the Abbey — but in order to carry this point, that body had recourse to a plan which was at least questionable in a legal point of view, and obviously open to great abuses: that is, during the height of the Wilkes controversy — when the popular sympathies were with them — they ventured to create, in one day, 500 honorary freemen, of the borough, at the head of whom were Horne Tooke and other popular leaders. Whether this move answered its intention, it is not the province of this work to inquire; suffice it to say, that its legality or illegality remained for a while untested by any regular issue in a court of law.

In a few years, however, the public excitement wore away — the patriotic fervor declined — and the authority of the corporation fell into the hands of a clique of persons, who employed their power over the honorary freemen of their creation for selfish and unworthy ends. The recent move had placed influence in their hands; and they used it for their personal profit and aggrandizement, just as the lords of Woburn Abbey had done when their power was in the ascendant. Supported by these new votes, they disposed of the representation at their pleasure. But voters who did not belong to the clique were far from being satisfied with this state of affairs. They charged the corporation with venality and tyranny. Within the town itself, an opposition arose to the dictatorial policy of the municipal body; though for a time this opposition did not assume a distinct form and organization. But at length the signal was given — and the two parties stood in presence of each other. At the point in the narrative of Howard's labors at which we have now arrived, Bedford was on the eve of an election. Reposing on its numerical strength, and confident from its long undisputed supremacy in the politics of the borough, the corporation — at least so it was said and generally believed — put up the representation for public sale. At first there was some difficulty in procuring candidates on the terms demanded; but they persevered, and success at length crowned their patriotic search. They found their men, and having made their bargain, presented them to the proposed constituency. The buyers were Sir William Wake, Bart., and Mr. Robert Sparrow — persons of great wealth, but strangers to the neighborhood, and publicly as well as personally unknown to the electors.

It is not to be supposed that so shameless an attempt to trade with the rights and liberties of freeborn men would be quietly endured by a whole constituency; even Bedford contained a number of spirited inhabitants, who could not tamely sit down while such things were being done in their name. The enlightened portion of the public of all parties — churchmen and dissenters, reformers and ministerialists — joined together for resistance; and casting about them for persons to lead in the matter, naturally fixed their eyes on Howard and his intimate friend and relative Mr. Whitbread — men of whose private worth and public spirit they were well aware. As the entire opposition was improvised, the invitation to come forward as a candidate came upon the former quite unexpectedly. As soon as he arrived at Cardington from his western tour, a deputation waited upon him with the proposal. The day of the election was then only a fortnight distant, and the position of the two parties extremely unequal. Besides the aid of the corporation, the rival candidates had availed themselves of the ordinary machinery of corruption in a wholesale manner — and had had all the advantage of a long personal canvass. The entire constituency was only about 1100; and the municipal faction, a compact and well-organized party in itself, could count, in addition to its own resources, upon the great majority of its 500 creatures. The chances of success for the reformers were therefore not very great. The justice of their cause, and the reputation of the patriotic candidates, were however no mean advantages. There was little time for deliberation — and Howard decided at once. He threw himself into the scale. His motives for so doing can hardly be considered personal. The thought which chiefly actuated him, was a desire to open up to Anglican Dissenters a path to public employments and parliamentary honors. As in the case of the shrievalty, there was a principle at stake — and Howard in the House of

Commons, would have been, in respect to the law or fashion of exclusion, a wholesome example to the country at large. It is a pleasing instance of the great respect in which his character was held by those who knew him most intimately as a neighbor and a magistrate, that we find men of all ranks and creeds forgetting their petty jealousies of him and of each other — a thing less easy and less frequently done in those days than now — banding themselves together, to fight, under his banner, the common battle against injustice and corruption. Some of the most orthodox ministers and members of the English Church did themselves and their denomination credit, on this occasion, by cordially acting with Howard's committee to secure his return.

A country town election is very amusing to those engaged in it, and very exciting while it lasts. In this case, as there was little time for preparation, the excitement was only the greater for being crowded into fewer days. For a small borough, party feeling ran mountain high. An extempore contest is usually a rough one; and here was a sudden stand-up fight between venality and respectability. Wake and Sparrow were regarded as purchasers of their expected honors; the fact was gravely recognized, even in the pulpit. During the height of the election-fever, a patriotic clergyman of the established church, startled his hearers on Sunday morning, by taking for his text — "Are not two *Sparrows* sold for one farthing? Fear ye not, therefore, ye are of more value than many Sparrows."

At length came the day of trial. Each party went to the poll confident of victory — the most knowing being well aware that the contest would be a hard one. The faction of the municipality had a manifest advantage over the opponents, in the fact of having the working of all the machinery of the election in their own hands; and it was generally expected that whatever might be the result of the polling, they would declare their own candidates returned. In the subsequent scrutiny, it appeared that they were not slow in availing themselves of this chance of success. The returning officer was charged with gross partiality in rejecting certain votes, tendered for his political opponents, which had never before been objected to; and with receiving many others, for his own friends, which ought not to have been received. Thus worked, there is little wonder that the popular candidates — neither of them men to stoop to any indirect means of gaining a vote — should have been placed at the bottom of the poll. The results published were: — Wake, 527; Sparrow, 517; Whitbread, 429; Howard, 402.

Considering the sudden way in which the contest had been got up on the part of the patriots, and the corrupt influences which the corporation had brought to bear upon it, this return was not discreditable to the losers. That Mr. Whitbread should have commanded a few more votes than Howard, admits of the simplest explanation. His property in the neighhood was immense, that of his friend was comparatively insignificant; in addition to which he was a member of the Church of England, and on that score alone would receive the support of many persons, to whom all the virtues of Howard could not atone for his heterodoxy. And at the bottom, this election was considered, not only by his immediate supporters, but by many congregations throughout the country — and also by himself — as in some sort a Dissenters' affair, — as a species of manifesto, or demonstration, of their reviving power and influence in the councils of the nation. A letter which will be quoted by and by, is decisive on this point.

The two gentlemen at the head of the poll, were of course returned as duly elected, the other two, convinced that they had been excluded only by the grossest unfairness, resolved to petition against the return, and thus bring the question of the legality or illegality of the proceedings of the corporation to an issue. In the interval which elapsed between the election and the time when his presence would be required in London in support of the joint petition, the Apostle of Suffering did not waste his time in vainly brooding over his imagined wrongs. Ere the bustle of the contest could well be over in the streets of Bedford, we find him traversing with great rapidity the large manufacturing counties of York, Lancaster, and Warwick; investigating the criminal state of those important districts, and revisiting on his way many other, to him now well known, abodes of misery, — particularly the bridewells. As a specimen of the condition in which he found some of these latter, we transcribe his account of one at Follingham, in Lincolnshire:—"In this prison, under the keeper's house, are five damp rooms; two of which were used for a lunatic, who was confined here for some years. The men's lodging-room, (18 feet by 9¾, and 6 feet 9 inches high,) has only an aperture in the door, a foot square, into the work-room. The women's room is 13 feet by 8, and 6 feet two inches high. In another room, 20½ feet by 12, you go down by a trap-door in the floor seven steps into a horrid dungeon, (10 feet square, 5½ feet high;) no chimney; small court; no pump; no sewer. Yet a woman, with a child at her breast, was sent hither for a year and a day! The child died." His reports upon the others do not call for any particular observation in this place. At the end of November he again reached home, having done much good,—and bringing back a new mass of valuable facts and observations.

On the 6th of December dates the commencement of a new tour of observation,—this time taking the direction of the principal towns and cities of Essex, Suffolk, Norfolk, Cambridge, and Hertford. After a rest of a few days, this journey was continued into Ireland, Scotland, and the northern counties of England. Few memorials of these various investigations remain. With the state of prisons in Ireland, the Philanthropist seems to have been much gratified, especially, with the facts, which soon came to his knowledge, that in most of them no liquors were suffered to be sold — that the clergyman was empowered to order the felons' bread for the parish in which he resided — that the separation of male and female convicts was generally provided for and enforced, — and with some minor points of discipline, all favorably contrasting with the arrangements in similar places in the sister country. His visit to Scotland was very brief, but was nevertheless honorable to himself and of signal service to that part of the kingdom. The magistrates and people of Glasgow seem to have been the first to pay the tribute of public honors to the extraordinary man who now appeared amongst them. He was kindly received by all ranks and classes in that place — was invested with the freedom of the city, and in every respect treated as became his distinguished merits. From this distant part of the kingdom, he moved rapidly southward — still visiting and re-visiting the gaols and bridewells in his route — to London, where his presence was required to give evidence in support of his petition.

Besides the joint petition from Mr. Whitbread and himself, another had been presented from a large body of the electors — their political supporters — praying for an inquiry into the truth of certain facts alleged to have taken place during the recent contest. A committee was consequently appointed, and the whole matter was gone into in the presence of the unsuccessful candidates, their counsel, and friends, on the 14th of March, 1775.

For the reasons already hinted at, this scrutiny excited at the time a good deal of interest in the country at large; and its various stages were watched and noted with anxiety. There were two principal points on which the verdict must necessarily turn: — the first was, the acceptance or rejection of the votes of the honorary freemen, most of whom had recorded their names in favor of the corporation candidates; and the second, the sanction of the claim of certain burgesses of the town, who, in various ways, received benefit from a munificent bequest of Sir William Harpur — a native of Bedford, who about a century before had removed to London, had become a great merchant and lord mayor, and at his death had left a large portion of his property to his old townsmen — and some other charities. Before the present election, the votes of this latter class had never been objected to, and they were obviously now challenged only because the majority of them had been tendered for Howard and Whitbread. Curiously enough, these two points were finally determined by the committee in favor of the respective claimants — the votes of both were pronounced good. The honorary freemen were held to be legally qualified; participation in the benefits derived to the town from Harpur's bequest was ruled to be no bar. This decision reversed the numerical order of the poll: Whitbread and Howard were now at the head, and for several days it was believed that they were returned. During this interval of supposed success, Howard wrote to his friend Symmonds, detailing the principal facts as they had transpired; but declaring that could he have defeated the corporation agents on the question of their right to make freemen at will, for such evident purposes of jobbing, even at the expense of his own seat, he would have done so with pleasure. These agents, however, adepts in all the mysterious arts of electioneering, were not to be so easily beaten. Driven from one line of defence, they hastily took up another. Fresh objections were started; and they at length gained, in part at least, their object. The committee had laid it down as a principle that persons residing in Bedford under certificates from other parishes, or receiving advantage from Harpur's testament — and some other charities — were legally qualified to vote; but in a subsequent part of the proceedings, they drew a nice distinction between these endowments and another charity — whether a just distinction or not, it were idle now to inquire — the effect of which was to alter materially the relative position of the candidates. When the changes caused by this new decision were made, the poll stood thus: — Whitbread, 574; Howard, 542; Wake, 541; Sparrow, 530. The patriots were still at the head of the poll — though their majority were small; but now the committee, in its last sitting, finally ruled that the vote of every elector who had accepted parochial relief within six months of the polling day, should be struck out of the lists. This decision excluded Howard; for when the figures were finally made up, they presented the following results: — Whitbread, 568; Wake, 541; Howard, 537; Sparrow, 529.

Thus, by a minority, of four voices only, was the Philanthropist of the World saved from falling into the position of a common-place representative of a petty provincial town, and dwindling down into a mere item in the collective wisdom of St. Stephen's! That he was himself, for a time, disappointed and grieved at the result, there is good reason for believing; the more so as he did not enter into the contest in order to gratify his own pride and ambition. In the following letter, written to the reverend friend before named, only four days after the report of the committee was made, he expresses his feelings at the result in much stronger language than he was in the habit of using: —

"Dear Sir, — Accept of my best thanks for your kind assistance and zealous attachment in an affair in which it has pleased God to rebuke us — I may say *us* Dissenters; for having the honor of being supported by them, and for being myself a Dissenter, I was made a victim by the ministry. Most surely I should not have fallen in with all their severe measures relative to the Americans; and my constant declaration that not one emolument of five shillings, were I in parliament, would I ever accept of, marked me out as an object of their aversion.

Two or three of the members told me of it on Monday; but I insisted, as the committee were on oath, that they *must* be consistent in their resolution as to the charities; and, as ancient usage was the line they went on, they never could disqualify the freemen in the town, as *we* knew many non-residents who were paupers, but who never objected to them. Yet, alas! when one would not do, both must be brought — even resolutions tortured — sooner than one private, independent person have his seat. I sensibly feel for an injured people; their affections and esteem I shall ever reflect on with pleasure and gratitude. As to myself, I calmly retire. It may be promotive of my best interest. On account of my large and extexsive acquaintance, and the very kind part the Protestant Dissenters of *all* denominations took in the affair, the result hurts me not a little; yet, in the firm belief in an over-ruling Providence, I would say, — 'It is the Lord: let Him do what seemeth right. He maketh light arise out of darkness."

Knowing, as we do, the future of his career, and reflecting that his successful return to the House of Commons, *might* have put an end to his prison-labors, and *must* have interfered with them, it is impossible not to rejoice in the result, and to join in the pious sentiment of resignation here expressed. To many, who regarded the failure of his petition as a personal and party defeat, his rejection was a source of infinite mortification; but this only evinces how little prophetic are multitudes when under the excitement of strong passions. There is hardly a sectary in existence now who can really regret the apparently adverse circumstances which served to rescue from the purposes of party the time and talents which were of such pre-eminent value to mankind.

CHAPTER VII.

THE PRISON-WORLD OF THE CONTINENT.

WHILE the parliamentary inquiry was still in progress, Howard was not so much absorbed in it as to neglect his far more serious mission. The greater part of the time when he was at liberty from attendance on the committee, he employed in a series of visits to the metropolitan prisons. As we have before noted, the efforts of the Philanthropist were not confined to obtaining information, measuring weighing, and observing — his benevolence was not of that abstract character. His mind was, in fact, eminently practical — fond of realities — more powerfully inclined to apply than to assert principles. His feelings were peculiarly concrete and sympathetic in tendency. He was about the least of an idealist that can well be conceived. Certainly, *he* would not have whined over a dead ass while his mother was starving, as an eccentric contemporary was accused of doing; it is therefore much to be regretted that we have so few memorials of his private benevolence extant and known. That his private charities and benefactions were very considerable — that he carried not only light, and air, and consolation into hundreds of dungeons, but food and raiment also into many, and life and liberty unto not a few miserable captives — is beyond all question; though his singular modesty has caused almost every trace of these generous actions to be obliterated. On his return from his journey into Ireland and Scotland, it was his intention to have at once arranged his papers and given them to the world; had he been seated for Bedford he would probably have adopted this course. What would then have followed it is not easy now to say; but as Providence had otherwise willed in closing against him that particular career of usefulness, he wisely resolved to walk for the future in his own path — to devote his time, his talents, and his fortune, to a more thorough and systematic inquiry into the gaol system, at home and abroad, than it had ever yet received. To render his plan complete, even in its preliminary stage, he determined to travel into France, Germany and Holland, and inspect whatsoever was most notable on this subject in those countries; with this purpose he quitted England in April, 1775.

Paris was the first halting place of this journey — the different gaols of which he purposed to examine; but he soon found that this was by no means so easy a thing as he had at first thought it. The political prisons — and especially the Bastille — were inexorably closed against his humane researches. Nor could he obtain leave to visit even the civil prisons, until he fortunately discovered that there was an old law of the parliament of Paris which directed the keepers of prisons in that city to admit all persons who were desirous of bestowing a donation upon the prisoners, and to allow them to distribute their alms with their own hands, — except in the case of prisoners who were confined in the dark cells; to these the keeper was enjoined to present the gift himself, but in the presence of the donor. Provided with a copy of this *arrât*, Howard knocked at the gate of the Grand Chatelet; but the law had fallen into abeyance — so little had it ever been acted upon, it was not, in fact, known to the warder — and he was still refused admittance. Thence he repaired to the Commissary of Prisons, and pleading the provisions of the law and his own desire to relieve the wants of the captives, obtained an authorization to inspect not only that, but the still more dreadful prisons of the Petit Chatelet and For I'Eveque. This old regulation proved of the utmost service to Howard, for it enabled him to speak with, and examine, more or less, almost every inmate of these great prisons. Of course this advantage was procured at not a little outlay in charities. The two last-named places of confinement were amongst the worst and most revolting — always excepting the Bastille — in Paris, having under-ground dungeons, dark, damp, and noisome beyond description. The other chief prisons of the city were — the Conciergerie, the Abbaye, and the Bicetre. The first was an ordinary prison, having an airy court and a fine piazza, but dungeons very dark and offensive. The Abbaye was used for the confinement of the military and men of rank: in the debtors' rooms, a simple partition of lath and plaster detached from the brick wall, answered the purpose of an expedient to prevent escapes, for if the smallest perforation were made in the wall it was immediately discovered by the mortar falling: there were six small dungeons, in which, as the keeper told his visitor, fifty persons were sometimes confined at once. The Bicetre was rather an enormous hospital than a gaol, being used in both capacities, and also as a sort of poor-house. In this great lazaret were congregated the most revolting objects of the capital — the wretched, the criminal, the diseased, and the insane! Howard says the most common and fatal distemper amongst them was the scorbute, — which they contracted from never being allowed to go out of their rooms for air or exercise. Many lost their lives, and many more the use of their limbs by it. All the prisoners were sickly pale, and had a melancholy look. The establishment was very ill-managed and very dirty; there was no fire-place in any of the rooms, and in the severe winter of 1775, several hundreds had perished of cold within its walls.

We have mentioned the Bastille. If Howard had found it difficult to obtain access to other prisons, he found it impossible to penetrate the dark adyta of this celebrated and ominous fortress. The convenient *arret* did not extend to the state prisons of Vincennes and the Porte St. Antoine. He made many other efforts — but in vain. Neither his own reputation, the influence of the English ambassador, nor the efforts of his Parisian friends, availed to open to him the gates of the Bastille. It was not the custom of its janitors to permit any man to enter and leave it at pleasure. Once its gloomy portals passed, but seldom did the traveller return; and when such *was* the case he was rigorously forbidden to tell the secrets of his prison-house. It was dangerous to speak of the fortress even in the privacy of domestic society. The subject was prohibited. If there ever were a human habitation to which Dante's inscription over Hell's portal might be applied, it was the Bastille. It was a place of unknown horrors. Attracted by its reputation as the abode of wrong and cruelty unimaginable, —likely to act upon a pure and sympathetic mind with a powerful fascination — as much, perhaps, as from any reasonable hope of being able to render assistance to its victims, Howard exhausted every means of forcing an entry. But failing to obtain any sort of official authorization, he loitered round it for hours, vainly hoping that chance might effect what influence could not. Unsatisfied at leaving Paris without a glimpse of this dark world, he one day presented himself at the outer gate, at the end of Rue St. Antoine, — rang the bell loudly — and, on its being opened by the officer in charge, boldly stepped in —

passed the sentry — walked coolly through a file of guards who were on duty — and advanced as far as he could, that is, up to the great drawbridge in the inner court. While standing there, contemplating the dismal structure, an officer ran up to him, greatly surprised and agitated at the unusual apparition of a stranger in that place, — and, as his manner appeared portentous and suspicious, the Philanthropist thought it prudent to retreat on the instant, — which he did, repasssing the guard, who were mute with astonishment at his strange temerity, and thus regained the freedom which few ever saw again after having once crossed that fatal threshold. That this adventure was eminently dangerous, a less simple-minded man would have comprehended much more fully; and to those who are really aware of the peril, it is a matter of profound satisfaction that the Philanthropist, at the outset of his great career, so nearly escaped being added to the list of the Bastille's illustrious victims. Had the gate closed upon his intrusive footsteps, his career would have been much shortened; he would probably soon have died in its secret dungeons; his freedom-loving spirit would soon have worn itself away against the bars of its iron cages; and a nation's pride would have been buried under a menial's name, — as was always the custom with the Bastille's illustrious victims.

As may be supposed, this adventure did not diminish the interest which Howard felt in the Bastille. Having heard that a pamphlet had been written on the subject the year before, by a person who had been himself confined in it for several years, he endeavored to procure a copy; but as the rule was rigorously interdicted by the government, the work itself proscribed, and the printed copies bought up and destroyed, he was some time before he could meet with it. A diligent search, however, was at length rewarded. He procured a copy of the pamphlet, brought it to England — translated and published it in his own books — gave it the sanction of his name, and with that a European circulation. The following are a few of the chief passages of this famous pamphlet: "This castle is a state prison, consisting of eight very strong towers, surrounded with a fosse about 120 feet wide, and a wall 60 feet high. The entrance is at the end of the street St. Antoine, by a drawbridge and great gates, into the court of the Hotel du Gouvernement, and from thence over another drawbridge to the corps de garde, which is separated by a strong barrier, constructed with beams plated with iron, from the great court. This court is about 120 feet by 80. In it is a fountain. Six of the towers — which are united by walls of free-stone, 10 feet thick up to the top — surround it. Contiguous to it are the other two towers. On the top of the towers is a platform, continued in terraces, on which the prisoners are sometimes permitted to walk, attended by a guard. On this platform are thirteen cannons mounted . . . The dungeons of the tower of Liberty extend under the kitchen . . . Near that tower is a small chapel on the ground-floor . . . In the wall are five niches, into which the prisoners are put to hear mass, where they can neither see nor be seen. The dungeons at the bottom of the towers exhale the most offensive scents, and are the receptacle of toads, rats, and other vermin. In the corner of each is a camp-bed, made of planks laid on iron bars that are fixed to the wall, and the prisoners are allowed some straw to put on the boards. These dens are dark — having no windows, but openings into the ditch; they have double doors, the inner ones plated with iron, with large bolts and locks. Of the five classes of chambers, the most horrid, next to the dungeons, are those in which are *cages of iron.* There are three of them. They are formed of beams, with strong plates of iron, and are each 8 feet by 6. The calottes, or chambers at the top of the towers, are somewhat more tolerable. They are formed of eight arcades of freestone. Here one cannot walk but in the centre of the room. There is hardly sufficient space for a bed from one arcade to another. The windows, being in walls 10 feet thick, and having iron grates within and without, admit but little light. In these rooms the heat in summer is excessive, and the cold in winter. Almost all the other rooms [of the towers] are octagons, about 20 feet in diameter, and from 14 to 15 high. They are very cold and damp . . . If prisoners of note are dangerously ill, they are generally removed, that they may not die in this prison. The persons who die there are buried under the names of menials . . . One of the sentinels on the inside of the castle rings a bell every hour, day and night, to give notice that they are awake; and on the rounds outside the castle they ring every quarter of an hour."

The work from which these extracts are taken was brought to England, translated, and published by Howard, — and, with his other works, was read in every country in Europe. The government of France never forgave or forgot this offence; and by and by we shall see what shape their anger will assume. On the whole, however, our countryman saw much to admire in French prisons, when compared with those of England. The correctional science of France was then certainly far in advance of ours. The prisons were generally clean and fresh; they had no gaol-distemper — no prisoners ironed. The allowance of food was ample and regularly delivered. These important provisions shame us for the barbarities practised at home.

Leaving Paris, Howard bent his course to Brussels, where he found nothing in the line of his researches very remarkable — and thence to Ghent, a city famous in the history of correctional discipline. The Maison de Force, a prison built by the States of Austrian Flanders, excited a large share of his attention, and furnished him with some of his most precious observations. In fact, for the time, it was the model prison of Europe; in almost every department offering the most striking contrast to the arrangements of English prisons. The convicts were properly lodged — fed — clothed — instructed — worked. The utmost regularity, order, and cleanliness prevailed; there was no drunkenness ; no riot: no excessive misery; no irons; no starvation. The city was not, however, entirely free from gaol horrors. In all ages, the janitors of the Church have been remarked as severe custodians. Here they did not belie their usual character. The gaol belonging to the wealthy monastery of St. Benedict — which fraternity possessed a great number of lordships, and had no small part of Ghent itself within its jurisdiction,— adjoined the court-house of the Abbey, and consisted of three dreary dungeons, deep, close, foul, and dark. Howard descended into these wretched abodes, and according to his custom, began seriously to count the steps, measure the cells, windows, and so forth; all of which proceedings so alarmed and enraged the warder — who was unused to such doings in his office — that he somewhat gruffly turned his strange visitor out; and on his calling again, years afterwards, refused him permission to enter — to speak with or even to relieve, the inmates.

Through Bruges and Antwerp — the gaols of both which cities he carefully examined — the Philanthropist proceeded into Holland, by way of Rotterdam. Thence he passed on, doing his work as he went along, to Delft, Amsterdam, Utrecht, the

Hague, Groningen, and Lewardin — delighted with nearly everything he saw in this country. In all that related to the law and administration of penal science, Holland was at that time far in advance of the rest of Europe. Its general average of crime was remarkably low — of fraudulency, still lower. At Amsterdam, Howard learned with surprise that in the whole of that populous city there had not been a single execution for the ten years immediately preceding his inquiry; and that for a hundred years, one year with another, the average of the executions had not been more than one per annum! There was food for thought in this. Amsterdam then contained about 250,000 inhabitants — London about thrice the number; in other respects the elements of comparison between the two cities were not unfair; and fortunately we have some data for a comparison. In the year 1772, an elaborate table was compiled and published by Sir Theodore Janssen, showing the number of persons tried at the Old Bailey, and capitally sentenced, during the twenty-three years, 1749–71, with the number of those actually executed. In these twenty-three years, there were 794 persons condemned to death — of which number, 678 were hanged, the remainder died in gaol, were transported, or pardoned. Taking those only who actually came to the gallows — 678 gives an average for the city of London of about 29½ per annum; which again, allowing for the difference of population, gives about *ten* executions in London to every *one* in Amsterdam! Nor did the paucity of death punishment encourage the growth of crime in the Dutch city. At the period of Howard's visit, there were but *six* delinquents confined in the gaols of that rich commercial depot, and, what is perhaps still more remarkable, only *eighteen* debtors. The restraining agents were moral, not material; resulting from education and public opinion, rather than from fear of bodily suffering. To be in prison for debt was considered in Holland as an indelible disgrace. Howard, as usual, goes at once to the root of the matter:—"The principal cause that debtors as well as capital offenders, are few, is the great care that is taken to train up the children of the poor, and indeed of all others, to industry. The States do not transport convicts; but men are put to labor in the rasp-houses, and women to proper work in the spin-houses—upon this professed maxim,

'MAKE THEM DILIGENT AND THEY WILL BE HONEST.'

Great care is taken to give them moral and religious instruction, and reform their manners, for their own and the public good; and I am well informed that many come out sober and honest. Some have even chosen to continue and work in the house after their discharge. Offenders are sentenced to these houses according to their crimes, for seven, ten, fifteen, twenty, and even ninety-nine years; but, to prevent despair, seldom for *life*. As an encouragement to sobriety and industry, those who distinguish themselves by such behavior are discharged before the expiration of their term."

Entering Germany, our traveller examined the various prisons of Bremen, Coblentz, Mayence, Mannheim, and several other cities, without encountering anything very notable; except the fact, which must have struck the Englishman's heart-chords strangely, that few of them had any tenants. The gaols at Hamburgh were also nearly empty — and in some other respects commanded the approbation of their inspector; but he found that in the case of refractory criminals, there was an excess of severity employed, which admitted of no justification, even in that age; and which he heartily denounced. In a prison of this city called the Buttuley, the felons were heavily laden with fetters; while in some instances the most barbarous tortures were resorted to, to make a suspected offender confess his crime. "Amongst the various engines," says Howard, "of Torture, or the Question, which I have seen in France, Italy, Germany, and many other countries, one of the most excruciating is kept and used in a deep cellar of this prison. It ought to be buried ten thousand fathoms deeper!" It is said that the inventor of this horrid instrument was the first to suffer by it; a sort of retribution which has frequently happened to those who have given to the world the results of their demoniacal ingenuity. At

Osnaburgh — a city which has given its name to a peculiar and most horrible species of torture — and at Hanover, of which George III. was sovereign, the same inhuman and absurd method of criminal investigation was still used. Speaking of the principal prison in Hanover, Howard indignantly observes: — "The execrable practice of torturing prisoners is here used, in a cellar, where the horrid engine is kept. The time for it is, as in other countries, about two o'clock in the morning. A criminal suffered the Osnaburgh torture *twice* about two years ago; the last time, at putting to him the third question — the executioner having torn off the hair from his head, breast, &c. — he confessed, and was executed." This was in 1774, in the hereditary domain of the paternal prince whose tyranny drove the Americans into rebellion the self-same year.

Through Hanau and Hesse Cassel, the indefatigable Philanthropist passed on to Mannheim; where he found much to admire in the correctional science of this clean and pleasant city. A curious custom here attracted his attention: — Every person who was committed to the Maison de la Force for delinquency, was greeted at his entrance within its walls, with what was quaintly termed the *bien-venu* (welcome); that is, he was seized by the officers of the gaol — stripped, and fastened by the neck, hands and feet into a machine, which held him firm and tight; — and as soon as this little arrangement was made, he received on the spot — according to the enormity of the offence, or the discretion of the magistrate — from twelve to thirty stripes. After the due performance of this edifying ceremony, the culprit was allowed to kiss the threshold, and walk in. In peculiar cases, the same compliment was paid the fellow on his discharge!

Mayence was the last place which Howard visited in Germany during this tour, or at least it is the last of which any record has been preserved. He returned towards England down the Rhine. The following extract from a letter dated Bonn, is all that need be added to this sketch: — "Dear Sir, I flatter myself that a line will not be unacceptable. As one's spirits are tired with the same subject, it is a relaxation and pleasure to write to a friend; which indeed is my case at present, being just come from the prisons in this place. I had visited many in France, Flanders, and Holland; but I thought I might gain some knowledge by looking into the German police. I have carefully visited some Prussian, Austrian, Hessian, and many other gaols. With the utmost difficulty did I get access to many dismal abodes; and, through the good hands of God, I have been preserved in health and safety. I hope I have gained some knowledge that may be improved to some valuable purpose."

And now what was this knowledge? What experiences had the continent yielded up? Was there anything which distinguished the prisons of

France, Germany and Holland, from those of England?

Yes; one great feature.

In almost every country of the continent which Howard had yet visited, he had found the prisoners EMPLOYED. This was the strong point of contrast with the usage in England. In fact, *hard work* was the chief correctional agent at that time in operation abroad. In this country correction was hardly thought of — confinement was the one thing aimed at. In several foreign cities he found the offenders at work in sight of the general public. As their crimes had been aggressions upon society, so, under the surveillance of the corporate body which they had wronged, were they compelled to make atonement and compensation by their labor, — being employed in rough, hard, menial work. For the greater part, they were occupied in cleaning the streets, repairing the highway, cutting stone, and so forth. Nor did the humane and judicious inspector discover that any ill consequences flowed from these open-day punishments. The labor so obtained was useful in some degree to the state; it inured the culprit to habits of unceasing industry; and it had a wholesome effect upon those classes of the community from which the criminal population springs.

In the progress of the social sciences, and under the pressure of new necessities, this question of the advantages and disadvantages attending the public infliction of punishments by means of labor, has come again to occupy the attention of penal writers and statesmen in this country. In its treatment of its crime, England has exhibited a strange and cowardly disregard of all high moral and political considerations. It has not, at least since the reign of the first George, dared to grapple boldly with its gigantic social corruptions — it has never attempted to confront and deal decisively with the spirit of criminality festering in its population. To talk of the criminal *science* of England even now, would be absurd; it is nothing more than a system of makeshifts. It has two agents — alike unworthy of an age or country pretending to a high state of civilization — the gallows and the penal settlement; both of them repudiated, or nearly so, by every other enlightened nation. Unable, or unwilling, to reform our culprits, we have only sought for our own safety in their destruction; thus multiplying crime in the name of justice; and, under the cover of legal forms, ministering to the darkest and sternest spirit of vengeance. A conqueror has been charged with putting to death a number of prisoners whom he could not feed and dared not liberate, as a monstrous act; yet in what better position does our criminal code place us, when regarded from an ethical point of view? What are our felons, forgers, burglars and the like, but prisoners of war? Is not crime an aggression, a social war? Are not professed criminals in a state of open hostility to society — in point of fact, if not in law? Certainly. Between law and crime a civil war, of a deadly, unappeasable, exterminating character, is always raging. And as the common sentiment of mankind has declared that a soldier is not at liberty to murder his prisoners to escape a troublesome responsibility — to provide against a possible peril, — neither has the social administrator any right to deal in a barbarous and irreversible manner with the prisoners of the law.

With the results of a long series of years, and the workings of many penal systems before us, it may well be doubted whether our gigantic plan of hanging and transporting has not been altogether a profound mistake. At all events it has been a failure. We have exported vice — disease — lunacy, more largely than any other commodity; and yet the supply seems inexhaustible. We have hanged offenders ten times faster than other nations; and offences multiply, in despite of all our severity. — England herself has not been improved by the process; while colonies of men, worse than demons, have rapidly grown up in her penal settlements — after a time, it may be feared, to repay her in a coinage like her own. If we will plant the storm, we must expect to have to reap the whirlwind.

About the time that Howard began to devote his attention to this subject, the American colonies threw off the yoke, — and the old outlets for this peculiar product of the English soil were closed. For a while our convicts had to be kept at home.

The gaols filled rapidly; disease was engendered; and public attention was forced to the matter. Those publicists and statesmen who had courage enough to strip the question of its traditions — to study it from first principles without reference to the *practices* of the country — advised the abolition of transportation altogether. But their views were permature, and their voices found no audience. There was then no public for such discussions: philosophy and humanity could obtain no hearing. Ministers, whose minds had been formed in office, feared and scouted the idea of innovation. The subject was in itself beset with difficulties. The penitentiary system was unknown to the ideas and habits of the country; and the boldest official of that time hardly thought of a culprit except as a being to be coerced and crushed. Criminals, it was considered, had by their own act placed themselves out of the pale of the law; and no one was bound to think of their rights or wrongs: having set the law at defiance, of course they could have no claim on its protection. Certainly their voices could never reach, so as to influence, the public mind; no vote could well be gained or lost by doing justice to them, and a selfish estimate of the *practicable* interfered to prevent any large and fundamental reform being attempted. Keep your criminals in the country, and they are sure to be troublesome; send them to the antipodes, and you have done with them at once: —

such was the facile way of solving the problem of the day.

In this manner — to idleness, to fear, to incapacity, — another continent was doomed to be all but sacrificed. For fifty-seven years —1718–75 — we sowed crime broad-cast upon the great seaboard of North America, until the colonists themselves indignantly protested against and put an end to our insane policy. For a second term of fifty-seven years — 1788–1845 — we poured the same elements of moral and social corruption along the seaboard of Australia; until, arrested at length by the threatening magnitude of the evil, we have been compelled suddenly to suspend our system, to admit an element of uncertainty and indecision into our penal administration, to start afresh and reconstruct our whole science anew. The question has now returned to the precise point at which it stood in the days of Howard; and the solution for which *he* struggled — the adoption of a correctional system to be carried out at home — is the one most likely to be arrived at. It is no mean point gained, to have found out that we were wrong — to have got a basis, how far back soever, for a new progress. The knowledge of a disease is said to be half the cure; but by this is meant not the mere knowledge that we *are* diseased, as some imagine, bnt the precise nature of the malady; that is the knowledge that alone is of value.

The transportation system is now (1849) in abeyance; but what is to supersede it, is not yet determined upon. Amongst those most profoundly acquainted with general theories, and with the penal experience of various countries, there is an impression in favor of employing criminals on public works of great national utility, but such as would not be likely to be undertaken by private individuals at their own risk and cost: namely — havens, breakwaters, embankments, new roads, and so on. Objections, of course, are not wanting to this plan; but Howard's experience on the subject — and it will be remembered that *he* had no pet theory to maintain; *his* judgment was formed on the strictest induction from facts — is decisive, at least as to the chief objection. He says: — "I have been very particular in my accounts of foreign houses of correction — especially those of the *freest States* — to counteract a notion prevailing among *us*, that compelling prisoners to work, especially in public, was inconsistent with the principles of English liberty; at the same time, that taking away the lives of such numbers — either by execution, or the diseases of our prisons — seems to make little impression upon us. Of such force is custom and prejudice in silencing the voice of good sense and humanity!"

Howard no sooner landed at Dover, on his return, than he recommenced his English inspections by visiting the gaol of that port. It was in much the same miserable condition as those already described from his notes; if anything, a little worse. For the next three months, his footsteps cannot be traced; it is probable that he retired to Cardington, to repose after the great fatigue of his journey — travelling at that time was not so easy as it has since become — and to reduce his mass of papers into order. Only once during these three months does he seem to have quitted his seclusion; and then it was for the purpose of paying a visit to the prison at Chelmsford, where the gaol-distemper had just been raging with great fury, the head keeper himself falling a victim to its ravages. The building was close, and subject to the fatal pest; from which, indeed, it was seldom entirely free. When Howard arrived, the whole establishment was in such disorder, that divine service had not been performed within its walls — except upon the compulsory occasion of an execution — for more than a year. The gaoler had no salary. In the tap-room a copy of regulations was hung up — one of which ran as follows: — "Prisoners, to pay garnish, or, *run the gauntlet!*" The keeper of this prison was a *woman*, by no means a solitary instance of the kind; for at that time the county gaols of Worcester, Horsham, Monmouth, Gloucester, Exeter, Bodmin, and Reading, were all under the custodianship of women!

Howard had now collected such a mass of materials for his work as no human being had ever gathered on the same subject, — the result of unwearied toil, time, devotion, and expense. Any ordinary man would have considered that at length he had seen enough to enable him to make a report to the world; and, had his desire been merely to astonish mankind by the extent and disinterestedness of his labors, he certainly had made ample provision; but he had other objects, higher views, before him. On coming to put his papers into order, he still found, or feared, that there were many gaps which ought to be filled up. As the sphere of his inquiries enlarged, he discovered new prisons, courts, houses of correction, and bridewells, of which he had previously never heard, — and all of which he considered it necessary to include in his accounts. To take in these, and to revise and correct his former observations, he resolved to undertake another complete tour of the country, and inspect or re-inspect the whole gaol-system of the kingdom. The mind is almost faint with following in the track of these multiplied and multiplying labors, though it can compress the efforts of a year into a line; what then must have been the devotion, the sacrifice, the grandeur of purpose of the man, who, without personal interest — nay, at the cost of his time, health, repose, property, and life — shrank not from the perils and privations with which his almost superhuman task was environed!

From the beginning of November, 1775, to the end of May, 1776 — seven entire months — was spent in this manner. One of the petty gaols which he then visited for the first time, was St. Brievell's in the Forest of Dean — a small, inconvenient building for the confinement of debtors, greatly out of repair, having no yard, no water, no firing, and no allowance of food. At the period of Howard's visit, two individuals, both sick, were there detained; one of whom told him that he had been immured in his close, dismal room for twelve months, never having been once suffered to go out of it! Another was at Penzance, in a stable-yard — thus painted by the Philanthropist: — "No chimney; earth floor — very damp. The door had not been opened for four weeks when I went in; and then the keeper began to clear away the dirt. There was only one debtor — who seemed to have been robust, but was grown pale with ten weeks' close confinement, with little food, which he had from a brother — who was poor and had a family. He said, the dampness of the room, with but little straw, had obliged him (he spoke it with sorrow) to send for the bed on which some of his children lay. He had a wife and ten children — two of whom died since he came thither, and the rest were almost starving." It is not easy to imagine a situation for an honest but unfortunate man more terrible than this.

Such scenes were, however, now become rarer than they had been two years before, when Howard commenced his labors. Though not invested with any official power, his influence was soon felt in the world of action which he had made his own. The ascendancy of his personal character, added to an instinctive and somewhat mysterious respect for his assumed mission, proved a higher and more useful credential than one bearing the royal seal could have been. No neglect could escape his vigilance; and petty tyrants soon learned to quail before an eye as stern as it was mild. In many of the prisons formerly remarkable for riot and distress, great improvement was evident in consequence of his suggestions having been carried out. On bringing these new examinations to a close, he felt so conscious of the advantages which he had derived from this laborious revision of his old observations, that he resolved to make another extensive journey over the continent for a similar purpose, and to visit the gaols of some countries not included in his former programme, before committing his work to the press.

Without resting for a day, he put this project into act. Arriving in Paris early in June, he began his work there, and after so consuming two or three weeks, proceeded to Lyons, where he found, in the prison of St. Joseph, twenty-nine individuals crammed into four small and horrid dungeons, though the heat was so intense and noisome that they had all stripped themselves naked to the shirt for ventilation. In the Pierre-en-Oize, a state-prison of the same city, Howard conversed with an old man who reported himself in the fiftieth year of his confinement!

In the republic of Geneva, the Philanthropist found only five criminals in durance — be it remembered, too, that Geneva did not send her convicts out of the country — and no debtors whatsoever. The latter was usually the case; the laws against bankrupts and insolvents, contrary to the general character of the civil code of the republic, being particularly stringent. They were deprived of their burgher rights, and rendered incapable of holding any public office of honor or emolument. Even the children who should refuse to pay their just portion of their parent's debts were subjected to the same rigorous laws. This regulation, if severe, was highly salutary. No great evil flowed from it, — but much good. The results were — an empty gaol; a more healthy system of private credit; greater confidence in the dealings between man and man. Nor, in reality, can these laws be pronounced unjust. Fraudulent trading is felony in morals, if not in law; and in treating insolvency as a social offence, fittingly punishable by social degradation, we suspect the Genevese were wiser in their generation than we are in ours. If insolvency in England were made to involve the suspension of certain civil and political rights, for a greater or less period, according to the amount of culpability — in every case and under all circumstances — we should have much less of it. At present, there is a premium tempting to extravagance, over-trading, over-living, and so forth. It is but seldom that a debt is more of a misfortune than a fault. Debts can hardly arise without some degree of culpability, which it would be no wrong to punish; and were that culpability more closely assimilated to other violations of the social law, it is fair to suppose that it would soon decline. The person who gets into debt without the prospect or intention of payment, acts as villanously, robs his creditor just as much, as the felon who empties his till, or the burglar who carries off his plate. The distinction drawn by our law between these crimes is one without a difference. The first, it is said, wrongs you with your own knowledge and consent, — the other, without it. This is a quibble: the first cheats under a form — which the requirements of commerce have introduced — but certainly *not* with the knowledge and consent of the party. The creditor is not aware of the fraudulent intent. He deals with his customer on the conditions which society has sanctioned, and trusts him with his property much as he trusts his servants and assistants. The moral guilt of a breach of that confidence, we hold to be equal in the one case to the other. While our present laws of debtor and creditor exist — while such facilities remain for escaping from the inconveniences of bankruptcy, a reckless, wanton, gambling spirit may always be expected to pervade our commerce, throwing obstacles in the way of legitimate exchanges and the prudent combinations of the conscientious merchant.

Throughout the whole of his tour in Switzerland, the Philanthropist saw no person in fetters — a state of things to which England presented a striking and mournful contrast. The separate system of correction was generally employed in these healthy republics. They had a cell for each prisoner — it is true they did not require many — warmed artificially, and strongly built. The scale of punishment was regulated by light: the greater the crime, the darker the cell. In several of the cantons there were no culprits at all; the gaols were empty — a circumstance attributed, and no doubt justly, to the great care which was taken by the state to give a sound moral and industrial education to the children of the poor. At Berne, Howard saw and conversed with the learned Dr. Haller, who gave it as his opinion that the gaol-fever in England was owing entirely to the over-crowded state of the prisons: — in conjunction with filth, misery, irregular and insufficient diet, and want of fresh water, this was no doubt its most prolific source. In that important city, all the prisoners were kept to hard, servile labor; indeed *work* was the principal element of the Swiss system of punishment and reform. The greater part of the men were employed in cleaning and watering the streets, removing the rubbish from buildings, and carrying off the snow and ice from the public thoroughfares in winter. Howard describes Berne as at that time one of the cleanest places on the continent. It is so still. These servants of the state wore a livery in the shape of an iron collar round the neck, such as in the feudal times was worn as the badge of serfdom. In every part of this land of real freedom, the average of crime was surprisingly low, and the correctional discipline commendable. The state began its care for the criminal in the germ. The child was sent to school to learn good before he learned evil. If he nevertheless passed the rubicon of crime, his welfare was still looked to; the dangers of association and contamination wisely provided against. The gaols were generally built with great strength, but attempts would nevertheless be sometimes made to escape. Howard relates an incident of this kind which is highly characteristic of the intense love of freedom in the Swiss heart, and the deep respect which is felt for that love, however it may be manifested.

The gaoler of the Schallenhaus, the principal prison of Berne, having one day accidently left the door of one of the men's wards open, twelve of the inmates, seeing their chance, rushed forth, and forcing the outer gate, effected their escape. The people in the streets, fancying they were going off to work, suffered them to pass. For the time, every man of them regained his liberty; but subsequently four or five were retaken and carried back to their ward. No punishment was inflicted. The magistrate who tried them for breaking prison resolved that — inasmuch as every man naturally loves liberty, and desires above all things to obtain it, the culprits, seeing that they had not made use of violence, ought not to be punished for obeying the greatest and noblest instinct of the human heart; however, as the keeper had been guilty of negligence in leaving the door open, the punishment fell upon him, — and justice was not denied her victim.

Our traveller proceeded from Berne to Soleure and Basle ; the gaol of which latter city was in one of the towers. There were separate cells, but no prisoners. Howard particularly noticed one very strong room, situate near the great clock. It was 6 feet high only ; the door, a trap, was in the roof, through which the inmate had to descend by means of a ladder, which was then removed.

On descending into this cell, the Philanthropist, remarking to the keeper on its extraordinary strength, was informed that a short time before a man had actually escaped from it. In fact, it was a very daring and remarkable attempt. The only instrument by which the prisoner effected his liberty, it would appear, was a spoon, which he was allowed to have to take his soup with. This utensil he contrived to sharpen, so as to be able to cut out a piece of timber from the wall of his room with it. With this second instrument he cautionsly proceeded to make experiments upon the tight fastenings of the trap. He knew, moreover, that the officers — well aware of the penalties with which the Swiss law visited *their* negligence in case of an escape from under their charge — were constantly on the alert, going about the galleries, and would immediately discover his plan if they overheard any noise. It was, nevertheless, quite impossible to strike the bolts without making a noise. Here there seemed an insuperable bar to his design. But the tower clock was near to his room; this suggested a chance. By proceeding cautiously, he gradually acquired the knack of hitting the bolts with his log just as the great clock was striking the hour, with such nicety of operation that the boom entirely overpowered the sound. In this way he in time made himself master of his immediate cell, the trap of which he could now open and shut at pleasure — that is, at the strikiug of the hours. So far all went well. He had, however, some other doors to force, and two or three galleries to pass; all the while running the greatest risk of detection from the patrolling guards. Nothing daunted by his numerous perils, he pushed his outworks further and further daily; securing his retreat as he went along, and returning to his cell whenever he expected the officers to be about. In this fashion he worked his way till at the end of fifteen days he emerged on the roof of the tower, in the open air and sky, — but at a frightful distance from the ground. Unchecked by this new and terrible difficulty, he instantly cast about him for the means of descent. Fortunately, there was a long rope coiled up in a corner. Of the altitude of the tower he had no knowledge, and consequently no means of ascertaining whether or not the rope was of sufficient length to reach the ground. Moreover, there was no time to deliberate; it was already on the edge of dawn, and daylight would prevent his flight even if he reached the ground in safety. So, taking all the chances of his dangerous adventure for freedom, he fastened one end of the friendly rope to a projecting part of the balustrade, threw the remainder forward into the air, waited for favorable moment when all was silent in the street below, and then committing himself to its frail holding, began to descend. Fortune does not always favor the brave. He had descended a considerable part of the fall when the rope suddenly gave way, or broke, and down he came with a frightful crash to the ground. Although some time elapsed before he was picked up, he was still quite insensible. So many of his ribs and limb-bones were broken, the surgeons declared it impossible for him to live. His fractures were, however, reset; and he did, nevertheless, in time, recover. As might be expected under the circumstances in Switzerland, on his recovery, he received a free pardon.

From Switzerland, Howard proceeded into Germany, in one of the cities of which he minutely inspected a torture-chamber; thence into Holland, which country he grew more and more partial to, as he became more intimately acquainted with it. He returned to England still more profoundly impressed with the superiority of the continental nations, generally, in the science of prison discipline over his own. "When I formerly," he says in summing up the results of his gains in knowledge and experience from foreign lands, "made the tour of Europe; I seldom had occasion to envy foreigners anything I saw, with respect to their situation, their religion, manners or government. In my late journeys to view their prisons, I was sometimes put to the blush for my native country. The reader will scarcely feel from my narration the same emotions of shame and regret as the comparison excited in me on beholding the difference with my own eyes. But from the account I have given him of foreign prisons, he may judge whether a design of reforming our own be merely *visionary* — whether *idleness*, *debauchery*, *disease*, and *famine* be the *necessary* attendants of a prison, or only connected with it in our ideas for want of a more perfect knowledge and more enlarged views."

There were still a few obscure prisons in England which Howard had not seen; and, on his arrival on its shores, without allowing himself a moment's rest, he proceeded to search them out. Of the places thus visited for the first time, a couple of gaols at Knaresborough were the most detestable. The one for felons consisted of but a single small room, in which it was customary to lock up, day and night, seven or eight persons, men and women, together, for a day or two before the time of holding the quarter sessions. This disgusting circumstance admits of no comment. The other was a place of confinement for debtors, but, in its different fashion, no less revolting. It is thus described by the humane inspector: — "No fire-place; earth floor; very offensive, a common sewer from the town running through it uncovered!" Only a short time before Howard's visit, an unfortunate officer had been cast into this horrible kennel. Having some knowledge of the place he had the precaution to take his dog in with him, to defend him from the vermin, which the stench, arising from the open sewer, produced in myriads. In a few days the dog was destroyed, having been actually devoured by its insidious enemies; and, at the same time, its master's hands and face were so bitten as to present to the eye nothing but three great and loathsome sores!! But enough of horrors at which the heart sickens. Let us pass in silence over the remaining details of this journey.

The Philanthropist had now been occupied upwards of three years, without intermission, at home and abroad, in amassing materials for his great work, in the course of which he had travelled not less than 13,418 miles! Coming up to London, he obtained the assistance of his friend, the Rev. Mr. Densham, in arranging the various observations which he had made — the enormous mass of rough notes which he had written down on the spot, visited and described — into something like systematic order. As they gradually assumed a methodical shape, Howard felt, or fancied that he felt, some chasms still in the work; and as any suggestion of this sort occurred to him, he lost no time in laying his papers aside, mounting his horse, and sallying forth to examine and re-examine, to compare and re-compare — that no wrong might be omitted, no wrong committed, through his negligence or haste.

A series of such trips, in different directions, and another complete course of inspection of the metropolitan prisons occupied his attention, until the beginning of the year 1777. In the intervals of these movements, with the assistance of his friend, Howard got all his rough memoranda fairly copied out, and the matter put into the necessary form before it could be subjected to the more competent literary supervision of Dr. Price. Price was now become a famous and a busy man. He had won the respect and friendship of Washington and Franklin, and as an ultra-politician had begun to excite the stupendous ire of Burke. Deeply engaged in polemics, he was a public man, and his time was of great value; but, nevertheless, he did not hesitate to assume the laborious office of reviser of his friend's multitudinous papers. He went through the whole mass with great care, and suggested many improvements as to style, arrangement, and so forth. Thus prepared, Howard went down to Warrington, to have the work printed — attracted thither by the reputation of Mr. Eyre's press, and the advantage of having the literary assistance of a young man, then rapidly rising into fame as an elegant writer, who was at that period settled in the town as a surgeon — Dr. Aikin. The latter gentleman at once divined the great and original character of his visitor, and entered into his plans perfectly *con amore*. Aikin himself was far from being an ordinary man; he was a scholar, a poet, and a critic of some pretensions. Everything he did was good — though nothing perhaps was great. He also belonged to a family of celebrities. His sister — afterwards Mrs. Barbauld — and his daughter, Lucy Aikin, have both left their names upon the page of their country's literary history.

With Aikin, the author read over his sheets as they issued from the press, taking his opinion upon them, and adopting his suggestions with readiness and gratitude. He was so extremely modest, and so diffident of his literary abilities, as to be unwilling to allow a single phrase of his own to stand, even though the young critic assured him that, in a literary point of view, it could not be improved. Even in this last stage of his great work, after all his journeyings and re-journeyings, doubts would sometimes occur to him as to the correctness of some observation, or hints would suggest themselves to his mind for more particular investigation; and then, such was his thorough conscientiousness, he would start off on a fresh expedition — sometimes hundreds of miles in distance, and of several days' duration — the results of which he would incorporate with the text or throw into notes. At length the great work was completed, and given to the world; we might almost literally say *given*; for he not only presented copies to the press, to public bodies, and to every considerable person in the kingdom whose position or pursuits enabled him to assist in mitigating the evils which it laid bare, but fixed the price of the remainder so low, that had the whole of the impression been sold, the proceeds would not have paid the outlay on the mere printing and paper.

The contents of this celebrated book have been already so fully drawn upon in the course of this narrative, that it will be unnecessary in this place to do more than present a few of the general observations — which enshrine the spirit of the whole — from its singularly modest introductory chapter. The want of a fixed amount of food — a proper supply of air and water — the dark, damp, noisome dungeons — the inconvenient sites — the tyranny of petty officers — the extortion of interested keepers — the want of room and of bedding, or straw — the pernicious custom of selling spirits in the gaol — the promiscuous intercourse and contamination of age and sex, tried and untried — the use of irons — garnish — gaming — fees, — such are the chief points in our gaol system to which attention is specially addressed, with a view to their modification and improvement. As his bold suggestions and innovations have now become, to a great extent, the common-places of our correctional science, they do not require to be here particularly noticed. The reader so deeply interested in the inquiry as to desire ampler details, will do well to consult Howard's work for himself. We cannot conclude this chapter better, or indeed otherwise, than in the solemn and impressive words of the Philanthropist himself:—

"Those gentlemen," he writes, "who, when they are told of the misery which our prisoners suffer, content themselves with saying, *Let them take care to keep out,'* — prefaced, perhaps, with an angry prayer — seem not duly sensible of the favor of Providence which distinguishes *them* from the sufferers; they do not consider that we are required to imitate our gracious Heavenly Parent, *who is kind to the unthankful and the evil.* They also forget the vicissitudes of human affairs, the unexpected changes to which men are liable, and that those whose circumstances are affluent may in time be reduced to indigence, and become debtors and prisoners. And as to criminality, it is possible that a man who has often shuddered at hearing the account of a murder, may, on a sudden temptation, commit that very crime. LET HIM THAT THINKS HE STANDETH TAKE HEED LEST HE FALL — AND COMMISERATE THOSE THAT ARE FALLEN."

CHAPTER VIII.

THEORIES OF CRIME.

On the first appearance of the work on The State of Prisons, it created an extraordinary sensation. It had been long and anxiously looked for. The fame of its author's labors — his disinterestedness — the purity of his motives in undertaking such a missionaryship — the courage and devotiou with which he had executed it — the sublime confidence in which he had penetrated dark and pestilential dungeons, in order to carry thereinto light and hope; and to bring the fearful secrets of the prison-house before the world — also, some intimation of the sterling worth and originality of his private character, had reached, through various channels, the knowledge of his countrymen; and there was consequently a strong desire on the part of the public to follow his fortunes more minutely, and to trace the lines of his apostleship from his own hand. The interest here indicated was, however, chiefly of a personal or biographical nature, and such as would have attached to the record of any other series of striking adventures. Many others, though not so large a multitude, perhaps, felt a deep interest in the subject of his inquiries; and there would necessarily be many whose curiosity would be excited by the Philanthropist's examination before the House of Commons, and the vote of thanks which that body had so publicly and honorably offered him for his valuable communications to it. Expectation was thus generally and highly raised; nor, on the publication of the work, was it at all disappointed. The critical reviews of the day received it with great favor, and welcomed it with that most flattering of all receptions from such authorities — an ample share of notice, comment and criticism. One and all, they bore the highest testimony to its author's commanding merits. The reading world — it was rather a limited one then compared with what it is now — appears also to have perused its contents with universal satisfaction and admiration. The meed of praise and acknowledgment was without stint of reservation — was free and full, as it was richly merited. It is pleasant to chronicle such facts. Services to the world are not always so recognized and honored. Neglect is too often the portion of the apostles of new ideas or new sentiments. But the greatness and novelty of Howard's ministry overcame in his case the common tendency to ignore high service. In no period, it is probable, could such private heroism, such generous self-sacrifice, such distinguished public services, have failed to extort the applause and gratitude of mankind.

A curious counter-movement in the theory and practice of criminal justice was taking place at this time, which also contributed not a little to increase the utility and importance of the labors of Howard. Throughout Europe, and in England especially, there were then two distinct and opposing currents of ideas and sentiments on this topic. The initiative — that is, the thinking, guiding, and ultimately, controlling mind of the country, was arrayed against the legislative, executive, administrative mind. Criminal science was then a chaos; its very elements had been thrown into a state of antagonism and confusion. Parliamentarians pulled one way — philosophers another. The first proposed to render punishments more penal — the latter to modify and mitigate them. Between the two tendencies their was a perpetual war. A race of powerful thinkers and learned jurists had recently arisen to contend against penal barbarities being administered under the names and forms of law and justice. Montesquieu, Johnson, Beccaria, Voltaire, Eden, Mably, Paley, and a host of minor publicists, marshalled the intelligence of Europe against the cruelties and fictions of a system of jurisprudence unworthy of the age; and a conviction that there already existed a necessity for a radical and widely-spread reformation — in fact for an entire reconstruction of the whole science of theoretic and practical criminal law, had begun to assert itself in all the higher circles of European mind. But the men to whose wisdom was committed the actual government of nations — *id est*, lawyers, politicians and administrators generally — were not penetrated by these humane ideas. On the contrary, as has just been said, they powerfully opposed the tendency thus manifesting itself, and urged, with disastrous success, the course of penal enactments in the opposite direction.

The simultaneous development of these counter-legislative ideas in England, is not a little curious; and, from its intimate connection with the life and labors of the Philanthropist, is well worthy of a brief elucidation and comment in this place.

The sanguinary measures of the English government for the repression of offences, date from about the middle of the eighteenth century. At that epoch, the Jacobite troubles had just been brought to a close — armed opposition to the House of Hanover was finally put down, — and, in consequence of these events, a vast number of idle and profligate adventurers, for whom the distractions of the times had found military employment, were turned loose upon society, without occupations and without resources. War had accustomed them to license, and made labor distasteful. The natural results ensued — they took to the roads, and robberies became more and more frequent. To repress these disorders, the executive power adopted a system of terror. The safeguard of the public services obtained its first attention; a provision was introduced into a bill (3 Geo. II. c. 25) making it a capital crime to rob the mail — in those days, it should be remembered, carried by a single horseman — whether violence were used or not; as also the robbing of any house, office, or place used for the reception or delivery of letters.

Another enactment, (originally 9 Geo. I. c. 22; but enlarged and draconized by 6 Geo. II. c. 37, — 10 Geo. II. c. 32, — 31 Geo. II. c. 42,) commonly called the Black Act, rendered capital the offences of hunting, wounding, stealing, or destroying any red or fallow deer in any park or forest; killing, maiming, or wounding any cattle; breaking down the head of any fish-pond, so that the fish might be destroyed; cutting down, or otherwise destroying any trees planted for profit, ornament, or shelter, in any garden, avenue, or orchard; and a still more reprehensible law (6 Geo. II. c. 3, 37) denounced the penalty of death against any person who should be found guilty of cutting a hop-band in any hop-plantation! A little later on, the legislature — as if, like the lion which has once lapped blood, it longed for it more and more — passed other acts, (14 Geo. II. c. 25, and 15 Geo. II. c. 34,) making it capital to drive away, steal, or wilfully kill any sheep or cattle with intent to steal any part of the carcase, or to be found aiding and abetting therein! Nor were these severities in any way exceptions to the general course of legislation. They were only parts of a uniform system. Every department of our punitive law was gradually and rapidly assimilated to the spirit which actuated these changes. Not only were forgery, smuggling, coining, and uttering base coin, made capital; but likewise shop-lifting, stealing from a barge or vessel on the river to the value of 5*s*., or from a bleaching-ground to the value of 10*s*.! These diabolical laws were in existence in the time of Howard — many of them in daily process of execution. The judge, it is true, had a discretionary power to transport in certain cases — but the exercise of this power depended upon his private feeling, and death sentences were constantly pronounced and carried into execution for the most trifling offences. Tyburn had its weekly victims.

George the Third — determined to walk in the bloody path of his predecessor — (when he ascended the throne,) is said to have expressed his resolution never to exercise that prerogative of Mercy which the Estates of Great Britain have confided to the sovereign; and his subsequent conduct did little to shame this act of his virgin royalty. The valuable table published by Janssen, and already referred to for another purpose, shows us the working of the sanguinary code, then in full force in the number of persons tired and convicted capitally, in London only, during the twenty-three years, 1749–71, both inclusive:

Crime.	Number capitally convicted	Died in gaol, transported, or pardoned.	Actually executed.
Murder	81	9	72
Attempt to murder	17	2	15
Sodomy	2	2	—
Bestiality	3	1	2
Rape	9	7	2
House-breaking	208	90	118
Robbing the Dwelling	74	40	34
Highway Robbery	362	111	251
Private Thefts	80	53	27
Horse-stealing	90	68	22
Shop-lifting	23	17	6
Forgery	95	24	71
Coining	11	1	10
Riot	2	1	1
Returning from Transportation	31	9	22
Enlisting for Foreign Service	4	—	4
Robberies on the Thames	4	2	2
Smuggling	20	4	16
Defrauding Bank	1	1	—
Defrauding Creditors	3	—	3
Sacrilege	1	1	—
	1121	443	678

Of the 678 executions, 72 only were for murder; the remaining 606 persons were put to death by the law for offences which the more enlightened spirit of the age pronounced to be unworthy of so terrible a punishment, in one single city of the empire! What a startling comment these horrible lines of figures make upon the "bloody letter of the law" as it then stood! What an awful vista they open up into the arcana of the social history of that vaunted era, when George the Third was king! But that inauspicious reign was, in fact, of one dark, uniform, and sanguinary texture. By laying aside his most royal and revered prerogative, the young monarch had taken, at his accession, the initiative of his rule — had prepared his mind to deluge two great continents with blood in a senseless struggle against the progress of the world, in a futile attempt to put down liberty in America and France! Of the 443 persons who died in gaol, were transported, or received pardons, 401 were transported, — the separate numbers of those who died in gaol or were pardoned are unfortunately not given; the last of these items would otherwise, we suspect, have been found miserably small; for with the demoniacal disregard for the holiness of human life which then characterized the councils of St. James, it would be in vain to expect clemency for legally convicted offenders.

It has been remarked before, that the difficulty of rendering any system of secondary punishments effective, was one of the chief causes of this reckless use of death-sentences. The administrators of the law were often at a loss what to do with their culprits, — so they hanged them out of the way. According to the notions of that day, it was at once the easiest, cheapest, and quickest method of escaping from a troublesome charge; for even then they had had some experience of the cost and difficulty of governing a convict population. Judge Heath — the great judicial doomsman — used boldly to avow the principles on which he pursued his victims to the halter. "If," said he, "you imprison at home, the criminal is soon thrown back upon you hardened in guilt. If you transport, you corrupt infant societies, and sow the seeds of atrocious crimes over the habitable globe. *There is no regenerating a felon in this life.* And, for his own sake, as well as for the sake of society, I think it better to hang." Here the assumption is as gratuitous, and the logic as false, as the inference to which they are made to lead is unjust; we cannot stay, however, to argue with his lordship — and will leave his dictum to the moral sense of the reader. If he can admit the force of the reasoning, the practice will of course be intelligible and consistent — not else. And we may fairly suppose that some such sophism impressed upon every mind which then advocated severe punishments a conviction of their political necessity. We must assume that the question was considered by statesmen entirely apart from its morality. No sense or sentiment of justice could, however, indwell in such legislation; for it is impossible to believe that any man in a healthy state of mind could conceive of the idea of death as a moral equivalent for breaking a hop-band or cutting down a tree! Under the peculiar circumstances of the time, rigor was considered a political necessity. Society was thought to be in peril, and the philosophy of statesmen suggested nothing but terror as the restraining agent. It failed however — failed signally. The completest evidence of this is to be found in the rapid augmentation of the offences against which these rigorous enactments were directed. The criminal returns for the first few years of the reign of George III. are very striking as illustrative of this remark. In 1760, there were only 14 capital convictions; in 1761, there were 22; in 1762, 25; in 1763, 61; in 1764, 52; in 1765, 41; in 1766, 39; in 1767, 49; in 1768, 54; in 1769, 71; in 1770, 91. These results are not a little curious; and without assuming that there was in this case a distinct and necessary connection between the increasing stringency of the law and the fearful accumulation of crime — for we all know how much local and incidental causes tend to prevent uniformity of effects, even under general uniformity of conditions — considering the changes in the amount of criminality thus indicated year by year, we are certainly led to adopt the converse of the proposition as an indisputable truth; that is, if the increased amount of terror employed did not *create* crime, as the first inference would naturally be, it utterly failed to *check* it. Some go beyond this, and maintain the first proposition — not without reason either: the whole history of jurisprudence suggests that disproportionate punishments *produce* the offences which they are enacted to *prevent*. The human mind revolts at injustice. When the law itself assumes an unjust form and expression, it cancels the sense of guilt in the lower order of minds — sets the example — furnishes the type and the pretext of violence and wrong. The first forged note upon the Bank of England was presented almost immediately *after* the crime of forgery had been declared capital!

If a counter-current had not set in strongly about the same period as the wild and reckless spirit to which we have here alluded, it is impossible to conceive to what a height of sanguinary cruelty our penal law might not have been carried. But fortunately, the great thinkers for the world — they who rule it most supremely, if only indirectly — had taken their stand against it early. One of the first and greatest of the men who attempted to wrestle with the retrograding efforts of the age, was Montesquieu. He may almost be said to have taken the initiative in the work of treating crime and its punishment as a real substantive science. Since his time, penal law has always been studied from a philosophical, as well as from a legal, point of view. His "Spirit of Laws," published in 1748, made a profound impression upon the mind of England — then far better prepared for its fine and comprehensive views than that of his own country — and marshalled other writers and thinkers into the way of reform. It is not requisite in this place to dwell upon the principles and merits of a work so universally known; but we may notice in passing that, according to Montesquieu, the element of punish ment most potent to deter, is its *certainty* — not its *severity*.

In 1764, Beccaria published his celebrated "Essay on Crimes and Punishment," in Italian. Its profound, luminous, and original views, at once commanded universal attention. It was translated into almost every language, and was certainly read and admired in every country in Europe. Perhaps no single publication ever did more for any study than this short but masterly brochure did for penal science. In Italy alone — the writer was a Milanese, but as, under Austrian rule, men are not permitted to think for the public to so bold a tune as he had taken, the work came out anonymously — six editions were sold in eighteen months. The principles it contains were universally seized upon and responded to. The work was cited by Blackstone, and commented upon by Voltaire; in France it was openly copied by Mably, and was secretly cribbed from by Paley in England. Like all real books on subjects of science, it must, however, be read by the light of its own age; for that age it was remarkably liberal, enlightened, and advanced. As yet, little had been done towards the elaboration of a philosophy of law; it is true, a few daring iconoclasts had ventured to assault the whole framework of the political and judicial system then prevailing in Europe; but these men were mere destroyers, and the salutary work of evoking light and reconstructing order out of the chaos which they had made, and were making, was hardly thought of until Baccaria wrote his treatise. The Italian thinker was endowed by nature with a finely organized, practical, and creative mind. His style is lucid, picturesque, and eloquent — his principles are stern and large — his thought weighty and original — his reasonings profound, and for the most part logical in form — his love of liberty and human good is a consuming passion. Within our limits, it is impossible to render more than the faintest outline of his chief doctrines; for although brief, his book is set thick with thoughts, and is well worthy of the student's most careful study. The master-idea presented to the mind by Beccaria is — that society can only deal with crime according to its results. Human tribunals are incompetent, he says, to pronounce upon motives; or upon opinions which have not developed themselves in positive acts; and, consequently, the only true standard of crime is the injury actually done to society. The scale of this injury furnishes the one correct measure of the offence; and supplies criteria by which to determine the nature, as well as the amount of punishment to be inflicted. For example, in a really philosophical system of law, the penalty for robbery should be partly pecuniary and partly corporeal: pecuniary, to counteract the cupidity; corporeal, to restrain the violence. On the other hand, for offences against honor, nature herself suggests the infliction of degradation — infamy. The same code would dictate that fanaticism should be subjected to a mental, not a physical discipline; because bodily pain always increases the maladies of the mind. As a rule, pecuniary punishments — except for theft, where the obvious motive is *gain* — are bad; for they almost always assume either the shape of a favor from the judge to the culprit, or that of an exaction — never a punishment, such as would lie within the intention of a righteous law. The criminal who has injured society, has thereby become its debtor; the state holds a lien upon his wealth and his services; and no system of jurisprudence can be considered perfect which does not provide for his atonement, *by his labor*, for the wrong which he may have done. The penalty of death, because it cuts off the life of the criminal, instead of sequestrating it for the benefit of the state; and transportation, because it removes the criminal from the scene of his offence, and throws a doubt over the reality of his punishment — are equally impolitic to the state, and unjust to the culprits. *Certainty* and *swiftness* are, accordingly to Beccaria, the most deterring elements of punishment; while, on the contrary, undue severity produces impunity, and transforms the culprit into a vulgar martyr.

Such is a short synopsis of this famous essay. No reader ought to be unacquainted with it. The chapters on capital punishment and transportation are especially deserving of study, — by those who support as well as by those who assail the institutions commented on. Beccaria's work was a great favorite with Howard; he studied it deeply, quoted it frequently, and appears to have coincided in almost every point with its humane and philosophical principles ; — it is highly probable that his reading of it had something to do with his assumption of his great mission.

The impetus given by this work to the study of law as a branch of moral science, was ably seconded by the lectures—commenced at Oxford in 1753—of Blackstone ; the Commentaries, which contain the substance of his researches on the subject of English law, were published at the end of the year 1765. Apart from his opinions—which were too uniformly in favor of the powers and things as they were—the peculiarity of Blackstone and the fact that removes him from the category of merely legal writers into that of philosophical jurists, is his attempt to give the rationale of the laws which he undertakes to explain. By lawyers this is considered his fault — inasmuch as that fraternity takes no cognizance of the reasons for an enactment, but only of its letter — the philosophical reader will properly regard it as the reverse.

While Blackstone was rousing attention to such studies at Oxford, Paley was delivering his lectures at the rival university on the general subject of morals. The chapter which this logical writer devotes to Crimes and Punishments, is one of his finest pieces of special pleading. He had no philosophy of his own on the subject ; and his social science, as therein developed, is neither true nor consistent with itself; yet the case is made out with great art and tact, for the writer was one well skilled to make the worst appear the better reason. Paley was a strong partisan. His mind and conscience were alike surrendered to his patrons. One object only was before him when he wrote — to defend existing abuses; and it must be confessed that he was accomplished in the necessary craft. He was the best of advocates, but the worst of judges. He examined institutions and moral systems in the spirit of an interested party; if he possessed the judicial faculty at all, his prejudices deprived him of its use.

With him, to be — was to be right. Nevertheless, his work contains some fine thoughts — all the finer that they are not his own, but Beccaria's. Bending the general scope of his argument into the conservative grooves, a man like Paley could not altogether resist the temptation to adorn his subject with the ideas of a more liberal and advanced philosophy than belonged to the cause which he had himself espoused. Hence a certain inconsistency between some of his aphorisms and his inductions; hence also the entire want of order and system in his ideas. There is in Paley absolutely no co-ordination of thought. His single sentences are pellucid as a running water; but collate and contrast them, and they become turbid as a ditch. Starting out with the assertion of a great principle — *id est*, that the end of penal discipline is not to punish, but to prevent crimes — he immediately proceeds to falsify it by commending the atrocious provisions of the penal laws to which reference has lately been made. He argues — as did the promulgators of the draconic code which he undertook to defend — that the severity of punishment should be measured, not by the injury sustained, as Beccaria contends, and common sense dictates, but by the amount of the temptation! This maxim is now repudiated by general consent of mankind; and the force of the temptation and the facilities offered for the committal of crime, are the ordinary elements for extenuation of the offence and mitigation of the punishment. Paley strongly advocated an increase in the number of death penalties. About the same period, Eden's work on the "Principles of Penal Law" made its appearance, and became a great favorite with the Philanthropist. Bentham was also rising before the world as a promising writer on the same important topics. Competent leaders were therefore not wanting in the crusade against the progressive cruelty of the law.

This decided setting in of the intellectual tide in the same direction as Howard's labors, tended to create a larger public for his works. Starting with no particular theory, and tracing his path through an entirely new set of experiences, he nevertheless arrived in the end at pretty nearly the same general conclusions as his more learned but less practical compeers. And his curious and complete observations upon the great variety of penal systems which he had encountered, furnished the theorists with materials for correcting and utilizing their hypotheses. That they should, therefore, be highly valued by the most competent judges is not wonderful: even as the *visits* of this Pilgrim of Humanity had been welcomed by the poor captives to whom he had brought hope and consolation — even where he could not carry light and freedom — was their *record* received in the scientific and political world as the groundwork of an entire new social and administrative science. The publication of the "State of Prisons" made and marked an epoch in the history of social jurisprudence. From that date the attempt to reform our criminals acquired a substantive form and character. Before then, the felon, the misdemeanant, the lorette — all who had offended against the law of society, — were abandoned, cast away, as so much humanity absolutely lost. If God had only judged the world as harshly as man judged it!

But the reign of finer feelings, nobler ideas, began to dawn. As usual, however, thought — theory — far out-ran experience; and although the elements of a new science had gradually evolved themselves, its hypothetical part had advanced a long way ahead of its facts. Howard's labors at once reversed this order. The impetus given by him to practical reforms has caused the perfection of discipline to be achieved while the theory of punishment still remains unsettled. In the year of grace, 1849, we have the most fundamental disagreement among publicists, statesmen, and judges, as to the principles and purpose of penal inflictions, and as to the relations and duties of society to its criminals: yet we have in the separate system of discipline, as administered at Pentonville, and in the silent system as it is carried out under the superintendance of the able Governor of Cold Bath Fields Prison — almost everything which the mind can conceive of perfection in the practical administration of the science. This not incurious result is almost solely attributable to Howard, and the method which he adopted. Fortunately, he commènced his acquaintance with the subject in the cell. He entered the prison perfectly untrammelled by previous notions. No false knowledge impeded his progress. He had no hypotheses to support — no pet crotchets to warp his judgment. Happily, too, he was not embarrassed by the refinements of legal learning. The evils which he saw he proposed to remedy in the most simple and unstatesmanlike fashion. If he found captives starving, he proposed that they should be fed; if sick, tended; if in irons, unmanacled; if unjustly detained, set free, —and so forth. On these subjects he had no paradoxes — no subtleties. With a sublime unconsciousness of the complicated difficulties, moral, social, and political, which beset the question of criminal treatment in the minds of mere reasoners, Howard always accepted the obvious and common-sense view of the case. The horrors which he encounterred were of the most tangible sort, and required, as he thought, the simplest of remedies, — and such he proposed. The method thus initiated, has, with intervals of neglect, been ever since followed; and the result is indicated in the fact, that notwithstanding the labors of many eminent writers on the theory of the science, the branch which deals with the disciplinary part of the subject is far in advance of that which relates to its ruling principles.

In following the career of Howard, from the period of his appointment to the High Shrievalty for the county of Bedford, to the date of his first publication we have preferred to keep the attention of the reader fixed upon the course of his public labors; but having now arrived at a point where the narrative as it were suspends itself, we may pause for a moment to relate a few particulars of his manner of life at this period. After that memorable journey into Italy — which it is hoped the reader has not forgotten — and the striking course of mental discipline to which he then voluntarily subjected himself, his mind seems never again to have lost its calm and steady tone — the equable and healthy activity which enabled him to carry on, without intermission from either mental or physical causes, the harrassing work to which he was devoted. Considering that his health had previously been so delicate, it is not a little astonishing that no fatal effects should have followed his daring intrusion into so many fever-haunted dungeons. In truth, he appeared to bear a charmed life. Whatsoever the danger into which he entered in the cause of the wretched, he came out unscathed. God was about his footsteps. His trust was in Almighty aid, and in the holiness of his own intention; and his Father, the Friend of the Wretched, did not fail him in his hour of need. The secondary reasons for his impunity are also well worth considering. Howard ate no flesh — drank no wine nor spirits — bathed in cold water daily — ate little, and that at fixed intervals — retired to bed early — rose early. Such was the programme of his personal course. This regimen enabled him to penetrate fearlessly dungeons into which gaolers, and physicians even, dared not follow him. From his youth upward — the lesson of abstinence had no doubt been learnt in his father's puritanical household — his diet had always been of the simplest kind, and as he advanced in years the habit of temperance grew stronger and stronger. Some details of his way of living while at Warrington have been preserved — which, as they were of a kind with his usual habits, are not unworthy of record in this history. Every morning — though it was then in the depth of a severe winter — he arose at two o'clock precisely, washed, performed his orisons, and then worked at his papers until seven, when he breakfasted and dressed for the day. Punctually at eight he repaired to the printing office to inspect the progress of his sheets through the press. There he remained until one, when the compositors went to dinner. While they were absent, he would walk to his lodgings, and, putting some bread and dried fruit into his pocket, sally out for his customary exercise — generally a stroll in the suburbs of the town — eating, as he trudged along, his hermit fare, and drinking therewith a glass of cold water begged at some cottager's door. This was his only dinner. By the time that the printers returned to the office, he had usually, but not always, wandered back. Sometimes he would call upon a friend on his way, and spend an hour or two in pleasant chat — a recreation he rather liked; for though anything but a gossip, he had all the social instincts largely developed in his nature. At the press he remained until the men left off their day's toil, and then either retired to his modest lodgings, took a simple dish of tea or coffee, performed his household religious services — a sacred duty, which he never under any circumstances, whether at home or abroad, suffered himself to omit — and retired to rest at an early hour; or, repaired to the residence of the Aikins, to consult with the future doctor upon any corrections or alterations which might have occurred to him during the day; in which case also he retired at his regular hour.

Beyond the safeguard of this severe and patriarchal regimen, the precautions taken by Howard to repel contagious diseases were very simple at first, — such as smelling a phial of vinegar, while in the infected cell, and washing, and changing his apparel afterwards; but, in process of time, even these expedients were abandoned as unnecessary. The question of how he preserved himself free from contagion being often pressed upon him, he replied — and his words are eminently note-worthy, — "Next to the free goodness and mercy of the Author of my being, Temperance and Cleanliness are my preservatives. Trusting in Divine Providence, and believing myself in the way of my duty, I visit the most noxious cells, and while thus employed, 'I fear no evil.'" And in this belief and fearlessness of ill, he passed all perils — like Shadrach, Meshach, and Abed-nego of old through the fiery furnace of the Persian king — without a hair of his head being injured. In all ages of the world such had been the defensive armor of heroes and martyrs — such the inspiration and the impulse of all great thoughts and holy deeds!

In his first journeyings through the United Kingdom — and in those countries alone, he travelled during the year 1773–4–5–6, 10,318 miles! — he was accompanied by his trusty esquire, honest John Prole. Well mounted, and not over fastidious tourists, they usually progressed at the rate of about forty miles a day. Though the roads in unfrequented parts of the country were not so well furnished then as they became in the more palmy days of stageing, our travellers were never at a loss for entertainment. Hardly a cabin which they passed, even in out of the way tracks in Ireland and Scotland, failed to furnish all the luxuries which they required. Some dried biscuit was easily carried in a wallet; and it was a poor hut indeed which could not supply a draught of fresh milk, or a cup of spring water, for a good round sum, which on these occasions was always tendered. The ascetic habits of the Philanthropist were such as he believed suited to his constitution; they were not adopted as matters of parade. On every occasion he carefully avoided making any display of his simple diet, and was particularly careful not to offer it as a pretext for parsimony. When he arrived at any town where he intended to rest for the night, he would go to the best hotel, order his dinner, with beer and wine, just like any other traveller, and stipulate that his own servant should wait upon him at table. When the cloth was laid, the viands spread out, and the host withdrawn, honest Prole would quietly remove the costly luxuries from the table to the sideboard, while his eccentric master would busy himself in preparing his homely repast of bread and milk, upon which he would then banquet with gusto,—equally to his own satisfaction and that of the landlord. Waiters, postilions, and all persons of their class, he was in the habit ot paying munificently, being unwilling to have his mind disturbed or his temper chafed, by paltry disputes about a few pence. He used to say that in the expenses of a journey which must necessarily cost three or four hundred pounds, twenty or thirty pounds extra were not worth a thought; and his liberalities in these matters not only procured him the good will of those who were the humble, but not unimportant instruments of his rapid progresses from place to place, but often accelerated his transits, and saved that time which was of so much more value to the world than money.

Travelling so much as he did, he came at length to be pretty well known on the roads, and his humor to be appreciated; indeed, considering the practical way in which his lessons were enforced, it was not easy to misunderstand them. A gentleman who travelled with him by post from Warrington to London, told Dr. Aikin a charateristic anecdote of his method of regulating postilions. The master of the whip on one of the stages appeared to have a theory of driving of his own — which was by no means agreeable to the travellers. To Howard's remonstrances, he turned a deaf ear only. Confident in his own system, he would receive no instruction, but went on, fast or slow, roughly or smoothly, as best suited his humor. All plagues, however, come to an end. When the travellers arrived at the post for change of horses, Howard requested the landlord to send for some poor and industrious widow from the village, and then placing her face to face with the amazed follower of Jehu, counted out to the latter his full fare — telling him at the same time, that he should not bestow upon him the usual gratuity given to postillions, on account of his misconduct; but, to convince him that he withheld it from a sentiment of justice, and not from any meaner motive, he would make a present to the poor widow of double the sum; and having counted the money out to her, dismissed them. This was his usual custom; and without violence or angry words it soon produced, wherever he was known, a ready compliance with his wishes.

In his earlier tours of prison inspection on the continent of Europe, he was alone — for his faithful follower having married, he felt a strong objection to separate him from his family. Subsequently, he promoted a youth named Thomasson, who had entered his household in some menial capacity while quite a lad, into the companion of his pilgrimages. Amongst other things, Thomasson had been employed to romp and play with young Master Howard, and his hearty affection for the child had procured him the notice and favor of its father: henceforth he becomes his almost constant attendant — is with him in some of his most trying situations — and the only one of his country's name and race who will stand near his dying bed, when he finally falls a martyr to his appointed mission in a strange and distant land.

In no way — as has been sometimes falsely assumed — was Howard a stranger to the amenities and social charities of life. His mental and moral organization eminently fitted him for domestic scenes. No man ever had a nicer perception of, or a keener relish for, elegant social intercourse; no man was ever more beloved and respected within the social circle. Not his reputation — the pressing demands on his time and attention to which his public labors gave rise — his long and frequent absence from home — the constantly enlarging sphere of his acquaintance and duties, — nothing, in fact, could interrupt the steadiness of his affection for his old Cardington friends, or theirs for him. In the intervals of the journeys which henceforward — as already — follow quickly upon each other, we shall find him always returning to his home — the scene of so much bliss and so much sorrow — as the dove to the ark — in search of love, seclusion, and repose. But even there his sense of duty did not sleep. His tenants and dependants still claimed his paternal care. He still continued to build model cottages, as of old, for the more deserving of his poor neighbors. There was still the same desire and competition to inhabit them. Sobriety, peace, cleanliness, and religion, still characterized them and their occupiers. The schools which he had established, thrived also, and brought forth their abundant fruits. When at Cardington they were amongst the foremost objects of his care and regard. For the young, he had always a particular affection ; and his intercourse with them was such as would be predicated from his character — grave, gentle, and thoughtful. For the children of his intimate friends, his affection appeared uniform and touching — especially when the magnitude and seriousness of his pursuits are borne in mind. He rarely visited the family of the Rev. Mr. Smith without carrying a pocket full of fruit for the younger urchins — and he seldom returned from one of his European tours, without bringing a cargo of foreign toys for his little favorites.

His son John, who was now in his fourteenth year, was under the tuition of the Rev. Mr. Robins, of Daventry — and his further academical career was a subject of much and anxious thought to the father; as yet, he had betrayed no sign of that dreadful mental malady which soon after this date began to embitter so much his parent's life.

But within this interval of rest, another shaft was sent into the Pilgrim's heart. In the August of this year, 1777, he was suddenly called to London to the death-bed of his only sister — but arrived too late to take a loving farewell of the departing spirit. This stroke fell heavily on the affections of Howard ; she was almost the last tie of blood which bound him to the selfish troubles of existence. But his mind had now been sternly schooled. The ordeal of private suffering was almost passed; his religion had become to him a thing of life; and henceforth, resigning himself more and more to the duty which seemed appointed unto him of God, prepared to carry on the work, even to the end. In one respect, her demise was not without its share of good: — her somewhat ample fortune was bequeathed to her illustrious brother, and this timely accession to his means enabled him to go on with his projects, without employing thereupon any part of the property to which his son had a natural right to expect to succeed.

With a better comprehension of the man and his appointed work, we may now advantageously resume the threads of our narrative.

CHAPTER IX.

PERILS BY SEA AND LAND.

We have already had occasion to speak of the suspension of the transportation system, on the breaking out of the American war of Independence. As England had then no penal settlements besides those in the States, convicts had to be kept at home as a matter of necessity. Of course, something had to be done with them. At first the Hulk-system was tried, but not fairly; for, on the part of the government, it was never considered more than a temporary expedient, until the old markets could be re-opened, or new ones created. Nevertheless the idea was gradually gaining ground that, as a plan or criminal discipline, transportation was radically vicious, and in the end would have to be abandoned; consequently, rude and imperfect as the Hulk-experiment was, it was watched by penal reformers with very considerable interest. Howard was an earnest advocate of home-cure, or at least home-treatment, of crime; and we may be assured that this new trial would not escape his close observation.

The "Justitia" was stationed at Woolwich and prepared for the reception of male convicts; but the discipline adopted was eminently calculated to defeat the trial — being loose, cruel, irregular, and tyrannical in the highest degree. Seeing these things, Howard was little pleased with the working of the affair; but as it was new to the country, and conducted under the immediate orders of the ministry, he refrained from embarrassing them by making public his fears and his objections. On his first visit to the "Justitia," he found the men looking very sickly and wretched; many of them had no shirts, others no shoes, some no waistcoats or stockings; all were ill-lodged, — even the sick had only the bare decks to lie on; and the broken biscuit given to them for food was green and mouldy. They had no drink allowed them except water — no beer, coffee, or chocolate — and their meat was tainted. No wonder, then, that the rate of mortality was high, and that the vessel had a strong pestilential smell, like a close prison. Although Howard did not publish these disgraceful particulars, his remonstrance with the officers in charge was so effective, that, from that day, things began to improve. Cruel and careless officials had learned to fear his prying eye. Such abuses will not bear the light, — and the mere knowledge that a bold and conscientious observer was near them, whose business it was to see their faults, whose representations would go forth to the world with a sort of gospel authority, acted as a certain check upon maladministration. Without moving government to take any steps in the matter, he had the pleasure of seeing the aspect of affairs improve — though they never assumed that perfect shape which it was his wish to see. The plan, as has been said, was only adopted at the first as a makeshift; and the bill authorizing it was now about to expire. However, as the Colonial markets had not yet been re-opened, something of an interim character had still to be done, and a committee of the House of Commons was appointed to inquire into the practical working of the Hulk-system, with a view to its provisional continuance. On the 15th of April, 1778, Howard was examined before this committee. At the request of honorable members, he spoke of his impressions of the plan, how far it could be held to have succeeded in spite of all obstacles, and how much its success had been neutralized by bad management. He described his earliest and latest visits, and contrasted them. The first we have noticed. In the other, he found the men treated more humanely; they were looking healthier; their food was good — though insufficient in quantity; they were still ill-clothed, and many of them very dirty; mats had been provided for them to sleep on; the sick were carefully attended to — had separate beds, and were released from their irons. Altogether the establishment was greatly improved, and he did not now find that fatal smell which he had formerly noticed with alarm. His opinion being asked by the committee, he declared that he thought the Hulk-system, with good management, capable of being made infinitely preferable to transportation. On this report, therefore, being made to the House, a bill was brought in and sanctioned, continuing this method of punishment. With Howard, however, as well as with the legislature, the Act was still regarded as a temporary measure. His own idea was to confine convicts in a great penal work-prison — something like the rasp-house of Holland — where the security would be greater, the labor more productive, the punishment more severe, and the reform more certain, than they could possibly be in a dock-yard. In fact, he wished to see introduced into this country, a *discipline of work* — an idea which has been carried out, to some extent, in our own day, in such gaols as Milbank and Cold Bath Fields. Influenced by his arguments and by his experience in many countries, these notions of his gained some favor with the government; and Sir Wm. Blackstone and Mr. Eden — the effect of whose writings on the progress of similar ideas has been referred to — were commissioned to make out the draught of a bill for the creation of such an establishment. As, however, there was no gaol in the kingdom at all adapted for the trial, it was necessary to think of erecting one — and on this intimation being conveyed to Howard, he at once set out for Holland with a view to procure more precise information as to the construction and regulations of the spin and rasp-houses of that country. Landing at Helvoetsluys on the 19th of April, he proceeded on this mission to the Hague and Amsterdam — where he met with an accident which for some time interrupted his labors and placed even his life in peril. A horse, which had taken fright and was running away with a dray, dashed against him in the street and threw him on a heap of stones with great violence. His sides were so severely bruised as to render him unfit to be removed for several days. As soon as he could bear it, he was carried to the Hague for better medical attendance; there the injury rapidly developed itself; an inflammatory fever supervened — and for more than six weeks his recovery was almost despaired of.

During this severe illness — as was his usual custom when unable to leave his room — Howard made frequent memoranda in his note-book, on his own internal and spiritual history — in tracing which they are of the utmost value. One or two of these fragments run thus: — "Hague, May 11th. Do me good, O God, by this painful affliction. May I see the great uncertainty of health, ease and comfort; that all my springs are in Thee. Oh, the painful and weary nights I pass! May I be more thankful if restored to health, more compassionate towards others, and more absolutely devoted to God. . . . . 13th. — In pain and anguish all night; my very life a burden to me; help Lord! . . . 14th. — This night my fever abated, my pains were less. I thank

God I have had two hours' sleep; prior to which, for sixteen days and nights, I had not four hours' sleep. Righteous art Thou, O Lord, in all Thy ways, and holy in all Thy works; sanctify this affliction, and show me wherefore Thou contendest with me; bring me out of the furnace as silver seven times purified. . . . 16th. — A more quiet night and less fever; yet much pain until morning. If God should please to restore me to days of prosperity, may I remember the days of sorrow, to make me habitually serious and humble; may I learn from this affliction more than I have learned before, and so have reason to bless God for it."

From this date he recovered fast. In ten days more he was able to go out; and in due course he prepared to resume the inquiries which had brought him again into Holland. These he accomplished to his own satisfaction, by making a regular and laborious tour of all the chief towns and cities of the country. Everywhere he was profoundly impressed with the superiority of the criminal police of Holland over that of England. The average of crime was always low — public executions rare — transportation unknown. In Utrecht, for example, he was informed that not a single person had been put to death in that city and the province, of which it is the capital, for fourteen years. We have already seen the contrast which England presented to this.

Entering Germany by way of Osnaburgh and Hanover, Howard passed on through Brunswick and

Magdeburg to Berlin, with the prisons of which city he was on the whole much pleased. They were clean, airy, healthy; the prisoners were properly fed, instructed, and employed. Unlike the rest of Germany, Prussia had no torture chambers. The Warrior King had a short time before abolished this barbarous mode of trial throughout his dominions.

Howard's reputation had now spread over Europe, and wherever he went, he was received with the most distinguished honors. While on his present visit to the capital of Prussia, Frederick William was at the head of his armies in Silesia, where a decisive battle was every day expected; but the following extract from one of the Philanthropist's letters, bearing date, Berlin, June 28th, 1778, shows that he was properly appreciated in the highest quarters. . . . "The pain and fever brought on by the accident I met with in Holland, made me almost despair of accomplishing my journey, or even of ever returning to England; but, through sparing mercy, I am now recovered, and have that pleasing hope before me. I was presented on Friday to Prince Henry, who very graciously conversed with me ten minutes. He said, he 'could hardly conceive of a more disagreeable journey [than Howard's], but the object was great and humane.' . . . . We are here just on the eve of an important event. The King of Prussia is in Silesia, and the emperor is encamped within a few miles of him; 40,000 men are ready to destroy one another, as the passions or prejudices of an arbitrary monarch may direct! This would be a matter of great concern to a thinking mind, had it not a firm belief in a wise and overruling Providence. In about a fortnight I hope to be at or near Vienna. . . . I have both parts of this day joined in worship with the French Protestants — a pleasure I shall now be debarred of for many weeks. I am here nobly lodged; I drank tea this afternoon with Prince Dolgoruky, the Russian Ambassador; — yet I thirst for the land of liberty, my Retreat and Cardington friends."

From Berlin our traveller proceeded to Spandau — the castle of which was, and still is, the Bastille of Prussia. That famous place of durance, and also that of Magdeburg — so well known as the prison-house of the chivalrous Baron Trenck — Howard tells us were not so dreadful as their reputations. It is true the men were badly lodged, and seemed to have little attention paid to them, except as to their security; but the prisoners generally were not kept in cells of 4 feet square and 6 feet high, loaded with heavy irons and fed on a miserable allowance of bread and water — as had been the case for six long years with the adventurous soldier whose revelations have made the name of the latter fortress a word of terror to all Europe.

At Dresden, our traveller saw the slaves and culprits strongly bound in fetters — even those who were sick. When not at work, both men and women were fastened by a staple to the walls of their cells, all of which were dirty and filled with noxious stenches; a circumstance which Howard did not fail to represent with great plainness to the grand baliff of the city, on calling to thank him for the permission which he had courteously granted to inspect them. Across Silesia — through the ranks of the opposing armies of Austria and Prussia, commanded in person by the Emperor of Germany and Co-regent of Austria, the celebrated Joseph II., and the still more notable, gray-haired warrior, Frederick the Great — through Bohemia and Moravia, our traveller proceeded to Vienna.

While making a short stay at Prague to visit the prisons and hospitals, he was induced to make a call at the principal monastery of the order of Capuchins in that ancient city. A very curious observer of men, Howard liked to see the effect of various kinds of discipline upon the mind and character; and in this instance he was perhaps attracted by the ascetic reputation of this order of friars. It was a fast-day when he made his visit; but judge of his surprise and indignation when, on entering the great hall, he saw the holy fathers seated at dinner round a table sumptuously furnished with the most delicate and costly viands which the season and country could furnish! Being known to some of the principal personages present, he was politely invited to sit down and partake of the feast. Had it been a palace instead of a monastery, he would have refused, it being contrary to his usual habits to indulge in such dainty food ; but to see such costly extravagance in a religious house, was more than his severe sense of fitness could quietly brook. He therefore not only declined their proffered hospitalities, but, turning to the elder monks, read them a pretty sharp lecture on the subject ; telling them he had been led to suppose that they had retired from the world in order to live a life of abstemiousness and prayer; instead of which he found they had turned their dwelling into a house of revelry and drunkenness. The jolly fathers, whatever they may have thought of their heretical reprover, deemed it politic to appear alarmed at the tone which he had taken, especially when he told them he was going to Rome, where he would see His Holiness, their master, and could ascertain if such loose discipline met with his approval. This threat went home. Next morning four or five of the penitent fathers waited upon him at his hotel, to beg his pardon for the offence which he had witnessed, and to implore his silence on the subject at head quarters. Howard answered that he would make no promise; on the contrary, he would be guided entirely by circumstances. He would take the necessary means to be well informed as to whether the offence was repeated or not, and would be governed by the result. If it were not repeated, he would use his own discretion as to what course he should take; if it were, they might be certain that he would do as he had said.

With this, after giving a solemn promise that such disorderly violations of their rules should not again be permitted, the deputation withdrew.

Of the prisons at Vienna the Philanthropist speaks in mixed terms of censure and commendation. The culprits were all kept at work — chiefly in the manufacture of woollens — and paid the full amount of their earnings; but the prisons were over-crowded; the inmates had no coverlids to their beds; and altogether far too little attention was paid to their health and morals. La Maison de Bourreau, the great gaol of Vienna, contained a number of horrid dungeons; into most of these the inspector descended, and thus he speaks of one of them: — "Here, as usual, I inquired whether they had any putrid fever, and was answered in the negative. But in one of the dark dungeons down twenty-four steps, I thought I had found a person with the gaol-fever. He was loaded with heavy irons and chained to the wall. Anguish and misery appeared with clotted tears on his face. He was not capable of speaking to me; but on examining his breast and feet for *petechia*, or spots, and finding that he had a strong intermitting pulse, I was convinced that he was not ill of that disorder. A prisoner in an opposite cell told me, that the poor creature had desired him to call out for assistance, and he had done it, but *was not heard.*" Consequently no relief came to the unfortunate wretch in his dire necessity. What mind can realize the misery endured in such a case? Seldom does such a dungeon find a tongue.

But let us listen for a moment to the voice of a more recent victim of the Austrian court — the young and patriotic Count Confalonieri, whose crime it was to be an Italian and to love his country. In a few of the most awful lines ever penned, thus wrote he the story of a life: — "I am an old man now; yet by fifteen years my soul is younger than my body! Fifteen years I existed (for I did not live — it was not *life*) in the self-same dungeon, ten feet square! During six years I had a companion; nine years I was alone! I never could rightly distinguish the face of him who shared my captivity, in the eternal twilight of our cell. The first year we talked incessantly together; we related our past lives — our joys forever gone — over and over again. The next year we communicated our ideas to each other on all subjects. The third year we had no ideas to communicate; we were beginning to lose the power of reflection. The fourth, at intervals of a month or so, we would open our lips to ask each other if it were indeed possible that the world went on as gay and bustling as when we formed a portion of mankind. The fifth year we were silent. The sixth, he was taken away — I never knew where, to execution or to liberty; but I was glad when he was gone; even solitude was better than the dim vision of that pale, vacant face. After that I was alone. Only one event broke in upon my nine years' vacancy.

One day (it must have been a year or two after my companion left me) the dungeon door was opened, and a voice — I know not whence — uttered these words: 'By order of his imperial majesty, I intimate to you that your wife died a year ago.' Then the door was shut; I heard no more. They had but flung this great agony in upon me, and left me alone with it again."

During his present sojourn in Vienna, Howard paid frequent visits to the hospitals and alms-houses, in which he found many things to approve. There was a curious mode of punishing bakers who were convicted of adulterating their bread or giving short weight — namely, by means of the ducking-stool. This engine of terror was fixed at the edge of the water, on the Wien or Danube, and consisted of a long pole, or plank, extending some distance over the surface of the river. The culprit was fastened in his own bread-basket, and, being placed at the end of the plank, was soused a certain number of times, according to the gravity of his offence. The punishment was at once severe and disgraceful; the fraternity of bakers would gladly have purchased immunity from the infliction; but the law or custom was rigorous, and the magistrates were compelled to punish the delinquent.

During his stay in the capital of Austria, Howard was introduced to Maria Theresa, the martial Queen of Hungary, and so far relaxed his usual custom with regard to courts, as to accept an invitation to dine with her. At the table of Sir Robert Murray Keith, English Ambassador at Vienna, he was a frequent guest, and sometimes not a little startled diplomatic and courtly company by the frankness of his observations. One day the subject of after-dinner conversation happened to be the *torture*; a German nobleman boasted that to his imperial majesty — Joseph II. — belonged the glory of having abolished it in every part of his estates; to which Howard rather warmly replied, — "Pardon me, Sir, his imperial majesty has only abolished one species of torture to establish in its place another still more cruel; for the torture which he has abolished lasted at most only a few hours, but that which he has appointed lasts many weeks, — nay, sometimes years. The poor wretches are plunged into a noisome dungeon, as bad as the black hole at Calcutta, from which they are not taken until they confess what is laid to their charge, and then only to be executed." "Hush!" said the ambassador, somewhat alarmed, well knowing his guests; "your words will be reported to the Emperor." Sir Robert knew how vain Joseph was of his darling institutions. Howard however, valued them at their proper worth, and cared no more for the Emperor's opinion on such a matter, than he would have done for that of an alderman. "What!" he replied, without noticing the consternation of the company, "shall my tongue be tied from speaking the truth by any king or emperor in the world? I repeat what I have asserted, and will maintain its veracity." Perhaps he had that day spoken to the man whose cries of agony had been unheard execept by his fellows in distress, and whose voice had now lost the power of utterance. His heart was full, and, like the prophets of old, he spoke out boldly. The words fell upon the ears of that courtly circle — unaccustomed to such sounds, — like thunder-peals; there was danger in them. A profound silence ensued. In Vienna, it was not then — nor is it yet — permitted to any one to speak of the acts or words of the sovereign, otherwise than in terms of superlative adulation. No rejoinder was made, and the subject dropped. Some amongst that assembly would no doubt admire the boldness of the speaker, but no one dared to acknowledged it; and the greater number feared his words as if they had been of that rankly treasonous kind, which it is almost as perilous to have heard as to have spoken.

Taking his departure from Vienna — where, notwithstanding a few escapades like the above, his high character and great reputation had made him a general favorite — our traveller continued his journey through Styria and Carniola into Dalmatia. In the castle of Trieste, the capital of the province, the convicts were confined and employed in the harbor about ten hours daily. They appeared healthy, clean, and strong; and labored cheerfully, because, when employed, each of them received about three farthings a-day wages.

Embarking at this port in a small shallop, he experienced a rough passage of two days and nights in crossing over the Adriatic to Venice. He entered Italy with high expectations of seeing much that would forward the objects of his journey; and in this he was not altogether disappointed. The celebrated prison of Venice, situated as every reader of Childe Harold knows, on the Grand Canal, near the Rialto, and over against the ducal palace, Howard describes as one of the strongest he had ever seen, and as containing, at that time, between three and four hundred prisoners. Hundreds of illustrious men — true patriots as well as false traitors — have been confined in this prison under the equally withering rule of the ancient Oligarchy and the modern Austrians. Who does not remember the touching plaints of the young and gentle Silvio Pellico, as he listened in his melancholy cell in *i Piombi* to the voices of the children in the campanile of St. Mark's, in the quiet of the summer evenings?

Except for political offences, death-punishments were foreign to the ideas of the Venetian people and to the genius of their laws; great crimes were consequently punished by imprisonment for long terms — often for life — the culprits being immured in dungeons horribly loathsome and perfectly dark. On inquiring from these wretches whether they would not prefer work in the galleys to idleness in the cell, the answer was invariably in the affirmative.

Padua, Bologna, and Ferrara were the next places visited by Howard; after examining which he proceeded to Florence, the prisons, hospitals, and workhouses of which city he inspected under orders from the Grand Duke. A simple incident occurred in one of the prisons, which, as it is characteristic of the man and of the country of his sojourn, is worth relating. According to his usual custom where he considered the allowance of food rather too low, Howard, on his first visit to the gaol called *Delle Stinche*, left a small sum of money to buy a quantity of beef and mutton to be distributed in rations to the men, and some tea and sugar for the women. He thought no more of it; but on paying a second visit two or three days after, he was unexpectedly greeted at his entrance with hymns and choruses of thanks from the grateful recipients of his bounty. The motive of his liberality — a thing to them, outcasts of society, shut off from all gentler charities of life, so unusual — they could not comprehend, otherwise than by referring it to a supernatural cause. As he walked in, they fell down at his feet, and would have worshipped him, had he not taken pains to convince them that he was only a poor mortal creature, like themselves, whose sole object was to do them good, but not to receive their homage.

By way of Leghorn and Loretto, our traveller continued his journey to Rome, where he found much to approve, but still more to condemn, in the criminal institutions of the States of the Church. Paramount was his desire at that time to inspect the dungeons of the Inquisition, and all his influence, personal and otherwise, was exerted to that end. But in vain. The gloomy portals of the Holy Office could not be opened to a heretic — unless to close on him forever. Baulked in this earnest desire, he haunted the ominous building for hours, as he had formerly done the Bastille in Paris; until his appearance began to excite the suspicions of its janitors, and he was warned of the peril which he ran.

It is only in our own day that the fearful secrets of this famous prison-house have been brought to the light. Howard lived to see the Bastille levelled to the ground; we, more fortunate still, have lived to see a deeper and more fatal dungeon broken into; and we cannot help appending here a few notes from the official report published thereon:—

"In consequence of a decree of the Roman Constituent Assembly, the suppression of the tribunal of the Holy Office, was resolved. The doors were then carefully sealed by the Roman notary Caggiotti, and the inventory was commenced. The first place visited was the ground-floor of the edifice, where were the prisons, and the stables, coach-houses, kitchen, cellars, and other conveniences for the use of the assessor and the father inquisitors.

"Some new doors were opened in the walls and part of a pavement raised; in this operation human bones were found and a trap-door discovered, which induced a resolution to make excavations in certain spots pointed out by persons well acquainted with the locality. Digging very deep in one place a great number of human skeletons were found, some of them placed so close together and so amalgamated with lime, that no bone could be moved without being broken. In the roof of another subterranean chamber, a large ring was found fixed. It is supposed to have been used in administering the torture. It still remains there. Along the whole length of this room, stone steps, rather broad were attached to the wall—these probably served for the prisoners to sit or recline on. In a third underground room was found a quantity of very black rich earth, intermingled with human hair, of such a length that it seemed women's rather than men's hair; here also human bones were found. In this dungeon a trap-door was formed in the thickness of the wall which opened into a passage in the flat above, leading to the room where examinations were conducted. Among the inscriptions made with charcoal on the wall, it was observed that many appeared of very recent date, expressing in most effecting terms the sufferings of every kind endured in these chambers. . . . The person of most note found in the prisons of the inquisition was a bishop named Kasner, who had been in confinement for above twenty years. He related that he arrived in Rome from the Holy Land, having in his possession papers which had belonged to an ecclesiastic there. Passing himself for that person, he succeeded in surprising the court of Rome into ordaining and consecrating him a bishop. The fraud was afterwards discovered, and Kasner being then on his way to Palestine, was arrested and brought to the prison of the Holy Office, where he expected to have ended his days, less, as he expressed himself, to expiate his own fraud, than the gross blunder of the court of Rome which had no other means of concealing his character of bishop, its own absolute laws preventing his being deprived of it.

"Passing to the upper flat, the attention of the government was especially directed to the chancery and the archives; the first containing all the current affairs of the inquisition, the second jealously guarding its acts, from its institution until now. Before commencing the catalogue of the contents of the chancery, it was resolved to remove such papers as might disturb or compromise the tranquillity of those persons who had had relations with the Holy Office.

"Attention was especially directed to the book, called of 'Solecitazione' (it contains reports), and to the correspondence. There results from a careful examination of these documents, that the past government made use of this tribunal, strictly ecclesiastical in its institution, for temporal and political objects, and that the most culpable abuse was made of sacramental confession, especially that of women, rendering it subservient both to political purposes and to the most abominable licentiousness. It can be shown that the cardinal secretaries of state wrote to the commissary to the Assessor of the Holy Office to procure information as to the conduct of suspected individuals, both at home and abroad, and to obtain knowledge of state secrets by means of confession, especially those of foreign courts and cabinets. In fact, there exist long correspondences, and voluminous processes, and severe sentences, pronounced upon *La Giorine Italia*, *La Jeune Suisse*, the masonic societies of England and Scotland, and the anti-religious sects of America, &c. There is an innumerable quantity of information and processes on scandalous and obscene subjects, in which the members of regular religious societies are usually implicated.

"Passing from the chauncery to the archives, which is in the second floor, it appeared on first entering as if everything was in its usual place, but on further inspection it was found, with much astonishment, that though the labels and cases were in their places, they were emptied of the packets of papers and documents indicated by the inscriptions without. Some conjecture that the missing packets have been carried to the convent 'Della Minerva,' or were hidden in the houses of private persons, while others supposed that they were burnt by the Dominican fathers. This last hypothesis receives weight from the circumstance, that in November, 1848, shortly after the departure of the Pope from Rome the civic guard came in much haste to the Holy Office — from having observed great clouds of smoke issuing from one of its chimneys, accompanied by a strong smell of burnt paper. But, whatever were the means, the fact is certain, that in the archives of the Inquisition the most important trials were not to be found; such, for instance, as those of Galileo Galilei and of Giordano Bruno; nor was there the correspondence regarding the Reformation in England, in the 16th century, nor many other precious records."

To return to Howard and his inspections. All the dungeons of the castle of San Angelo — the Spandau of Rome — were empty, except one, in which a bishop had been confined twenty years, and had now become insane from the effects of his punishment. Convicts were sent from Rome to work in the galleys of Civita Vecchia; for simple theft the term was never less than seven years, for forgery the sentence was invariably for life; and if the forgery was of a bank note, or any instrument by which a large sum of money had been lost, the offender was compelled to wear, in addition to his other punishments, an iron glove. Prisoners condemned for life were chained two and two together; those for shorter terms worked separately. All however, carried fetters, the weight of which was gradually diminished as the term approached expiration, until a ring round the leg — like that now worn by convicts in the dockyard at Woolwich — was all that remained. Juvenile offenders, were sent, not to the galleys, but to the great hospital of San Michele; an institution which, in some respects, may be considered as the archetype of our present Penitentiary at Parkhurst, in the Isle of Wight. It is thus described by its inspector: "The Hospital of San Michele is a large and noble edifice. The back front is nearly 300 yards long. It consists of several courts with buildings round them. In the apartments on three sides of one of the most spacious of these courts, are rooms for various manufactures and arts, in which boys who are orphans, or destitute, are educated and instructed. When I was there, the number was about 200, all learning different trades, according to their different abilities and genius. Some were educated for printers, some for bookbinders, designers, smiths, tailors, carpenters, shoemakers, and barbers, and some for weavers and dyers — a cloth manufactory being carried on there in all its branches. When boys arrive at the age of twenty, they are completely clothed, and a certain sum of money is given to set them up in the business they have learned."

Public executions in Rome, as in all other parts of Italy, were rare; not an incurious circumstance when it is considered how much more passionate and sanguinary are the genius and temperament of the Italian people than our own. When they did take place, however, they were conducted with much pomp and solemnity. The ceremonies upon such occasions were served by the Confraternita della Misericordia, or Brotherhood of Mercy, of the order of San Giovanni di Fiorentini, composed of about seventy members, selected from the first families in Rome. This institution was of ancient standing; the church of San Gio Battista Decollato belonged to the order in 1450. Whenever a malefactor was condemned to suffer death, one of the heads of this order — sometimes two of them — would go to him at midnight, inform him of his sentence, serve him with the choicest viands, exhort him to confession, and remain with him until the appointed hour. When the fatal moment approached, the whole order, robed in white, would repair in solemn procession to the place of execution, where they would stay until the wretch expired. Then they departed, leaving him hanging until night, — when they returned, and one of their order, generally a prince, cut down the body, which was conveyed to a handsome cemetery appropriated to the purpose of such burials. Such a ceremony must have an impressive effect upon the spectators, as also upon those who read of it at a distance; but a doubt may fairly arise whether, in the very solemnity of such a scene, there is not a most dangerous element — an air of grandeur and importance most seductive to the imaginations of the young, and very consoling to the mind of the hardened criminal. It is, we fear, a capital mistake, under any circumstance, to lend an air of importance to the death of a criminal; and to invest or environ it with anything like beauty, dignity and romance, infinitely mischievous. There should be nothing of the heroic about public punishments — nothing which the vulgar mind could possibly deem desirable, or in which the most depraved heart could sympathize.

Only a few months ago the writer was present at the execution of Sale the murderer. The crowd collected to see the exhibition was enormous. Amongst that crowd was the *mother* of the culprit. When the wretched man came forward on the scaffold, he looked pale and ghastly; but his bearing was insolent, and he died with the apparent insensibility of a dog. "Bravo!" cried his mother, as the drop fell, and the murderer was launched into eternity, "I knew he would die game!" A woman who had lived in adulterous intercourse with the malefactor was with her; they had made up a party to come and see the last of "poor Tom," and when the tragedy was over, sallied off to a public house and made a day of it. Nor was this all. Among the party was another of the Sales, — brother to the murderer, son of the woman who, instead of shame, had found a glory in his death; he had been liberated from gaol only two or three days before the execution. His history is the moral of the gallows. Within a few weeks he was again arrested on a charge of robbery; the crime was clearly brought home to him, and he now lies under sentence of transportation. Another brother had been already sent off to a penal colony, these terrible warnings — hangings and transportation — were inoperative, even to the blood of the sufferers. From the altitude of its own scaffold, to hurl defiance in the face of society, in the presence of thousands of witnesses, is a point of honor and of pride with the criminal class. It is being *game.* Within its own sphere the family of which we speak enjoys a sort of high pre-eminence — a heroism in guilt. Dr. Moore is not far wrong when he says that our mode of punishing murderers is such as to warrant the idea that our object is *not* to prevent any one from following their example. Death punishments should be secret, but at the same time swift and certain; surrounded by all the terrors of an unseen but inexorable doom. When he passes from the court in which he receives condemnation the culprit should be seen of the world no more. This arrangement would be merciful to him, for no sufferer can be wholly unmindful of the vast tribunal before which he is now called upon to die, and a thousand thoughts of who may be there, what eyes may gaze upon his fall, and how he must and will deport himself in presence of these exacting judges, rush into and occupy his mind, to the exclusion of all better and more needful thoughts: at the same time, it would be far more terrible to his compeers in guilt — as much more terrible as the dark mystery of a doom which leaves no room for hope, and yet much scope for fear, always is, — than an end which we have seen, a worst which we have known.

In Naples, to which city Howard next proceeded, he found the crime of assassination alarmingly common. He does not hesitate to assert, as the result of his observation, that more murders and attempts at murder take place annually in the city of Naples, than in the whole of Great Britain and Ireland. The hospitals he found crowded with the victims of the secret stiletto, and the prisons and sanctuaries (churches) full of the culprits. The criminal statistics of all countries prove that the frequency of the atrocious crime of murder bears no kind of relation to the nature of the penalty assigned as its equivalent, but rather depends upon the genius and education of the people. From Naples, Howard returned towards Northern Italy, by way of Civita Vecchia, where he embarked in a vessel bound from that port to Leghorn.

Coasting pleasantly along, on the evening of the second day the captain put into a small creek, as was the custom in these days of leisurely travelling; and, the night being magnificently fine, — as autumnal nights only are in Italy, — pitched a tent for his traveller on the land, who was only too grateful for the opportunity of quietly enjoying the beauty of the scene. Surrounded by all that is most beautiful in nature — at his feet the calm blue waters of the Tyrrhene Sea — around him Europe's most romantic and historic lands — above him the balmy and delicious air of the sweet south, he lay down to rest, and, lulled by the sighing music of the winds and waters, was soon wrapt in a profound and tranquil sleep. On awaking in the morning, all was changed. The delicious beauty of the scene had vanished. The air was hot, the sky clouded, the waters angry. They put to sea, nevertheless, but had hardly lost the sight of land, when a sudden and tremendous squall arose. The white squall of the Mediterranean is proverbial for its violence and peril: the thunders rolled and roared, and pealed and crashed alternately; and the lightnings burst and blazed as they only do in southern climates. Every moment the excitement of the elements increased. The sea ran mountains high, and the frail bark was dashed about in the tempest like a piece of wreck, entirely at its mercy. For that whole day the mariners were tossed and torn, the sport of every wave and gush of wind — driven about, just as the waters would, with little or no power to help themselves, and dreading the approach of darkness as of certain death. To their infinite joy, however, just as the night was falling, the force of the storm carried them into a harbor of one of the small islands lying off the Tuscan coast. Soaking wet, and exhausted with their terrible struggle, they were anxiously preparing to land, when a fresh difficulty beset them. The inhabitants refused them permission to go on shore! A rumor had broken out that the plague had made its appearance at the port from which this vessel had sailed before it put in at Civita Vecchia, and, so great was the terror of the pest, that notwithstanding all their entreaties, neither sailors nor passengers could obtain leave to quit it. This refusal must have been doubly trying to Howard, to whom it revealed a new and additional danger.

Whether the ship was infected or not, he was obliged to remain in her with the rest; so making the best of their misfortunes, they anchored for the night in a sheltered nook under the walls of the town, and next morning put out again to sea.

No change of weather came that day. The violence of the storm went on increasing hour by hour. The bark was in fact given up to the wind, and drifted on before it at a tremendous pace, as may be judged from the fact that in the afternoon they were thrown upon the African coast,—where, however, they were again doomed to be cast off by their brother men. Even the piratical Algerines, governed more by their fears of infection than by their love of booty, refused them permission to enter their harbors. So, resting a short distance from the shore for the night, they again departed at daybreak, and were soon upon the wide waste of waters once more.

For three weary and nevér to be forgotten days and nights they were out again at sea. The toils, and perils, and privations then undergone may be conceived, but cannot be described. Never before had Howard suspected the terrible significance of that word — PLAGUE. By merely raising a doubt, it had caused them to be twice rejected by their fellow-creatures in their direst need — in Europe and in Africa, by Christian and by Mohammedan, — their cries of distress heard but not heeded, their persons driven back upon what appeared at the time to be an inevitable doom. Howard certainly never forgot it: and when hereafter, we find him undertaking a special mission to the East, in order to discover the causes of this dreadful pestilence, and the best methods of preventing its spread, we shall do well to trace its first suggestion to the personal suffering now undergone. After three days of sleepless and exhausting anxiety, they sighted the island of Gorgona, but on account of the strength of the current, could not succeed in making port that night, and were obliged to cast out the anchor until dawn. The weather had now calmed a little, but the sea was still too rough for the exhausted sailors to manage their craft. As soon, however, as it was light, the governor of the island sent his long-boat with four-and-twenty men, with oars, to take Howard and his servant, Thomasson, on shore, and with their assistance the vessel was got round in the course of the day to a good and convenient anchorage in front of the island. In this hospitable place, the guests of the governor, the voyagers remained about a week, reposing after their severe toils, and recovering their worn-out strength. As soon as it was prudent, the Philanthropist took leave of his courteous host and sailed for Leghorn, which he reached in safety and without farther peril.

From this city he passed through Lucca, Lerice, and Genoa, to Milan, which afforded a fine field for prosecuting his inquiries. To give a trait of national character, curiously distinct from one already exhibited on the other side of the Swiss Alps, — it was the custom in the capital of Lombardy, when a person broke prison and was afterwards re-captured, to renew his sentence, with the addition of half the original term; thus if a fourteen years convict escaped at the end of ten years of service, he would receive as punishment for obeying what the magistrates of Berne considered a natural and noble instinct, twenty-one years more. Such is the difference between Swiss and Austrian notions! Much of the prison discipline of Milan met, however, with the approval of the inspector. The Casa di Correzione — then building — was precisely such an institution as he was desirous of seeing introduced into England; and in its chief ideas was not materially unlike our present establishment in Cold Bath Fields, blending the two great features of labor and instruction. Consequently, being deeply interested in the working of this Casa di Correzione, Howard visited it very frequently, entered into conversation with its inmates, and always made them happy on retiring by means of a small present, measured by his opinion of their deserts. Some remarkably fine and skilful work was turned out by these prisoners. One, whom he particularly noticed, was a youth of about five-and-twenty, a gold brocade worker, of very superior talents. Howard spoke with him, and found him highly accomplished, being able to speak four or five different languages with great fluency and correctness. His crime was bigamy, an offence redeemable in Italy by a fine; and as Howard considered, both from his conversation and the reports of others as to his habits, that he was a person of some worth who had been guilty of an indiscretion through the prompting of passion, and seeing that he had already suffered a very severe penalty, he purchased his release, gave him some fatherly counsel, together with sufficient money to carry him to his native place, and set him at liberty.

On leaving Milan our traveller passed into Piedmont, and thence through Savoy once more into Switzerland, where he assiduously prosecuted his examinations, and on their completion re-entered Germany. We have before traced his footsteps through the Faderland, and noted the general character of the criminal institutions their prevailing; we shall therefore only add one note from his present observations. It is an account of the prisons of Liege — then an ecclesiastical city — and runs thus:

"the two prisoners near La Porte de St. Leonard, in Liege, are on the ramparts. In two rooms of the Old Prison I saw six cages, made very strong with iron hoops, four of which were empty. These were dismal places of confinement, but I soon found much worse. In descending deep below ground from the gaoler's apartments I heard the moans of the miserable wretches in the dark dungeons. The sides and roof were all stone. In wet weather, water from the fosses gets into them, and has greatly damaged the floors. Each of them had two small apertures, one for admitting air, and another, with a shutter strongly bolted, for putting in food to the prisoners. One dungeon, larger than the rest, was appropriated to the sick. In looking into this with a candle, I discovered a stove, and felt some surprise at this little escape of humanity from the men who constructed these cells. The dungeons in the New Prison are abodes of misery still more shocking, and confinement in them so overpowers human nature as sometimes irrevocably to take away the senses. I heard the cries of the distracted as I went down to them. The cries of the sufferers in the torture chamber may be heard by passengers without and guards are placed to prevent them from stopping and listening!"

Towards the end of the year, Howard arrived in England, having travelled on this continental tour 4,600 miles. As he came homeward through France his attention was again arrested by the sufferings inflicted upon prisoners of war, and in making complaints on the subjects to persons in authority in that country, he was told that French prisoners in England suffered still greater hardships. On reaching London, therefore, his first care was to call upon the Commissioners of Sick and Wounded Seamen, as well to report what he had seen and heard, as to inform them that he had determined to go round the country to every town where war-prisoners were kept, to personally get at the truth or falsehood of the statements which had been made to him in France. The Commissioners received him with courtesy, and expressed their desire to assist him in his inquiries; to that end they furnished him with letters to their agents throughout the country. Thus prepared for ulterior measures, he went down to Cardington to spend the Christmas with his boy; and as soon as the holidays were over, set out on this new tour of inspection; re-visiting as he went along, gaols, bridewells, and houses of correction; noticing, in particular, the effect of the new laws, and completing the collection of material for an appendix to his great work.

This home-journey was, in fact, one of the longest and most laborious which he had yet undertaken — occupying from January to the end of November, of the year 1779, in the course of which he traversed almost every country in England, Ireland, and Scotland, — travelling, to and fro, 6,990 miles. The results of all these labors were given to the world at the end of the year. On the whole, notwithstanding that many bad practices still obtained in our gaols, this new inspection satisfied him as to the utility of his labors. Some of the more flagrant abuses which he had formerly noted had been removed; the spirit of reform was aroused — the gaols were almost universally cleaner, more orderly, more healthy. One person only did he find ill of the gaol-fever; he was in Newgate, lying under sentence of death. That disgusting den at Knaresborough had been so far improved as to have got the open sewer — up which the rats were wont to come and banquet on their victims — boarded over. A few other outrageous matters of this kind were remedied; but still the work of improvement went on slowly, especially in the episcopal gaols of Ely, Durham, and other places. At Ely, things had grown so much worse since his last visit, that they had actually placed debtors and felons together, though formerly they had always been kept separate!

Whilst the Philanthropist was thus employed at home and abroad, his fellow-laborers in the work were not idle in the legislature. An act — (19 Geo. III. c. 74) — had been obtained for building two penitentiary houses in Middlesex, Surrey, Kent, or Essex, to try the great experiment of Home Correctional Discipline. The Government, as a matter of course, named Howard first supervisor of this undertaking; but there were several difficulties in the way of his acceptance of office. In the first place, it was an official appointment, and Howard was conscious that he would lose rather than gain influence by it. On this point his objections were overruled by his friend Sir William Blackstone — who, as the legal promulgator of the scheme, and having it much at heart, showed him that its successful issue depended solely upon his acceptance of the post. Then there was the selection of his two colleagues; to ensure his entire devotion to the plan, he was himself allowed to name one of them. He chose Dr. Fothergill; the minister nominated as the other Mr. Whatley, treasurer of the Foundling Hospital. Still there was an obstacle — the officers were *salaried*; and he was resolved in no way ever to receive *money* in exchange for his services to humanity. He had frequently expressed a belief that if proper steps were taken, hundreds of competent men would come forward and devote themselves to labors like his own. Alas! Howard fancied the world much better than it is. But these points were at length arranged to his satisfaction, and the three Commissioners commenced their labors. The fact of this appointment was made known to the public in his second publication, which he concludes by saying that he had formerly determined, as soon as he had brought the inquiries in which he was then engaged to a termination, to retire from public life; but that he had been induced by the urgent requests of others to accept a new series of labors, and it only remained now to see whether the humane intentions of the legislature could really be carried out. Thus began a fresh chapter in his history.

CHAPTER X.

AN EUROPEAN PILGRIMAGE.

Even before he accepted his ministerial appointment, Howard had a prophetic feeling that his official labors would prove unpleasant, and he found them so, to a greater extent than his fears had forewarned him. After a most minute investigation of every part of London and its neighborhood, Dr. Fothergill and he decided upon a spot of ground in Islington for the site of the contemplated building; but their colleague Mr. Whatley, fixed upon a site at Limehouse. His reasons for such a choice were anything but satisfactory. Nothing, however, would induce him to give it up, and a long, intricate, and tiresome dispute arose upon the point. The referees in the matter were the twelve judges. Sir William Blackstone strongly supported Howard's proposition; others took the opposite view. There was no end of running to and fro, of weighing and comparing evidence, of agitation and diplomacy; until the Philanthropist, seeing that no progress could be made in the work, and that his own priceless time was being rapidly consumed in useless disputes, grew tired of it altogether, and began to think of surrendering his post. While the controversy was it its height, his friend and chief supporter, Sir William Blackstone, died. Dr. Fothergill had waited upon the great jurist, a few days before his demise. Though ill, he found him keenly interested in the affair, and anxious to know the exact position in which it then stood. The doctor explained that every attention having been paid to the question of site, and opinions being still divided, recourse must of necessity be had to the judges for a final decision. "Be firm in your own opinion," was all that the dying jurist was able to reply. The conversation was not renewed, for he expired soon after, Feb. 14, 1780. Howard was at Warrington when these words were reported to him, and he instantly wrote to his colleague thus: "Mr. Justice Blackstone's dying words, *Be firm in your own opinion*, seem to me to be the most important direction for our conduct. We are fixed upon as the proper persons to determine upon a plan, situation, &c. of a penitentiary house. Why then transfer the office to other persons, whose station in life and other engagements must render them very unfit for entering into such a matter? Let us, when we meet, *absolutely* fix upon *one* situation, as the best on the whole, according to our ideas; and specifying our reasons, let us submit the approbation or rejection of this *one* plan to those in whom the law has invested such a power; but not give *them* the unnecessary trouble, nor *us* the improper degradation, of determining in our stead the respective advantages of several different plans. I am sensible that many amendments will occur in the execution of every part of this plan: but these must be the result of experience, as we go on. At any rate, *we* are the proper judges of that part which the law has committed to us, and ought to follow our *own ideas* with firmness, without depending upon the superior judgment of others." Whatley could not, however, be brought to concur in this, and so nothing was done. Time, meanwhile, passed on; and towards the end of the year death removed another actor from the scene, in the person of Dr. Fothergill. This second warning determined Howard to give up his post; and his resolution was thus signified to Earl Bathurst, Lord President of the Council: "January, 1781. My Lord,—When Sir William Blackstone prevailed upon me to act as a supervisor of the buildings intended for the confinement of certain criminals, I was persuaded to think that my observations upon similar institutions in foreign countries would in some degree qualify me to assist in the execution of the statute of the 19th year of his present Majesty. With this hope, and the prospect of being associated with my late worthy friend, Dr. Fothergill, whose wishes and ideas on the subject I knew corresponded exactly with my own, I cheerfully accepted his Majesty's appointment, and have since earnestly endeavored to answer the purpose of it, but at the end of two years I have the mortification to see that not even a preliminary has been settled. The *situation* of the intended building has been made a matter of obstinate contention, and is at this moment undecided. Judging therefore from what is past, that the further sacrifice of my time is not likely to contribute to the success of the plan, and being now dedeprived, by the death of Dr. Fothergill, of the assistance of an able colleague, I beg leave to signify to your Lordship my determination to decline all further concern in the business; and to desire that your Lordship will be so good as to lay before the King my humble request that his Majesty will be graciously pleased to accept my resignation." So ended Howard's official career. With his retirement the project, which had probably never been seriously, entertained by the ministry, was abandoned. In its stead, the Botany Bay transportation scheme was adopted; and another of the fairest portions of the earth were given up to be defiled. Being a practical race, an evil, to us Englishmen, is not an evil, until it has been trebly demonstrated by experience. More than seventy precious years more was given up to be consumed in re-enacting former failures, until in our own day, as the diabolical machinery will work no longer, we have come to a dead set; and so having, at infinite cost and mischief, bought for ourselves the knowledge which the Philanhropist had at his own expense procured for us, we are now compelled to revert to his ideas — then ignorantly spurned — and build up our Pentonvilles and Parkhursts, turn to our Portland Islands and Portsmouths, and resume the work of reform exactly at the point where he left it off.

Fairly freed from these embarrassing and faultless engagements, Howard's thoughts again turned towards the continent of Europe. There were still vast regions unexplored — some lessons, it might fairly be presumed, still unlearned — certainly much suffering yet to be relieved — many consolations needing to be carried to the heart-wasted and the dying; and thoughts of this nature never appeal to minds like his in vain. In his travels thus far, he had only crossed and re-crossed the great central states of Europe — the settlements of the most civilized part of the human family. All the great lands lying upon the borders of the civilized system — Denmark, Norway, Russia, Poland, Turkey, Egypt, Sicily, Spain, and Portugal — beckoned him to their cities; and when he thought of the good he might be the minister of to their suffering or sinful children, and of the additional experience with which his visits would possibly supply him, — there is little reason to wonder that he should grow impatient at the dilatory proceedings of the peniten tiary commission, and earnestly wish to resign his share in it.

In May, 1781, Howard departed for Ostend, and immediately proceeded into Holland. In one of the prisons of Rotterdam, a number of Englishmen were at the time confined; a few weeks previously they had been treated to a public whipping for an attempt to escape in a body. To provide themselves with instruments, they had melted their pewter spoons, and by means of a mixture obtained from a chemist as a cure for the tooth-ache, hardened the metal sufficiently to enable them to form it into keys. In all probability they would have succeeded in their attempt, had not their intention been treacherously revealed by an English Jew who was in the secret, and who expected to receive his own pardon as a reward for his baseness. The dexterous rogues were seized and carried to the whipping-post, where, in sight of all the prisoners, they received a severe flagellation; while the rascally Jew was set at liberty — although he had been condemned for thirty years for a very serious offence. They managed these things better at Berne!

At the free city of Bremen, the first place at which he rested in Germany, he found no debtors confined; and there had been no execution for five-and-twenty years. The goals were certainly horrid places, — but they had the great merit of being almost empty. In one of them, there were six close dungeons, miserably small and dark; these had had but one inmate recently, and he had dashed his brains out against the wall, which was still spattered with his blood. An institution had just been established in this city, that much pleased the Philanthropist; namely, a workhouse for the children who were found begging or prowling about the streets — somewhat similar to the industrial schools now opened in Aberdeen. The appearance of the city was by this means quite altered. Formerly the streets had been crowded by dirty and riotous urchins; now there was hardly one to be seen. At the workhouse, Howard saw nearly 200 of these children — otherwise inevitably doomed to grow up into the future bandits of society — averaging from six to nine years old, clean, cheerful, and happy, whilst busily engaged in spinning under the care of proper instructors. The experiment had so far been eminently successful, and many other cities were beginning to look on it with interest. Whilst in Bremen, Howard spent an afternoon with Dr. Duntze, a medical gentleman who had been in England about forty years before, and still remembered it with horror. A German friend was with him at the time in London, and being desirous of seeing Newgate, they procured an order for admission and went; but in one of the rooms they encountered a smell so offensive, they were obliged to retire. Not soon enough, however; for next day both were violently indisposed. The doctor's complaint assumed the form of jaundice — from which he recovered; but his friend went worse from hour to hour, and in a few days died, with every symptom of the terrible gaol-fever. This incident had put an end to Dr. Duntze's prison visits.

Through Hamburg, Holstein, and Schleswig, Howard next proceeded to Copenhagen. At the entrance of Danish towns, he noticed that a whipping post was always conspicuously placed, — on the top of which stood an emblematic figure, holding in one hand a whip, in the other a sword. Gibbets and wheels were also erected upon eminences; and on these the bodies of malefactors were sometimes left after execution to rot, in order that the sight of them might infuse terror into the souls of their associates. Executions were however rare in Denmark. The chief idea in the criminal system of the Danes, was, to excite terror by the public exhibition of the suffering and ignominy poured out upon those who had once broken the laws. One of the most curious shapes which it assumed, was that of wearing the so-called Spanish mantle; a vestment more readily described pictorially than in words. The reader has seen one of those heavy, lumbering tubs, made of unbent staves,. narrowing towards the top, in which our grandmothers were wont to churn their own butter — just such a thing was the Spanish mantle worn by the felons of Denmark. A hole was made in the narrow end, through which the culprit's head was thrust; the bottom of the barrel came down to his knees — entirely covering his arms — the weight of the whole resting upon his shoulders. The head put through the aperture, a simple contrivance prevented the mantle from being thrown off; escape from it was therefore quite impossible. The face was completely bare and visible. In this way he was promenaded about the city, attended by two officers. On the whole, it was a severe punishment, as well as an indelible disgrace, and so much was it dreaded, that night robberies — for which offence it was especially inflicted — were almost unknown,

Beheading was the usual mode of capital punishment then in use in Denmark; but for some heinous crimes, the wheel was still used. Persons confined in the state prison were very rigorously guarded. There was only one at the period of Howard's visit, yet an officer and a soldier were in the same room with him, and another soldier was on duty at the door — although the guard-house was just below. In the room in which Counts Struensee and Brandt has been immured, in consequence of the charges which the King had made against the unfortunate Caroline of Denmark, sister to George III., he noticed that chains were riveted in the wall, to which they had been bound in order to render their confinement more irksome. When the first of these unhappy nobles was brought out of his dungeon, after rather more than three month's captivity — although in presence of a terrible death — he exclaimed, "Oh, what a blessing is fresh air!"

In the prison in which criminals from the garrison and slaves were kept, there were two rooms which, although but ten feet high, contained a double tier of beds, all of them dirty beyond description. Here were 143 slaves, who were never permitted to take off their clothes, night or day; and as they were only provided with a fresh suit once in two years, many of them were entirely naked. All of them wore chains, and one was fastened to a wheelbarrow — the ordinary punishment in Copenhagen for an attempt to escape. The whole place was dirty and disgraceful to the officers in charge; a fact which the Philanthropist did not fail to impress upon those functionaries in good round terms. Singularly enough, his remonstrance had all the effect of a royal command; for when, two or three days later, he went again, the rooms had been put in order, and the floors well swept — which had perhaps never been so treated before. This circumstance, with its characteristic difference, reminds one of the story of the monks of Prague.

Crossing the sound at Elsimore, our traveller was soon delighted with the clean and cheerful aspect of the towns and villages of Sweden, and from their appearance hoped to find a striking contrast to the gaols of Denmark in Stockholm. In this, however, he was disappointed. The dwelling of the peasant proved to be no type of the condition of the prison. In the entire gaol system a remarkable uniformity prevailed throughout the Scandinavian nations; but their uncommon filthiness was their chief distinction. No irons were used in them. After condemnation the culprit, as in Denmark, could appeal to the parliament against his sentence, and without the special sanction of this high court no man could be legally put to death. The general mode of execution was by the axe. Women were beheaded on a scaffold which was afterwards set on fire and consumed with the body, — a striking and impressive addition to the ceremony. In the course of his researches at Stockholm, Howard discovered one of those practical falsehoods which his experience had taught him to believe not uncommon, and against which he warns all who may tread in his own footsteps. Gustavus III., the reigning king of Sweden, following the general example of enlightened Europe, had decreed the abolition of *torture* throughout his States, — and the dark and terrible dungeon which had been used for this purpose in one of the prisons of the capital, had been ordered to be built up. This was reported to have been done, and when our countryman visited the prison and asked to see the cell, he was also told that it was built up. Having learned, however, to distrust anything less than ocular evidence in such matters, he demanded to be shown it. The gaoler, thus pressed to an extremity, was at length forced to confess that it was still open!

The prisons of Stockholm generally exhibited the vices most common in English gaols — much more so than any others on the continent — which is about the severest thing that can be said of them: — namely, idleness, drunkenness and uncleanliness on the part of the inmates; filth, insecurity, closeness, dampness and darkness on the side of the gaol.

In the courts of law, which were opened to the public, Howard observed some customs which pleased him greatly. In a prosecution of a man for beating his wife, one of the senior magistrates pleaded the cause of the woman, and when his statement was completed, withdrew with the other parties concerned in the trial. The judge then consulted a book of laws, and having satisfied himself of the legal bearing of the point at issue, called them in again, and after causing the law to be read to them aloud, passed sentence; whereupon the parties bowed and retired. Domestic disputes amongst the poor were almost invariably settled in this way, to the mutual satisfaction of the parties — man and wife not unfrequently shaking hands in court, and going off together crying for joy.

Personally, Howard had no reason to like Sweden. To say nothing of the coldness of the climate, — which, to his constitution, was in itself a severe punishment — he could obtain nothing to eat which his previous habits had rendered agreeable. The bread of the country was coarse and sour; the milk was also sour: while fruit and garden stuff — the staples of his diet — could seldom be procured. Tea, a quantity of which, and the necessary apparatus for cooking it, he always carried with him, was nearly his sole support; but these privations, of great importance to almost any other man, were considered by Howard as of very small consequence compared with the sublime purposes of his journey.

Russia, then dominated by the iron will of the imperious Catharine, was the country next visited. The reputation of Howard had now spread so widely, and public attention had so riveted itself upon his movements, that his visits became in some sort recognized in an extra-official manner by monarchs and governments. This fact was no doubt highly honorable to the individual; but it sometimes acted as a draw back on the usefulness of his labors. Wherever his presence was known or expected, preparations were made to receive him; prisons, hospitals, and houses of correction were turned the sunny side without, cleaned up and got ready for review. As an occasional good, this was in itself a point gained; but, at the same time, it was calculated to throw the inspector off his guard, and cause him at times to make a report not warranted by the everyday character of the place described. Against this source of error he took all possible precautions. In his earlier tours it had been necessary for him to obtain letters of introduction to men high in authority in the countries through which he had to pass; but having now become so universally known that his own card presented at the gate of a prison was generally a sufficient authorization, he gave up that practice. Indeed, pushing this policy still further, he now began to keep his intended movements as secret as he considered needful. Wishing to see the prevailing forms of criminal police exactly as they were — not made out in gala fashion — it was indispensable that some, if not all of his visits should be made unexpectedly. This was especially necessary in the case of Russia, for he had grave misgivings as to the value of that country's claim to the glorification which was at that time so industriously diffused in Europe by a few writers, who, dazzled and deceived by the material splendors and the factitious airs of civilization which a succession of able state constructors had bestowed upon the capital, had accepted without criticism or question the imperial government's version of its own good works. Howard was certainly not a man to take matters of such importance upon trust; he desired to see men and institutions for himself, and to make his own report.

In this spirit he approached St. Petersburg. Anxious to avoid recognition, he alighted from his carriage at some distance from the city, kept back his equipage, and entered the Russian capital alone and on foot. But, as may be supposed, this simple piece of strategy was useless. The imperial police were then, as now, almost omniscient, and he had no sooner taken up his abode at an hotel than a messenger arrived from the Empress, inviting him to appear at court. With his usual frankness he at once refused the invitation, and told the courtier who waited upon him that he had devoted himself to the task of visiting the dungeon of the captive and the abode of the wretched, not the palaces and courts of kings and empresses — and that the limited time which he had to stay in the capital would not allow of his calling upon her imperial majesty. How this reply was received by the Empress we know not; but, if honestly rendered, it could hardly fail to impress her with a sense of the stern and singular virtues of her visitor.

Howard found St. Petersburg abounding with prisons and hospitals, full of inmates of various kinds; the criminal discipline of the country being greatly complicated by the system of serfdom or slavery, universally prevailing. So inveterately had this institution — although not of ancient standing in Russia — become incorporated with the ideas of the people, that *debtors* were considered in much the same light as slaves; and were often employed as such by the government, in which case they were allowed as wages twelve rubles (about forty-eight shillings in English money) per annum, which went in liquidation of the original debt. Private persons who would undertake to pay this sum, and to produce the person of the debtor whenever it should be required, were also permitted to take the same class of unfortunates into service. All the Russian gaols were held and guarded by the military; they had no regular governors, and little or no attention was paid to the health or moral improvement of the prisoners. Most of their rooms were so over-crowded as to render them unbearably hot and offensive; they had no regular allowance of food; and they were generally manacled.

One of the great boasts of the philosophic admirers of the Russian system was, that capital punishments for all civil crimes were abolished in that country, and no one was liable to suffer death save for acts of high treason. Our traveller had always suspected the veracity of this statement, and now on the spot resolved to ascertain the precise facts. The governor of the police at St. Petersburg — probably in obedience to orders — displayed before him all the engines of torture formerly in use in that country, as well as those still employed; the former consisting of the axe and block, a machine for breaking the arms and legs, an instrument for slitting and lacerating the nose, another for branding, and so forth. The latter were simply the knout, and a whip called the cat. The inference intended to be raised by this exhibition was, that from a very barbarous nation Russia had become highly humane and civilized. The care taken, however, defeated the end in view. The ordinary punishment of the knout Howard availed himself of an opportunity of witnessing, and he thus describes the scene: "August 10th, 1781, I saw two criminals, a man and a woman, suffer the punishment of the knout. They were conducted from the prison by about fifteen hussars and ten soldiers. When they arrived at the place of punishment, the hussars formed themselves into a ring round the whipping-post, the drum beat a minute or two, and then some prayers were repeated — the populace taking off their hats. The woman was taken first, and after being roughly stripped to the waist, her hands and feet were bound with cords to a post made for the purpose, a man standing before the post to keep the cords tight. A servant attended the executioner, and both were stout men. The servant first marked his ground and struck the woman five times on the back. Every stroke seemed to penetrate deep into the flesh. But his master, thinking him too gentle, pushed him aside, took his place, and gave all the remaining strokes himself, which were evidently more severe. The woman received twenty-five, and the man sixty. I pressed through the hussars, and counted the number as they were chalked on a board. Both seemed but just alive, especially the man, who had yet strength enough to receive a small donation with some signs of gratitude. They were conducted back to prison in a little wagon. I saw the *woman* in a very weak condition some days after, *but could not find the man any more!*"

This latter circumstance confirmed his previous suspicion that the knout was in reality the Russian gallows, and that under cover of a mere whipping, death was sometimes, if not frequently, inflicted; while western Europe was abused with idle boasts of the superior clemency of Russian laws. It was, however, useless to think of making any inquiries on the subject amongst the courtiers of Catherine, or even amongst the ministers of justice: so in order to get further information he took his own characteristic course. Having ascertained the address of the executioner, he got into a coach and drove off to his house. The poor fellow was alarmed at seeing a person having the appearance of a noble and an official, enter his humble dwelling; domiciliary visits from the authorities of St. Petersburg rarely boding good to the host. Howard had calculated upon the man being surprised and thrown off his guard, and now endeavored to increase his confusion by his air, tone and bearing. The fellow probably remembered seeing him within the lines on the occasion just described, and of course supposed him to be a person in authority. Howard expected this. Assuming therefore an official tone, he desired the man to answer the questions put to him simply, and without equivocation; adding, that if his replies were found conformable to truth, he had nothing to fear. The executioner meekly declared his readiness to answer any questions that should be put to him. "Can you inflict the knout in such a manner as to occasion death in a very short time?" "Yes, I can," was the prompt reply. "In how short a time?" continued Howard. "In a day or two." "Have you ever so inflicted it?" "I have." "Have you lately?" added our countryman, going to the point he was very anxious to be satisfied of. "Yes, the last man who was punished by my hands with the knout died of the punishment." Even so! no wonder that the Philanthropist had not been able to find him. "In what manner do you thus render it mortal?" "By one or two strokes on the sides, which carry off large pieces of the flesh." — Hum! "Do you receive orders thus to inflict the punishment?" "I do." This was the substance of the extraordinary catechism, — and thus were Howard's doubts resolved.

The hospitals and educational establishments of St. Petersburg afforded Howard far more pleasure than the prisons. With one of the latter he was particularly struck. It was a stately pile of buildings, situated on a rising ground, on the southern side of the Neva, at a short distance from the city, originally designed for a convent, but converted by the reigning Empress into an institution for the education of a certain number of girls, the daughters of nobles and commoners in about equal proportions. About five hundred pupils, all of rank or wealth, lived in the establishment; and we may add, that they showed their appreciation of the merits of their visitor by presenting him with a very curious and elegant piece of their own work in ivory, which was long preserved in his favorite hermitage at Cardington. This highly creditable institution owed its existence and prosperity to General De Betskoi, a sort of Russian Howard. This truly good man was the soul of all Catherine's charitable undertakings; and our countryman has borne the highest testimony to his liberality and enlightenment, a circumstance which must have been highly gratifying to the gallant soldier. We know of no grander object of ambition than the approbation of such a man as Howard. And, on his side, De Betskoi entertained the most profound esteem and veneration for his visitor. Nor was he the only soldier of that military empire who felt thus towards the Friend of the Sufferer. His fine character, his frank bearing, his apostolic undertaking, revived in those who came into contact with him — especially in the fearless men whose lives had been spent in the camp and on the field of battle — something of that by-gone chivalry, which, in the olden time, warrior kings and armed knights were wont to display towards the acknowledged servants of God and mankind; a sentiment of which the world has lately almost lost the trace. A pleasing instance of this fine feeling — honorable alike to its subject and object — is recorded in this present visit to St. Petersburg. One of the most distinguished men of that day in Russia was General Bulgarkow, who, with a princely liberality, had endowed, or enlarged, a great number of noble charities. His benevolence soon attracted the attention of his countrymen, who, desirous of honoring themselves by honoring him, about this period made him a great present of a gold medal, as "one who had deserved well of his country." Perhaps the highest proof of his merit was his reply: he said, "*his* services to mankind reached his own country only; but there *was* a man whose extraordinary philanthropy took in all the world, — who had already, with infinite toil and peril, extended his humanity to all nations, and who was therefore alone worthy of such a distinction; to him, his master in benevolence, he should send the medal." And he did so.

During his stay near the Russian capital Howard made a trip to Cronstadt, to see the galleys. The slaves, who were employed in emptying ships of ballast, were healthy and robust. The hospital of the island, built by Peter the Great for a palace, was a magnificent structure, the cleanliness and comfort of which — unlike most of the public establishments of Russia at that time — was in some measure worthy of the exterior splendor. On his return to St. Petersburg, Howard was attacked by a fit of ague; but having no time to lose, he treated it with as little ceremony as he had done the message of Catherine, and set out immediately on his journey to Moscow. The following letter contains nearly all that is known of this trip: — "Moscow, September 7, 1781. Dear Sir, I am persuaded a line will not be unacceptable, even from such a vagrant as I am. I have unremittingly pursued the object of my journey; but having looked into no palaces, nor seen any curiosities, my letters can afford little entertainment to my friends. I stayed above three weeks in St. Petersburg. I declined every honor that was offered me, and when pressed to have a soldier to accompany me [to Moscow] I declined that also. Yet I fought my way pretty well 500 miles, over bad roads, in less than five days. I have a strong, yet light and easy carriage, which I bought for fifty roubles — about ten guineas. This city is situated in a fine plain, totally different from all others. Each house has a garden, which extends the city eight or ten miles; so that four and six horses are common in the streets. I content myself with a pair — though I think I have driven to-day near twenty miles to see one prison and one hospital. I am told sad stories of what I am to suffer from the cold; yet I will not leave this city till I have made repeated visits to the prisons and hospitals, as the first man in the kingdom assured me that my book would be translated in Russian. My next step is for Warsaw, about seven or eight hundred miles; but every step being homeward, I have a spirit to encounter it, though through the worst country in Europe. I bless God I am well with calm, easy spirits. I had a fit of the ague before I left St. Petersburg, but I *travelled it off*, the nights last week being warm. I thought I could live where any men did live; but this northern journey — especially in Sweden, where there was no fruit, no garden stuff, and only sour bread and sour milk — I have been pinched. But in this city there is every luxury, even pine-apples and potatoes."

In the course of this very rapid transit — 500 miles in five days! — though Howard never once paused to procure repose or refreshment, he found time to inspect the prisons of Wyshnei and Tver, both of which were in a fearful state; into the latter the medical attendant refused to follow the Philanthropist — always a fatal sign. Howard's mode of dealing with the race of Jehu has been already noticed; an incident on this road may be added to the subject. On one of the stages betwixt St. Peterburg and Moscow, he was so much pleased with his two drivers that he wished to mark his approbation by a rather large donation than usual — namely, about half-a-crown English money. The poor fellows had never before obtained so large a sum, and feared to take it. For similar services they were in the habit of receiving only a few copecs, of the value of two or three pence; and not until Howard had taken some trouble to explain to them that inasmuch as he had entrusted his life into their hands — as they had obeyed all his wishes, and saved some of his time, they were well entitled to his gift, could they be brought to accept it. In all essential respects, Moscow presented to our countryman the same class of prison vices as the metropolis of the country, if anything these vices were somewhat darker in shade.

Passing now rapidly through Poland — in the capital of which, Warsaw, he encountered some of the most miserable objects he had ever seen — and Silesia, which presented a most favorable contrast to the neighboring country, — Howard soon re-entered Prussia. The criminal police of Berlin had been vastly improved since his former visit; the streets were cleared of the beggars and thieves by whom they had formerly been over-run. The Orphan House was well regulated; and the children, being kept employed, were industrious and contented. On the way from this capital to Hanover, an incident occurred which is very characteristic of our countryman. It will be remembered by the historical reader that the sword of Frederick the Great then ruled in Prussia. The soldier prince, aware of the great political importance of rapid intercommunications, had established a system of couriers, who traversed the kingdom in all directions on the king's business, with matchless celerity: a celerity, however, procured at the price of much inconvenience to the king's lieges. These messengers, wearing the royal colors, commanded and compelled assistance of all persons whom they met on the great highways. The will of the monarch was known, and a Prussian would as soon have thought of bearding heaven as throwing an obstacle in the way of one of his fleet couriers. But Howard was not a subject of Frederick; nor was he a courtier either through hope or fear. The incident referred to is thus narrated by Dr. Aikin: "Travelling in the King of Prussia's dominions, he came to a very narrow piece of road, admitting only one carriage, where it was enjoined on all postilions entering at each end to blow their horns by way of notice. His did so; but, after proceeding a good way, they met a courier travelling on the King's business, who had neglected this precaution. The courier ordered Mr. Howard's postilion to turn back; but Mr. Howard remonstrated that he had complied with the rule, while the other had violated it, and he should therefore insist on going forwards. The courier, relying on his authority, to which in that country everything must give way, made use of high words, — but in vain. As neither was disposed to yield, they sat still a long time in their respective carriages ; at length the courier gave up the point to the sturdy Englishman, who would on no account *renounce his rights.*"

The Philanthropist was introduced to his royal highness the Duke of York — then prince-bishop of Osnaburgh — during his short stay in Hanover ; when he embraced the opportunity of speaking to the young prince on the subject of the torture, which still disgraced his episcopal seat. The royal youth was anxious to know *how* the torture was inflicted ; but his visitor refused to describe it, saying it would hurt his feelings too much ; but he begged that the prince would direct his ministers to inquire into the matter, and have the horrid instruments destroyed. The result was, that he promised, when he came of age, to abolish it altogether. Some time after, his royal highness was delicately reminded of this promise by receiving a handsomely bound copy of Howard's work, with the riband placed at the page on which the Osnaburgh torture is described, and a hope expressed that it will soon be put an end to.

From Hanover, by way of Holland and the Austrian Netherlands, our traveller returned once more to England, from one of the longest tours on which he had yet been absent. Arriving in London about the middle of December, his first care was to carry his son down to Cardington, to pass the holidays in each other's society. The future course of young Howard's education occupied much of his thought at this time. His first idea now was to send him to Eton; and he had made every preparation for his removal thither, when learning that at that institution no efficient moral and religious control could be exercised over him, he changed his plan, and at the advice of several friends, placed him under the charge of a reverend gentleman of Notts. This matter for the present set at rest, the Philanthropist commenced in January, 1782, a new series of prison inspection in England, Ireland, and Scotland — in which labor he was arduously employed the entire twelve months, with scarcely a day's intermission — concluding for the year with a visit to the Fleet on the 30th of December.

The memorials of this year's work are ample, and not without interest; but we can only dwell upon one or two of its incidents. When in Ireland, the University of Dublin marked its high appreciation of his services, by conferring upon him the honorary distinction of a Doctor of Civil Law; an honor of which he was duly sensible, though he had not sought it; and when it was thrust upon him, knowing that it was in reality the distinction of a scholar, to be considered which he had no claim, he always refused to add it to his style.

In the earlier part of this history, the circumstance of Howard's captivity led to some remarks on the treatment of prisoners of war; this subject was now present to the traveller's thoughts wherever he went, and many were the opportunities which he found of alleviating sufferings like those of which he had himself had such bitter experience. It was at that time the custom of European Governments to try every means in their power to corrupt the fidelity of their prisoners, with a view to induce them to enter their services — without reference to the peril to which they would thereby expose their victims. Under all circumstances, Howard set himself to oppose these base seductions. In France, in Holland, in England, in Spain, his counsel was ever the same. He reminded the captives of their allegiance — of the baseness of the renegade — of the danger in case of re-capture. He appealed to their fears as well as to their principles; and in some cases threatened to become himself the means of their punishment, if they succumbed to the guilty arts practised upon them. By his strong remonstrances he saved many a poor fellow from the rebel's crime and doom; but not without imminent peril to himself. Governments did not like the thwarter of their purposes. Certain proceedings of this kind were remembered against him in France with great bitterness — and did not tend to mitigate the crime ef reprinting the Bastile pamphlet. An incident of the same sort now happened in England; and the Philanthropist stepped between his own Government and its perfidious intention, as fearlessly as he had before done with that of France. A body of 338 Dutch prisoners of war, who were confined in a building on the banks of the Severn, were almost naked and starving, when their privations coming to the knowledge of certain benevolent individuals, a subscription was made to purchase for them some necessary articles of clothing — shoes, stockings, shirts, and so forth. The Government commissary, however, prohibited the offered donation. He had already practised upon their distress, to induce them to enter the English service, and fight against their native land; he even had an officer on the spot, ready to enlist them the moment his arts had procured their consent. As soon as Howard heard of these proceedings, he repaired to the spot — found the statement truc in all its particulars — and learned that an order had been issued to prevent any person having communication with the prisoners. He at once added his name and ten guineas to the subscription list, and requested that all the articles which had been bought might be sent to the prison at nine o'clock next morning. Howard knew that no prison gates in England could be closed upon him; and beyond this assurance, he bore a warrant from the central authority to inspect every place where prisoners of war were detained. He accordingly repaired thither early in the morning; and the commissary, somewhat awed, suffered him to take his own course. This was very simple and very effective. He called the poor Hollanders together, and after distributing amongst them the various articles, according to each man's need, charged them on no account to listen to any man who proposed to them to become traitors; as, if they did so he would take care to transmit their names to Holland, that they might be hung as soon as retaken. This settled the matter: Howard then left the commissary and his officer to make the best of their defeat.

In one of the hospital-ships then stationed at Portsmouth, in which there happened to be more than ordinary sickness, Howard was told that the surgeon very culpably neglected his duty to the sufferers. Seeing in the countenances of the patients, as well as learning from their oral complaints, that such was really the case, he sent for the surgeon, and spoke to him very strongly about his derelictions. The man confessed his neglect, and said, he thought the great danger of going on board was a sufficient excuse for it. Then, said Howard, you ought not to take Government wages for doing that which you are afraid to do; and I assure you, that when I return to London I shall represent your conduct to the admiralty, and have you dismissed from a station whose duties you do not choose to perform. And he was as good as his word. To be surgeon to an hospital-ship, is, no doubt, to be in a post of considerable peril; but when a man solicits or accepts an appointment of the sort, he must be fully aware of the danger, and prepared to take all the consequences which it may entail upon him. It is an heinous crime to sacrifice the lives of others to our own fears, be those fears real or imaginary.

Howard certainly was not a man to sanction such criminality. As the prisoners' friend, he was resolved to have justice done to them. More than one circumstance of this kind oozed out to public knowledge, and, together with his practical benevolence, gradually served to invest the character of Howard with something like superhuman influence. His power over criminals was very great, and was exercised on several notable occasions. Dr. Brown, the personal friend of the Philanthropist, relates the following as one instance of it: — When Ryland, the celebrated engraver, was under sentence of death for forgery, a gentleman came one morning to Mr. Howard, during one of his temporary visits to London, and begging pardon for his intrusion, informed him that some years ago a maid-servant in a house opposite to Ryland's had suddenly left her situation and could not be heard of. In her room however some scraps of his writing were discovered, and application was immediately made to him to learn what had become of her. But the only answer he would give was, that she was provided for; and with this, during the days of his prosperity, her friends were obliged to be satisfied. When, however, his fortune was ruined by his condemnation, they desired to be informed more particularly of her condition, in order that they might take her home, to prevent her from . . . . They accordingly applied to him in Newgate, but could get no specific answer to their inquiries; when hearing that Mr. Howard had great influence over persons in Ryland's situation, they had determined upon soliciting his assistance, which he was now come to ask, in the hope that he would be able to procure from the criminal the desired information. He promised that he would bring back an account of the poor girl's situation in four-and-twenty hours; and he fulfilled his promise. She had been kept by Ryland in a village at some distance from London, where she was found by her relations and restored to their protection." An incident of another description may be added. At the time of one of his visits to London, a most alarming riot took place at the Savoy — then used as a military prison — during which the infuriated prisoners broke loose, killed two of their keepers, and committed various other excesses. They were 200 strong. Having got possession of the building, no one dared to approach them until the intelligence reached Howard, when he instantly repaired to the spot, and trusting to his own singleness of soul for protection, undertook to encounter the wrath of the excited men, who had broken through every trammel of authority and cast away every fear of the law. Unarmed and alone, he entered the prison. In vain his friends attempted to dissuade him from his purpose — in vain the gaolers pointed to the murdered officers, and warned him of the peril; he went in, and effected his purpose. We know only the result. How he induced the furious mutineers to listen to his remonstrance — how he charmed their savage passions into submission, must be imagined by the reader. They presented to him their list of grievances; and finally suffered themselves to be quietly conducted back to their cells.

Thus passed the year 1782. Another Christmas spent at Cardington, ushered in new enterprises. Spain and Portugal — lands whose histories were dyed in darkest shades — were still unexplored; and thitherward his course was now directed. Leaving Falmouth on the 31st of January, he sailed direct for Lisbon, where he this time arrived in safety. In some respects the prisons of Portugal were superior to those of England; they contained only criminals — imprisonment for debt having been abolished since 1772. The sexes were completely separated: no garnish was allowed to be extorted. The bad custom of detainment for fees prevailed, but even these were generally discharged by a charitable order, composed of some of the chief personages of the kingdom — an order somewhat resembling the Confraternita della Misericordia at Rome. One of the most glaring faults of the criminal policy of Portugal, was the custom of keeping persons immured in gaol for months or even years, without bringing them to trial; a custom which had perhaps crept into the civil courts from the practice of the neighboring tribunal of the Holy Inquisition. Sometimes, after trial and condemnation, convicts were allowed to lie in gaol, or even to go out on parole for several years, before their execution. Until the vigorous administration of the Marquis de Pombal, it was not uncommon for the custodians of criminals to suffer their charges to leaving the gaols on giving their word to return when summoned to do so. Howard tells of a man who had been condemned to death in the usual manner, leave his place of confinement on these terms, and resuming his usual employments in the country. Years passed on, and the poor fellow fancied his offence had been forgotten or forgiven. But not so: when about seven years had elapsed, he learned with horror that an order had at length been issued for his execution. Whatever may have been his feelings, he at once returned to prison, and redeemed his word. A man who would do this, could not be unworthy to live; and it is pleasant to know that the magistrates, either struck with his honesty, or influenced by a sense of the cruelty of punishment under such circumstances, obtained for him a free pardon.

The dungeons of the Inquisition, notwithstanding all his endeavors, Howard could not obtain permission to inspect. Through Evora and Elvas, our countryman continued his journey from Lisbon towards the frontier of Spain. At Elvas, the Marshal de Vallere did the honors of the place —

carrying his guest over the barracks, round the ramparts, and to the other notabilia of the city. Howard did not fail to observe that the troops of the garrison looked sick and pallid; and he told the Marshal that he was persuaded it arose from the dampness and closeness of their rooms. A fountain, with a grandiloquent inscription in honor of the chief magistrate of the town, was being erected at the time; and Marshal de Vallere exhibited this piece of magnificence to his guest with a great deal of pride. Howard bluntly observed, that had he not seen several poor wretches in prison, who had been waiting three or four years to be put upon their trials, he might have entertained a more favorable opinion of the dignitary; but as it was ——!

Entering Spain at Badajoz — since made very memorable by the entry of his countrymen in a different fashion — he travelled through Toledo to Madrid, carefully inspecting all the prisons and hospitals on his route. He found the country abounding in charitable institutions, and containing few beggars. The regulations of the gaols much resembled those of Portugal. In some places, the rack and wheel were still in use as judicial instruments; irons were also common; and, except in the capital, the prisons were fearfully dirty. From Count Fernan Nunez, Spanish Ambassador at Lisbon, Howard carried letters to Count Campomanes at Madrid, who received him with distinguished honor, and furnished him with warrants to enter every prison in the kingdom — except those spiritual dungeons which the mandate of a minister of state could not then reach. In Spain, however, he was more successful in obtaining a glimpse of the Holy Office than he had been in Italy and Portugal. But what he saw therein will best be given in his own words: — "At Madrid, by the kind assistance of Count Campomanes, I got access to the inquisitor-general; but the day on which I applied to him being a great holiday, he appointed me seven o'clock the next morning. On this holiday, I saw the inquisitor, several of the nobility, and others, go in procession to church, carrying the insignia of the order, — which are, a cross between a palm and a sword. The next morning, the inquisitor received me at prayers, and in a few minutes conducted me to the tribunal, which was hung with red. Over the inquisitor's seat there was a crucifix, and before it a table with seats for the two secretaries, and a stool for the prisoner. I could not prevail on him to show me any other part of the prison; but he told me he went round once a month with a secretary, and asked every prisoner if he had any complaints to make. . . . The letters of the same kind friend, Count Campomanes, procured my admission at Valladolid. I was received at the inquisition-prision by the two inquisitors, their secretaries, and two magistrates, and conducted into several rooms. On the side of one room was the picture of an *Auto-da-fé* in 1667, when ninety-seven persons were burnt; at that time the

Spanish court resided at Valladolid. The tribunal room is like that at Madrid, but has an altar, and a door (with three locks) into the secretary's room, over which was inscribed, that the greater excommunication was denounced against all strangers who presume to enter. In two other tribunal rooms were the insignia of the inquisition. In a large room, I saw on the floor and shelves many prohibited books, some of which were English; in another room I saw multitudes of crosses, beads, and small pictures. The painted cap was also showed me, and the vestments for the unhappy victims. After several consultations, I was permited to go up a private staircase, by which prisoners were brought to the tribunal; this leads to a passage with several doors in it, which I was not permitted to enter. On one of the secretary's telling me, 'none but prisoners enter those rooms;' I answered, I would be confined for a month to satisfy my curiosity; he replied, 'None come out under three years, and they take the oath of secrecy.' . . . It is well known that from this court there is *no appeal*. I need not say how horrid the secrecy and severity of it appears. I could not but observe, that even the sight struck terror into the common people as they passed. It is styled, by a monstrous abuse of words, the Holy and Apostolic Court of Inquisition."

From Valladolid, Howard went through Burgos to Pampeluna. Before crossing the Pyrenees to Bourdeaux, he wrote the following letter, dated Pampeluna, April 17th, 1783, to his Cardington pastor:—"I am still in Spain. The manner of travelling with mules is very slow; I was fourteen days betwixt Lisbon and Madrid (400 miles). You carry all your provisions; the luxury of milk with my tea I very seldom could get; but I bless God I am well, and enjoy calm spirits. I received the greatest kindness from Count Fernan, Nunez, the Spanish ambassador at Lisbon, through whose recommendation to Count Campomanes, every prison has been flung open to me. I have a letter to one of the magistrates of every city that I pass. I have been here three days; but must stay a few days longer, before I cross the mountains. The Spaniards are very sober and very honest:—and, if he can live sparingly and lay on the floor, the traveller may pass tolerably well through their country. I have come into many an inn, and paid only fivepence for *the noise I have made* (as they term it) in the house; as no bread, eggs, milk, or wine do they sell. Peace has not been declared. Many will hardly believe it. They talk of General Elliot with a spirit of enthusiasm; never were two nations so often at war, and yet individuals have such esteem and complacency one towards another. . . . I go through Bayonne—stopping only one day; and shall pitch my tent at Bourdeaux, where I have much business, there being some horrid dungeons."

He now travelled leisurely homewards through the heart of France. At Lille he caught a violent fever by visiting some sick debtors in a noisome cell; it threatened at first to be fatal — but again he recovered. His expressions in his private memoranda are full of piety and gratefulness; the spirit being the same as pervaded the former extracts: — "God, do my soul good by this affliction. Make me more sensible of my entire dependence on Thee; more humble, more watchful, more abstracted from this world, and better prepared to leave it.' In about ten days he was able to continue his journey and his labors. His course lay through Amsterdam, Antwerp, and Brussels, where the rack and wheel were still in use, to Ghent. Here a sad spectacle awaited him. The Maison de Force of this city had, in former years, merited and obtained his highest approbation; it was a model of correctional discipline for all Europe. When Howard waited upon the burgomaster to obtain the usual authority to visit it, he was told that the emperor had given orders for no one to be admitted. "But you, sir," observed the magistrate, "are above all rules; you must not, however, impute to me the unhappy changes which you will notice." When our countryman entered the building, which not two years before he had seen full of clean, orderly, industrious workmen — all employed and instructed, and thus undergoing preparation for a better return to the world — he found filth where he had left cleanness, idleness were he had seen industry, sickness where he had known health. The word of one man had done it all!

Joseph II., Emperor of Germany, was by nature a revolutionary. He was fond of changes — in a thousand things his dominions much needed them — but he made them without knowledge, and for the most part in the wrong quarters. He was an innovator without being a reformer. Unlike almost every other prince of the conservative House of Hapsburg, he had a mania for disturbing everything. Scarcely was there an institution which he did not touch. During the early part of his reign, he never dropped the scalpel from his hand; and though his intention may be considered to have been good, he invariably applied it either at the wrong time or in the wrong place: consequently all his efforts to cut away the disorders of the state failed. His management of the Maison de Force at Ghent, was a fair specimen of his misgovernment. Under the impression that the works conducted in this famous establishment were injurious to the manufactures of the empire, he ordered them to be discontinued. The prisoners were thrown into idleness — and upon that rapidly supervened disease, disorder, and other gaol vices. More; — as if these stupid proceedings could not work their disastrous ends quickly enough, the imperial mandate declared that less care must me taken to keep the rooms clean and healthy; in the ignorant hope that by rendering them more disagreeable, he would thereby add to their terrors for evil-doers. No mistake could have been greater, as experience soon proved. The intimate connection of honesty with industry is now universally recognized — and was then; the relation of cleanliness to honesty was not so clearly perceived at that period as it is now. The common saying that cleanliness is a Christian *virtue*, contains a profound philosophical truth; for though apparently a mere physical attribute and not a moral state, cleanliness exerts a subtle and most powerful influence over the mind. In the whole range of sanitary science, no fact is better established than that a filthy condition of the body, insufficiency of light, or the inspiration of a polluted atmosphere, induces an unnatural craving for strong stimulants; thus creating at once the moral insensibility which makes crime possible, and the material wants and necessities which render it inevitable. And, in brief, such was the history of the changes in the policy pursued in the Maison de Force, at Ghent. The looms were all sold; the diet was reduced; and an entire quarter of the building had soon to be fitted up as an infirmary!

Returning to England in June, Howard commenced another series of home inspections, which occupied him until the end of the year, when his labors being completed, he gave the entire results to the public in a second appendix to his great work; and then, full of years and honors, and conscious that he had done his duty, he retired to his favorite Cardington to look after his schools and cottages, to enjoy the society of his friends, to assist in forming the character of his son, now growing up to manhood, as a fiery and somewhat irregular youth — and to repose both mind and body after his many years of unparalleled labor. Being so very domestic in his habits, some of his friends expected he would again marry; but the grounds for this idea were hardly conclusive. He himself related a pleasant anecdote to Dr. Aikin. He was travelling in Holland from one town to another, on a common packet boat — when he saw a young lady — very like the deceased Harriet, as it seemed to him — under the protection of an elderly gentleman, apparently her father. Whether it was her own beauty, or the likeness to his buried love, which so powerfully attracted the attention of the Philanthropist, he hardly knew, still less do we. He continued, however, to watch her; and we all know how the prolonged sight of any form on which the eye delighted dwells, will fill the mind with bland and affluent thoughts. He noted her manners and her movements with increasing interest, and when the boat reached its destination, sent his servant to watch them home and inquire who they were. Was he really touched? If not, what had the sage to do with such an arrant trick? Thomasson returned with the intelligence that the elderly gentleman was an eminent merchant, and that the young lady was — his wife! It could have been nothing more than the resemblance to the sainted Harriet. Another lady adventurer is upon the chronicles, relating to somewhere about this period.

While residing in London, in a house in Great Ormond-street, bequeathed to him by his sister, a lady whose admiration had been powerfully excited by the fame of his great labors, called upon him several times, but was so unfortunate as not to find him at home. At length, however, the worshipper of benevolence found admission, and was ushered into the library. On her entry, Howard was rather puzzled by her appearance. Her immense height, ill looks, masculine build and bearing, suggested to his mind the idea of some species of trick. He suspected his pertinacious visitor to be a man in female clothes, and consequently stood upon his guard. But his fears were quite groundless; the poor, harmless enthusiast poured only a flood of veneration and respect at his feet; and having completely tired out his patience — for he did not like such scenes — with her inflated praises, very meekly and quietly took her leave, declaring that she could then go home and die in peace!

CHAPTER XI.

THE CITIES OF THE PLAGUE.

WITH the publication of the last additions to his great work on prisons, Howard's labors seemed brought to a natural termination. Any other man would now have been content with what he had done, and reposing on his laurels, have given up his few remaining years to dignity and rest. At first such seems to have been the Philanthropist's intention. Thirty years had now elapsed since he had first become acquainted with the sufferings of prisoners in the military dungeons of France; and twelve had passed since he had commenced, in the cell of John Bunyan, those active inspections which he had subsequently carried on in every part of civilized Europe. During these twelve years his energies had been addressed to the one paramount object; he had traversed every country on the continent, with the exception of Turkey; had visited and minutely inspected the gaols of all their capitals and principal cities; had travelled upwards of 42,000 miles, and had expended upon these travels, or in relieving the sick, and in giving freedom to the captive, more than 30,000*l*. These labors, through sacrifices which the world has not been ungrateful for, were now closed, so far as the collection of knowledge and experience from other countries was concerned; the further progress of the work depended wholly upon the developments of time and the issues of new experiments.

His public career thus apparently ended, Howard retired to his estates at Cardington in the spring of 1784; but, like all men of the true apostolic stamp, he soon became aware that to his active temperament, rest was far more irksome than the most fatiguing work. While the man of action has within him great capacities still unexhausted, long voluntary repose is a thing impossible. Man must fulfil the destiny which his organization imposes upon him. Howard's sentiment of duty grew with him. With time, wealth, experience at his disposal, there could be no repose for him in the comparative idleness of ordinary life. The more he did for the temporal or eternal good of mankind, the more he felt he had always still to do.

In the calm of his present retirement at Cardington, it is probable that he would review the various scenes and incidents of his career, while deeply pondering on his schemes of future usefulness. At such moments of retrospection, no picture of his past life could occur to his mind more forcibly than that fearful incident of the frail Italian bark, driven alternately from shore to shore, from Italy to Africa, from Africa back again to Europe, the sport of the storm and the victim of the plague; and finding, whether in Christians or Moslems, only men unhumanized by their fears. This event would keep that terrible enemy of mankind—the plague—perpetually in his thoughts; and the idea of undertaking a crusade against it gradually assumed shape and character in his mind. In his later tours his attention had been incidentally attracted to the subject of Lazarettos in connection with his hospital researches, and he had expressed in his book a hope that some future traveller would obtain drawings of those of Leghorn and Ancona, with an account of their regulation. The hope remained ungratified, and he now resolved to obtain them himself. To render his journey still more useful, he got his friends, Drs. Aikin, Jeb, and others, to draw up a set of queries respecting the plague, which he undertook to submit to the most competent medical men who had had direct experience of the pest on the continent. Thus prepared, he set out towards the end of November, 1785—this time alone. He knew the gravity of the peril which he was about to brave, and he would not suffer even Thomasson to share it.

Mind of man cannot conceive a sublimer spectacle than is afforded by the Apostle, thus going forth voluntarily, to encounter perils from which other men are so eager to flee; for the good of strangers, to confront that deadly pest, in its chosen seats, and at the imminent risk of his own life, win, if possible, the important secrets of its causes, mode of propagation, and remedy.

His plan was to repair in the first instance to all those cities in which it had been found necessary to adopt precautions against the pest; Marseilles, Leghorn, Venice, Valetta and some others; and having obtained drawings and plans of their quarantine establishments, and collected all the information respecting the nature and treatment of plague which their experience afforded, to proceed to encounter it bodily in Smyrna and Constantinople, cities in which it is, or was at that time, permanently endemic, — and so obtain, if possible, such a knowledge of it as might enable him to suggest measures that would render the rapidly increasing intercourse of his countrymen with the Levantine cities less perilous to the health and safety of Western Europe.

It might be supposed that a mission like this — so dangerous to its subject — so important to all the rest of mankind — would have met with universal sympathy and assistance. But no, France had nourished an unsleeping resentment against Howard, and now the time had come for her to show it. At that period, the most celebrated, and in fact the most important quarantine establishment in Europe, was that of Marseilles, and it was essential to the success of Howard's investigations that they should commence at this point. The object which he had in view, having no political or commercial bearing, he thought it possible that the court of Versailles might not object to grant him the necessary authorization to inspect it; and Lord Carmarthen, our minister for Foreign Affairs, undertook to apply for it on his behalf. While the negotiation was pending, Howard passed over to Holland, and after waiting some time at the Hague, in expectation of hearing from his lordship, went to Utrecht, to see his friend, Dr. Brown, at whose house he received the expected letters; but instead of the hoped-for permission to proceed upon his tour, he was not only refused an authorization to inspect the Lazaretto of Marseilles, but was peremptorily forbidden to enter France, on pain of being sent to that Bastille which he had been so curious about. This reply seems to have for the moment embarrassed the Philanthropist. Marseilles was his chief point of inquiry, and to have abandoned that visit, would have been to abandon the whole scheme. On the other hand, to traverse France, and attempt to see it without permission of the government, would be to run the most imminent risk of imprisonment for life. He had a choice of difficulties. Danger stood upright in his path and tried to scare him back; but Duty rose beyond, and in spite of the remonstrances of Dr. Brown, he chose the path of peril and of glory.

Returning to the Hague, he procured a disguise, and then made the best of his way, by a rapid journey to Brussels, where he took a place in the diligence for Paris. It was a dark wintry night when he arrived in the capital of France, and so far favorable to his incognito. On reaching it, his first step was to carry his small trunk to an obscure inn, where he hired a bed, and paid his bill. A diligence started from a neighboring street early in the morning for Lyons, and having taken his place in this conveyance, he retired to rest, flattering himself that he had completely baffled the ingenuity of the police. Fatigued with travelling two whole days and nights, he was soon buried in a profound slumber. But he was not left to enjoy it long. An hour or two had hardly elapsed when he was suddenly aroused with a tremendous knocking at his bedroom door, quickly followed by a threat of breaking in if it were not opened. He was well aware that an unpleasant visit was within the range of chance, and he was therefore more alarmed than annoyed at the disturbant of his rest. The mischief, however, was now inevitable, and he resolved to meet it as became himself. He got up, unfastened the bolts, bade them to come in if they wished, and then coolly returned to bed. The femme de chambre, with a lighted candle in each hand, entered, followed by a tall fellow in black, with a sword dangling at his side, and his hands enveloped in a huge muff. Howard at once recognized an agent of the prefecture, and waited in silence for his interrogatories. The midnight visitor first asked if his name was Howard; to which the reply was promptly given

— "Yes; what of that?" The other took no notice of the retorted question, but continued his own by asking if he had come from Brussels in the diligence, with a man in a black wig. Howard answered sharply to the effect that he had come to Paris in the Brussels diligence, but as to the black wig, he neither knew nor cared anything about it. The man appeared to be satisfied with this information, and, without saying another word, withdrew. Our countryman already knew France sufficiently well to enable him to guess something of the purport of this nocturnal visit; he rapidly jumped to the conclusion that the police had been on his traces, but were probably baffled by his disguise — he travelled as a physician — and by his assumed name. He felt that he had only a moment for escape; so dressing hastily, and shouldering his trunk, he left the house. It was about one o'clock of a dark and piercing night. So far as he could see beneath the dim glare of the lamps by which Paris was then lighted, the street was clear, and he made a quick sortie from the hotel, knowing that in a few minutes it would be placed under strict surveillance. Keeping himself secluded for an hour or two, he then repaired to the diligence office, and long before daybreak, was rattling over the stony pavements of the suburbs of Paris towards the great southern highway — for the first time since he had left the capital of Holland free from the company of a spy.

Indeed, his position had been far more critical than he had supposed; and his escape from Paris was entirely owing to an accident. Howard's indomitable will was not unknown to the French authorities; and when the answer was sent to Lord Carmarthen, it was believed that the Philanthropist would disregard the threat held out, and enter France in defiance of it. The French ambassador at the Hague was therefore ordered to keep watch over his movements; and when he departed thence, the gentleman in the black wig was sent to bear him company to Paris. But being thus clearly brought to the capital, why was he not at once arrested? An incident prevented it. It had recently happened—just at the outbreak of the revolution, as France then was—that a great number of arrests had been made, as afterwards proved, on false or very frivolous grounds, and a vast amount of odium had thereby been cast upon the prefect and the government. This made them chary of using their unpopular power. Fortunately, too, it chanced that the very day on which Howard arrived in Paris, M. Le Noir had gone over to Versailles, after leaving word with his subordinates that no new arrests should be made until his return on the morrow. In this interval, Howard escaped towards the South; and though the bloodhounds of the prefecture were soon upon his trail again, he still succeeded in eluding their vigilance.

His physician's disguise no doubt contributed to his safety; but other dangers connected themselves with this assumption, which, had his previous studies not given him a nice acquaintance with physical ailments, and the nature of medicine, must have been very embarrassing. A lady in the diligence was suddenly taken ill, and as a doctor he was called upon to prescribe for her. The remedy given was entirely successful, which circumstance, while it confirmed his assumption and lessened the danger of suspicion, brought him a very troublesome accession of practice. Numbers of patients presented themselves — and altogether he had a critical part to play as a follower of Esculapius; but, as he afterwards remarked, as one of the empirics he perhaps did as little harm as the rest. In Lyons he remained a few days known only to M. Froissart, and one or two other protestant clergymen — but nevertheless venturing to visit the principal gaols and hospitals. Through Avignon he went to Marseilles, where he at once repaired to the house of his friend M. Durand — who already aware that the agents of the police were in search of him in that city, met him upon the threshold with a very dispiriting welcome. "Ha! Mr. Howard," said he, "I have always been happy to see you until now. Leave France as fast as you can. I know they are searching for you in all directions." But his visitor had not traversed the whole length of France, and run such imminent risks, to be frightened from his purpose at last. Captured, or not captured, he was resolved to remain in Marseilles until he had achieved his end. His inflexible will overcame all contrary counsels; the services of his trusty friends were put into commission, and, with great tact, he got into the Lazaretto — though even natives were strictly prohibited such a favor — obtained plans and drawings of it, and a minute account of the practical working of its every department, all of which may be seen in his work on the lazarettos of Europe.

Having now, to his own satisfaction, fulfilled the intention which had brought him into France, his next anxiety was how to get safely out of it. By land it was considered impossible to escape. The water frontier offered greater facilities. Dressed as an exquisite of the Faubourg St. Honore, and passing as a Parisian gentleman, he remained four days at Toulon, in the midst of perils, before he succeeded in bribing the captain of a wind-bound vessel to put to sea, and carry him to Nice. For some hours it blew a hurricane, and the frail bark was forced to shelter under the small island of Port Crosce, near the mouth of the harbor, after quitting which haven, they were tossed about at sea for several days, but ultimately reached their destination in safety. The following letter, dated Nice, January 30th, 1786, contains a few notes on his recent adventures: "I persuade myself that a line to acquaint you that I am safe and well out of France, will give you pleasure. I had a nice part to act. I travelled as an English doctor; and perhaps among the number of empirics, I did as little mischief as most of them. I never dined or supped in public: the secret was only entrusted to the French Protestant ministers. I was five days at Marseilles, and four at Toulon. It was thought I could not get out of France by land, so I forced out a Genoese ship, and have been many days striving against wind and tide — three days in an almost desolate island, overgrown with myrtle, rosemary, and thyme. Last Sunday fortnight I was at the meeting at Toulon. Though the door was locked and the curtain drawn, one coming in late put the assembly in fear, even to inquiry before the door was opened. I was twice over the arsenal, though it is strictly prohibited to our countrymen. . . . I am bound this week for Genoa, and thence to Leghorn, where a lazaretto has been built within these few years. I know that *you* will not treat my new attempt as wild and chimerical; yet I confess it requires a steadiness of resolution not to be shaken, to pursue it."

After visiting the prisons and hospitals at Nice, our countryman proceeded to Genoa, where he added considerably to his store of information, and thence to Leghorn by sea. Frederigo Barbolani, governor of the city, accompanied Howard on his visit to the lazarettos of San Rocco and San Leopoldo, then considered as the best models in Europe, and presented him with plans and ample descriptions of them. The Grand Duke Leopold, whose enlightened administration was an honor to Italy, happened at the time to be in Leghorn, and sent an invitation to the Philanthropist to dine with him, which the latter politely declined, on the ground that without forwarding the chief object of his journey, it would detain him at least three hours, then of more than ordinary importance, as he was anxious to proceed by the next diligence. These great and original men therefore did not meet; the Englishman, however, not only thought highly of the Italian reformer, but acknowledged it in ample terms. "The rapid visits," he remarks in a letter, "which I have paid to his prisons, hospitals, &c., have given me the fullest conviction that he is the true Father of his country." Praise like this, from the immaculate pen of a Howard, has a dignity which the loftiest might well be proud of.

From Leghorn our countryman proceeded through Florence to Rome, where he was grieved to find the noble hospital of San Michele suffering great neglect from the cardinals under whose care it was placed. The flourishing condition in which he found a charitable institution for the education of young females, patronized and protected by the reigning pontiff, the unfortunate Pius VI., did something, however, to redeem the character of the Eternal City. At the earnest request of the venerable Pope, Howard waited upon his Holiness at the Vatican, — but only after stipulating that the absurd mark of homage, kissing the foot, and indeed every other species of ceremony, should be dispensed with. The Christian Philanthropist and the Christian Priest spent some time in conversation; a nearer acquaintance more profoundly impressing each with respect for the distinguishing virtues of the other. It was a noble thing to see these two illustrious men — alike remarkable for their public virtues and their private sorrows — casting aside the traditional and religious antipathy which each conscientiously felt towards the creed of the other, and meeting together as men and as Christians on the common ground of human charity. At parting, the pious pontiff laid his hand upon the head of the distinguished heretic, saying good-humoredly, "I know you Englishmen care nothing for these things; but the blessing of an old man can do you no harm." A truly noble and catholic sentiment, which his visitor was too large-minded not to accept in a becoming spirit.

A fortnight spent in Rome, and about the same period in Naples, enabled Howard to collect all the information necessary to his purpose which those cities afforded. Sailing thence to Malta, as the vessel coasted slowly along the Sicilian shore, he had a fine view of the lazaretto of Messina; but as a terrific earthquake had recently overwhelmed that city, buried or driven away its inhabitants, and suspended its traffic, he did not attempt to land.

On the 19th of March, 1786, the vessel ran into the harbor of Valetta, the city and citadel of Malta, then the head-quarters and sovereign domain of the historic order of the Knights of St. John of Jerusalem, and the residence of its Grand Master. This guild of priestly warriors had already fallen from the splendor of their ancient position; but, even in their decline, they still constituted a power in the Mediterranean, — a power, however, far more prolific of evil than of good. The Knights were sworn, amongst other things, to make eternal war upon the Turks; to recognize no truce, no cessation of hostilities with the infidels, on any pretext: — and in the course of many centuries of armed conflict with the rival race and creed, they had contracted the intolerent spirit of the Moor, without catching any portion of his splendid virtues. In fact, by their interpretation, the religion of the Nazarene had become more vindictive than that of the Arab. Safe in their impregnable fortress, they carried fire and sword into the Mohammedan settlements of the Barbary coasts. All the usages of war in civilized lands were set at naught by these self-constituted soldiers of the cross. In the fulfilment of their adopted mission, they made descents on the shores of Africa, seized the natives — sailors, peasants, fishermen, all who fell in their way — and having burnt their habitations and destroyed their property, carried them off bodily into captivity. They were in fact a body of chartered pirates, more dangerous than the Algerines, because doing their work of infamy in the name and under the supposed sanctions of religion. Well might Howard exclaim, on becoming personally acquainted with their doings, " How dreadful! that those who glory in bearing on their breasts the sign of the

Prince of Peace, should harbor such malignant dispositions against their fellow-creatures, and by their own example encourage piracy in the States of Barbary." And well indeed might he suggest the inquiry — "Do not these Knights make themselves the *worst enemies* of the cross of Christ under the pretence of friendship?" In the face of history it would be difficult to answer this question otherwise than in the affirmative. Every department of this dark-age institution bore the sign and impress of an order of things which had long passed away with the rest of the world. Every church in the island where a sacrament was administered, was a sanctuary for criminals; and, although the worst offences were awfully frequent, the churches were so numerous that the most abandoned culprits could easily escape the sword of justice by taking refuge within them. Mediæval notions universally obtained in Malta, though Europe was just on the eve of the French revolution, — and the spirit of the crusaders, still floated about it. Altogether it exhibited the most perfect specimen then existing of the splendid barbarism of the twelfth and thirteenth centuries.

Next to the Lazaretto, the special object of his visit, the institution which most attracted the notice of our countryman in Malta, was the Great Hospital of the Order, the noble hall of which, with its marble pavement worn by historic footsteps — its lofty ceiling, black with time — its tall narrow windows — its sombre walls, darkened by the dusky forms of pictured priest and soldier — the vanishing traces of the Order's long-departed glories, had an air of dim and fading magnificence which well consorted with the spirit of the place. In this hospital the traveller found five or six hundred patients; but their condition was little creditable to the Knights, whose ancient soubriquet was Knights Hospitallers. He says the sick were served by the most dirty, ragged, unfeeling and inhuman wretches he had ever encountered, notwithstanding that his experience had furnished him with some strange specimens of that class of men. Once he saw eight or nine of these servitors of the sick amusing themselves with the delirium of a dying patient. In the days of their prosperity and glory, the Knights were required to attend in person to the relief of pilgrims and sick wayfarers: this was, in fact, the fundamental idea in the institution, and the condition on which it had been endowed by Godfrey de Bouillion and other Christian princes with rich lands and lordships. But since the Order had taken to soldiering and piracy, these militant priests had devolved their hospital duties upon the lowest menials; and it was even difficult to induce one of the body to act as governor of the hospital, though the term of service was only two years, and this important office was therefore generally filled by a young and inexperienced person. The food was bad, the rooms and wards insufferably filthy, and the number of attendants quite insufficient. The governor told Howard that for the entire establishment they had only twenty-two servants, and most of those were either debtors or criminals, who had fled thither for refuge, and were therefore ill adapted for the discharge of their onerous functions.

In the stables of the Grand Master of the Order were twenty-six horses and as many mules: these had forty servants for their especial tendance. The hospitals contained nearly six hundred patients: these had twenty-two fugitives from justice to attend them. The contrast did not fail to strike our countryman. The quadrupeds were sumptuously fed, and their dwellings kept scrupulously clean. The sick wayfarers were ill fed, and worse lodged. In the centre of the pile of stabling there was a noble fountain always throwing up a column of fresh water to cool the air for his Highness's brutes. In the court of the hospital there was likewise a fountain — but no water! Twelve years later the island was captured by Napoleon, and the Order became extinct as a political power.

After Howard had made his first series of visits, he presented his letters of introduction to the Grand Master, by whom he was received with distinction, and offered permission to inspect whatever he should think worthy of his notice in the island. At a subsequent interview, his Highness desired to know his visitor's opinion of the Great Hospital. With his customary frankness, Howard detailed the more striking faults which he had observed in it, and added, that if the Grand Master wished to have the various abuses rectified, he must personally undertake the duty of supervision. This language was thought too bold, and the petty potentate took offence. Nevertheless, before our countryman quitted the island, he was gratified in seeing that some of his suggestions had been adopted. On the 9th of April, 1786, we have a letter dated Malta, giving a number of particulars as to his past, present, and future movements.—"As the French minister thought proper to deny Lord Carmarthen's request for me, I travelled *incog.*, as on a physician's tour, and did my business both at Marseilles and Toulon. In the latter place. . . . I was informed that no stranger could enter the Arsenal, but particularly no Englishman. However, I passed several hours there on two days, but was advised to get off by shipping as soon as possible. . . . At Genoa and at Leghorn I was received in the most generous manner —was allowed to visit the lazarettos, the plans of which were sent to my lodgings to copy. I visited Florence, Rome, and Naples—about a fortnight in each place—to review the places in my line. I then took shipping for this island. We lay, by contrary winds, several days close to Messina, Catania, Syracuse, &c., and saw the dreadful effect of the earthquake which happened about two years ago in Sicily. Soon after, we met a sad storm, but happily for us it lasted only four hours, and we arrived here about ten days ago. I have paid two visits to the Grand Master: every place is flung open to me.

He has sent me — what is thought a great present — a pound of nice butter, as we are all burnt up here; yet peas and beans are in plenty, melons, are ripe, roses and flowers are in abundance; but at night one is tormented with millions of fleas, gnats, &c. We have here many Turks. I am bound for Zante, Smyrna, and Constantinople; the accounts from thence are not favorable. A ship arrived to-day from Tripoli; the plague now ravages that city. The crew, &c., went into strict quarantine. One effect I find during my visits to the lazarettos, viz., a heavy headache — a pain across my forehead; but it has always left me about an hour after I have come from these places. As I am quite alone, I have need to summon all my courage and resolution. You will say it is a great design, and so liable to a fatal miscarriage. I must adopt the motto of a Maltese Baron, '*Non nisi per ardua.*'"

Having now obtained the plans and other information which he considered necessary as bases for more dangerous inquiries, he set sail for the veritable cities of the Plague — calling on his way at Zante, where he was struck with the fact, afterwards fully confirmed by a larger knowledge, that the Turks have never descended to the reckless wickedness and folly of confounding *detention* and *imprisonment*. Debtors and criminals were carefully kept separate. The gaol at Zante stood at the back of the guard-house; the poor wretches confined in it were abominably filthy — though not more so than the Venetian soldiers who had them in charge. Somewhat more than three years before this time, a daring pirate had been captured and executed for an attack upon the Grand Duchess, bound from Leghorn to London. Three volleys of shot were fired into him without killing him — and he was only dispatched at length by a pistol applied to his ear. The heads of the gang were placed on the poles and exposed to the public view, and to the action of the atmosphere. In two months, the ruffian's companions were undistinguishable — the skulls only were left; but the chieftain kept his proud pre-eminence even in death. His was one of those firm organizations which time has scarcely any power over. Even at the distance of three years, the features were still quite perfect, and the superstitious Greeks of the island still looked up at the dark and frowning face with trepidation.

The quarantine regulations of Zante, like those of Malta, were strictly enforced.

Thence Howard sailed for Smyrna and for the first time trod upon Asiatic earth, about the middle of May, 1786. In this city, plague is permanently endemic — a fact easily accounted for by its awful sanitary condition. When our countryman arrived, no case of the more virulent kind had been known for some weeks; but the destroyer was still sufficiently active for the purposes of the inquirer, — who at once took a dragoman into his service and began his inspections. At the gate of the principal prison of the town sat three grave Turks, smoking their long chibouques, of whom he demanded permission to enter — a request which they treated with a surly silent contempt, until the dragoman informed them that he was a physician, upon hearing which they greeted him with respect and allowed him to pass. His professional skill was soon called into requisition: a young man was brought forward who had been so severely beaten at a bastinado, that his body was an enormous swelling, beneath which the human form could hardly be distinguished; this personage he was requested, with Moslem peremptoriness, to cure. It was not a little perilous either to refuse the task imposed, or to fail in it; but the assumed doctor examined the case with hearty good-will, and prescribed bathing in the sea, and the application of plasters made of salt and vinegar to the soles of the offender's feet. These remedies, assisted by two doses of Glauber's salts, soon brought the patient round — and the fame of the physician spread far and wide, and caused him to be courted by all classes of society — until the sudden breaking out of a fatal form of the ever-present disease, warned the more prudent to shrink from the company of a man who daringly intruded into the dwellings of the stricken, the dying, and the dead.

The reputation which Howard had thus acquired in Smyrna, preceded, or at least accompanied, him to Constantinople, in which city he remained, upwards of a month, visiting pest-houses, prisons, and hospitals. The plague was then raging with some virulence in the capital. On his arrival, Sir Robert Ainslie, our ambassador at the Ottoman Porte, kindly offered his distinguished countryman a home at his palace; but, knowing the many serious perils which he had come to encounter — perils which he had refused even his favorite servant to share with him — he felt that he had no right to subject the lives of others to the risks which he himself was willing to run for the attainment of his object, and therefore firmly declined to avail himself of the offered courtesy. On many accounts, he thought it desirable to take up his abode in the house of a physician — a man of courage, and of some experience of the pest, to whom he could communicate the general nature of his daily explorations — at once to put him on his guard, and to prepare him to act promptly in case of any fatal contingency arising. On commencing his visits, however, the scenes of horror which he witnessed, and the awful dangers into which he ran, still compelled him to keep the more perilous of his visits secret. For himself, he seemed as if conscious that he bore a charmed life. He sometimes saw the smitten fall dead at his side. He penetrated into pest-houses and infected caravansaries, whither physician, guide, and dragoman alike refused to follow. From these fearful visits he always returned with that scorching pain across the temples, which he had first experienced in the Lazaretto of Malta — though an hour's fresh air and exercise invariably carried it away.

At the commencement of his sojourn in the Turkish capital, an incident had occurred, which not only added vastly to his medical fame, but greatly facilitated his researches in the city. The favorite daughter of a powerful Mussulman, high in rank and office about the court, had been seized with a dangerous illness which baffled the skill of all the celebrities in the healing art at Constantinople; and the father was vainly struggling to reconcile himself to her loss, when he heard of the wonderful cures performed by the Frankish physician. Howard was immediately implored to come and see the great man's daughter. He went, and, seeing at once that her malady was not so desperate as to defy the science of the West, prescribed some medicines which gave her instant relief — the crisis of her malady passed over — and she soon afterwards recovered. The grave old Turk could set no bounds to his gratitude. He pressed upon the savior of his child a purse containing 2,000 sequins — about 900*l.*, which was of course, absolutely refused. Howard told him he never took money for his services — but would not object to receive a handful of grapes from his sumptuous garden. The fee solicited astonished the Turk not less than the skill exhibited; he evidently could not comprehend it; but with a pious ejaculation commanded his servants to furnish the Frank with a supply of the choicest fruits, so long as he should sojourn in that place. This incident, and the impunity with which he visited the plague-stricken, served to invest the simple character of our countryman with an air of mystery and interest. No human motive for his acts could be imagined by a race, which from a sentiment of fatalism abandoned their infected fellow mortals to their fate without help or counsel, while they regarded as sacred the ravenous dogs of the capital, and close to the splendid Mosque of Saint Sophia supported a large asylum for cats!

In most of the Turkish prisons there were few prisoners — a circumstance which at first rather puzzled the inspector, until he found how brief was the interval in that country between the detection of an offence and its punishment. A crime being committed, the bastinado or the bowstring settled the matter — and large penal establishments were rendered unnecessary.

Omitting nothing connected with the circle of his inquiries, in whatever place he found himself, Howard paid particular attention to the regulations of the assize of bread in Turkey. He obtained permission to attend the cadi and the officers of police, when they went their usual rounds to inspect the weight and quality of the bread of the various bakers; the delinquents in these matters he saw severely punished by the bastinado on the spot, or sent off to prison for a still severer punishment. The penalty, as he could see, was often unjustly inflicted, the cadi, generally a young, inexperienced man having a discretionary power to inflict any number of stripes. The superior officers of this department were held responsible for the quantity and quality of the loaf; and whenever a popular discontent arose, the grand chamberlain was sacrificed to appease the vengeance of the mob — just as an unfortunate grand vizier was generally made the victim of a political catastrophe. While Howard was in the Dardanelles, on his way to Constantinople, an instance of this kind occurred — and it formed one of the topics of conversation for some time after. One day the grand chamberlain — the functionary charged with the supply of bread to the capital — received a summons to attend the grand vizier; and surrounding himself with all the pomp and circumstance of his office, he repaired to the palace of the latter. "Why is the bread so bad?" asked the great Turk, with the laconism of his race. "Because the harvest has been bad," was the prompt reply. Apparently satisfied with this answer, the first speaker continued —"Why is the weight so short?" On this point the answer was not so ready — indeed, a good excuse was impossible. The minister did not dare to deny the fact, and tried the policy of extenuation. "That," he said, "may have happened in one or two instances out of the immense number of loaves required for so large a city; but care shall be taken that it does not occur again." No more was said. The grand chamberlain, dismissed, left the palace with his train, and was returning home in great state, when an executioner, sent after him from the vizier, overtook him in the street, and without a word of parley struck off his head in the midst of his followers. For three days his body lay in the public thoroughfare where it had fallen, to satisfy the people of his death — and three light loaves were placed beside it to denote the crime for which he had suffered so severe a penalty.

On the completion of his labors in Constantinople, it had originally been Howard's intention to return overland to Vienna — that route being much more expeditious, since the discontinuance of quarrantine at Semlin, formerly enforced upon all persons entering the Austrian dominions from the East, than by sea; but while we was making preparation for his departure, it suddenly struck him, as he calmly reviewed the scenes which he had witnessed on this important tour, and the accessions of knowledge which he had made, that all his information respecting the arrangement and discipline of the lazaretto was only second-hand; that he had not seen and experienced them himself; and, consequently, that many things had probably escaped his notice, which, should his inquiries lead to the formation of a great Quarantine Establishment in England, would be of essential import. The thought determined him to alter all his plans, and instead of returning homewards over the Balkan mountains, to sail again to Asia Minor. This step was perhaps the boldest — all things considered — which had ever entered into the heart of man to conceive for a purely philanthropic purpose, and threw even his own previous adventures into the shade; he deliberately went back to Smyrna, where the plague was raging, to go by an infected vessel to the Adriatic with a foul bill of health, in order that he might be personally subjected to the strictest quarantine, and thus become acquainted with the minutest details of a lazaretto! This unparalleled devotion has been deemed quixotic; it was so; it was indeed one of the sublimest pieces of quixotism in the world's history. Perhaps not more than once has such a sacrifice of self been seen — and then it was made by one who knew nothing of humanity save its virtues.

This design was no sooner formed than put into act. Howard took his passage in a vessel bound for Salonica, where were two famous hospitals to be visited; they had hardly quitted the Bosphorus, however, when the captain of the light Greek craft in which he sailed came to him, believing him to be a physician, and asked him to see a man in the forecastle who had suddenly fallen ill. He complied, and on feeling the poor fellow's pulse, knew by its motion, and by the rank odor of his breath, that he had been seized with a contagious disorder; and then looking behind his ear, found the black spot, the certain sign of plague. Convinced of the imminent peril to all on board — especially if the morbid fears of the Greek sailors should be excited — Howard instantly resolved not to exhibit any sign of uneasiness, and only to communicate his discovery to a French officer who shared the cabin with him, whom he cautioned to abstain from animal food and not to approach the sick man. He then placed the infected person in a separate cabin: fortunately the crew never suspected the proximity of the pest; and the ship arrived at Salonica without its spreading. The day after they landed the poor fellow died.

In a letter written from Salonica, Howard says, he visited all the prisons there, though his interpreter was very angry at being carried into such dangerous places. He expresses his intention to call at Scio, where was the most celebrated hospital in the Levant, on his way to Smyrna, and his wish to pass his forty days of quarantine in Venice — in which city were the oldest lazarettos in Europe, — having, in that expectation, obtained letters from the ambassador of the republic at Constantinople to the authorities at home, to facilitate his observations. He blesses God for the continued enjoyment of health and unflagging spirits — noting how much he needs, at times, a determined resolution, as he is quite alone; not having travelled a single mile with any of his countrymen since he quitted Helvoetsluys, or even seen an English ship. "At Smyrna," he remarks, "the Franks', or foreigners' houses, are shut up; everything they receive is fumigated, and their provisions pass through water; but in Constantinople, were many of the natives drop down dead, the houses of the Franks are still kept open. I there conversed with an Italian merchant on Thursday, and had observed to a gentleman how sprightly he was; he replied, he had a fine trade and was in the prime of life; but alas! on Saturday he died and was buried — having every sign of the plague."

Visiting the reputed birth-place of Homer on his way, our countryman went on to Smyrna, where he soon found a vessel with a foul bill of health bound for Venice, and in her he took his passage. The voyage was long, and would have been tedious had it not been chequered by the gravest perils. Howard had already had several hair-breadth escapes — but none, perhaps, so near as this. Shortly after leaving the port of Modon in the Morea, where the vessel had put in for fresh water, they were suddenly borne down upon by a Barbary privateer — the Venetian republic being then at war with Tunis — which fired into them with great fury. For a while the Venetian sailors defended themselves with desperate courage, for it was a question of victory or perpetual slavery with them; but their numbers were limited, their arms indifferent, and altogether the contest seemed too unequal to last long. It was the first actual fighting in which Howard had been present; but the imminency of the danger and the sight of conflict appealing to the strong combative instincts of his race, he fought on deck with the coolness of a Saxon and the courage of a knight templar. Indeed it was his self-possession which proved the salvation of the crew. There was only one gun of large calibre on board — and of this he assumed the direction — though he had probably never fired even a rifle in his life. This gun he rammed almost to the muzzle with nails, spikes, and similar charge, and then steadily waiting his opportunity, as the privateer bore down upon them with all her crew on deck, apparently expecting to see the Venetians strike their flag — he sent the contents in amongst them with such murderous effect, that, after a moment or two of consternation, the corsairs hoisted sail and made off at their best speed. Not however, until the enemy was beaten off, did our countryman know the extent of his danger — for he then learned that the captain, determined not to fall into the hands of the Tunisians, had made preparation to blow up his vessel as soon as it should have been boarded by the pirates!

Howard frequently refers in his private letters to this encounter, and mentions his own part in the affair with singular modesty. He does not, however, speak of his act of bloody heroism with regret; on the contrary, he speaks like a man, who, in a proper cause, would have sacrificed himself, like the Decii, on the field of battle, as readily as he did in the prison and the pest house. There was nothing puling or morbid in Howard's philanthrophy; he was a man of true courage; his work of charity arose out of the strength of his character — not out of its weakness. Had his ministry been of the sword — like that of Washington — he would have wielded it with the gallantry natural to his race. Devotion in man, is ever allied with valor.

After touching at Corfu and at Castel-Novo, in Dalmatia, at neither of which ports were they permitted to land on account of their foul bill of health, the vessel anchored in the roadsteads of Venice — having been sixty days on the voyage. Now came the personal martyrdom. Howard was placed in rigorous quarantine for forty days; of the daily experience of which, he has left a minute and interesting record. Being in the worst class of the suspected, the miseries, privations, and perils of the confinement were far beyond expectation.

Whilst undergoing this self-accepted, but still severe punishment, letters reached him from England which went like poisoned arrows into his heart — and one of them left a wound there from which he never recovered. One of these missiles brought him word that a number of well-meaning but ill-advised persons in London had commenced a public subscription for the purpose of erecting a statue to his honor. The project originated with a gentleman who had met with Howard some months before in Rome, and had seen the distinguished honors paid to him in every part of Italy. Thinking it a disgrace to England that no public recognition had yet been made of the virtues and services of her illustrious son, as soon as he returned to London, he made a proposal in the newspapers for a public memorial, and found a warm response to his appeal. A committee was formed, and money poured in upon them from all quarters. The press busied itself with the project — every day some new design connected with the main idea was started: an hospital, a service of plate, an alms-house, a statue, and many other forms of honor were suggested; and as soon as a statue was found to receive the meed of general approval, the site came in for discussion — St. Paul's, Westminster Abbey, and the Parks, being most in favor. The whole affair was improvised; and in a few days had already assumed a large proportion. The first intimation which the man whom it most nearly concerned received of such a scheme, was while buried in the lazaretto of Venice; and chained as he was to a spot so far from home, it occasioned him the most poignant distress.

The other letters spoke of the misconduct of his son, and darkly hinted at the true cause thereof — the unsoundness of his intellect. Had Howard been free, his first move would have been homewards — to put an end at once to the first subject of annoyance, and to ascertain the reality of the second. But he was a prisoner, and had forty days to serve before he would be permitted to leave the lazaretto. Confined to his apartment by a merciless janitor — consumed by a scorching fever, brought on by the intolerable, gaol-like stench of the establishment — that burning of the temples growing perpetual — and wasting with heart-sickness at the idea of the interval of dull, blank, motionless existence, which must intervene ere he could know the worst of his dearly-loved boy, Howard now felt in the bitterest form all the horrors of a prisoner's cell. He could only write to his friends to desire them to put a stop to the progress of the Howardian Fund — as the committee had called it — and to tell him at once and without reserve the simple truth with regard to his son. His letters of this date are filled with the most mournful ideas; the iron had entered deeply into his soul, and his sufferings were intense. In one of them, after describing the horrors of his place of confinement, he says that neither there in the lazaretto — nor once when at sea in a tempest his cabin had become filled with water — nor during the perilous encounter with the pirates, had his spirits or his resolution forsaken him; but he acknowledges that the contents of these despatches from England were almost beyond his strength, and put his fortitude to the severest trial.

It is imteresting to know the manner in which Howard spent these dreary days, "sick and in prison." Part of the time he passed in translating into English the regulations of the Venetian lazaretto — part in spiritual exercises — part in writing letters. Amongst the latter, dated from his prison-room, is a characteristic note to his faithful bailiff, John Prole, which runs as follows: — "It is with great concern that I hear the account of my son's behavior. I fear he gives you, as well others, a great deal of trouble. A great loss to children is their mother, who would check and form their minds, curbing the corrupt passions of pride and self-will, which are seen very early in children. I must leave it to Him, in whom are all hearts; trusting that the blessing of such an excellent mother is laid up in store for him. As to another affair [the projected statue] it distresses my mind. Whoever set it on foot I know not; sure am I they were totally unacquainted with my temper and disposition. Once before, on an application to sit for my picture to be placed in public, I hesitated not a moment in showing my aversion to it. . . . . . Now as to our Cardington affairs; but I hope everything goes smoothly on, and the cottagers do not get behind in their rent. When Rubin leaves his farm, if you choose, it shall not be raised; if otherwise, should it not be nearly the same as Smith's? I wish you to give a look on my garden, the edge in Close-lane, and clumps; I hope the sheep are prevented from jumping over. Walker's close and my closes I hope are neat; the latter were very indifferent when I last returned; there were many nettles and weeds. Take in John Nottingham, or William Wiltshire, for a month, to keep them down by spading them up. After Christmas, desire Mr. Lilburn to settle your accounts to the two Christmases, as it will be easier for me — separating the school-bills, donations, taxes, &c., from other things. Samuel Preston I hope is well; if not, I will do anything for the two widows. Mrs. Morgan I hope is well; tell her, if Nottingham's girl continues good, she shall lay out two guineas for her in any way she thinks proper. Some fine currants will, I hope, soon come, as I was about six weeks ago at Zante; and they are finer this year than usual. They are for my tenants, widows, and poor families at Cardington — about three pounds each . . . At Christmas, give Mrs. Thompson and Beccles, each 1*l*. 1*s*.; Rayner, what I usually give him, 10*s*. 6*d*.— if not given last Christmas, then 1*l*. 1*s*.; Dolly Basset, 1*l*. 1*s*.; the blind man's widow, 10*s*. 6*d*.; five guineas to ten poor widows, — that is to each half-a-guinea, where you think it will be most acceptable — one of which widows must be Mrs. Tingey, in memory of Joseph Tingey, whom I promised to excuse one year's rent; five guineas also to ten families that you think proper objects — one of which must be Richard Ward's. I think you said Abraham Stevens left a girl and a boy, one of which is dead; privately inquire the character, disposition, and circumstances of the other. *You* will accept of coat, waiscoat, and breeches. . . . . Is my chaise-horse gone blind, or spoiled? Duke is well; he must have his range when past his labor; not doing such a cruel thing as I did with the old mare — I have a thousand times repented it. . . . . When my confinement is finished, I have a long journey, over bad roads and snow; but through mercy my calm spirits and steady resolution do not forsake me — as the sailors observed during the action with Barbary pirates; and I well remember I had a good night, one evening when my cabin baskets floated in water." Referring to the memorial, he says in another letter: — "Why could not my friends, who know how much I detest such parade, have stopped such a hasty measure! As a private man with some peculiarities, I wished to retire into obscurity and silence. Indeed, my friend, I cannot bear the thought of being thus dragged out. I wrote immediately — and hope something may be done to stop it. My best friends *must* disapprove of it. It deranges and confounds all my schemes. My exaltation is my misfortune — my fall."

When Howard came out of his confinement he was greatly debilitated and ill of a strong intermittent fever; he was consequently obliged to remain in Venice for a few days, until he recovered strength enough to bear the fatigue of travelling. On making his appearance in society, he found he had become quite a lion, and his labors the general theme of conversation. During this forced stay in the Queen of the Waters, he paid a good deal of attention to its criminal police, illustrative of which two recent cases came to his knowledge, which he afterwards related to the following effect: A German merchant, who was staying for a short time in Venice on business, supped in the evening at a small inn, in company with a few other miscellaneous persons. One night, an officer of the state inquisition came to him at his lodgings, and desired him to seal his trunk, deliver it up, and then follow his conductor. The merchant wished to know why he was to do this; the officer only put his hand to his lips as a sign of silence, and muffling the head of his prisoner in a huge cloak, guided him through a number of streets to a low gate, which he was made to enter, and was then forced along several underground galleries to a small, dark apartment, where he was left alone for the night. The next day, he was conducted into a a larger room, hung with black, adorned with a crucifix, and lighted with a single wax taper. Here he was again left alone. After remaining in anxious suspense for two more days and nights, a curtain was suddenly withdrawn before him, without apparent agency, and the voice of an invisible personage questioned him as to his name, birth, business, the company he kept, and particularly, as to whether, on a certain day, he had not been in the society of persons, whose names were mentioned, and whether he had not heard an Abbe, also named, make use of expressions which were now accurately repeated. To these questions, the simple German gave the best answers he could. At length he was asked if he should know the Abbe again; and on his replying in the affirmative, another curtain was withdrawn, and the identical Abbe was discovered hanging on a gibbet, but quite dead. He was then dismissed.

The other incident happened only a few days before Howard's arrival in the city, and in the family of a distinguished senator of the republic. An officer of the state inquisition roused the said senator in the dead of night, and ordering him to step into a gondola, which was waiting for him at the door of his palazza, had him rowed out of the harbor to a lonely spot, where another gondola was moored to a post, into which second gondola he was commanded to step. There he was shown a dead body, with a rope still about its neck, and asked if he recognized it. He did, and trembled with horror as he gazed on a well-known countenance, now distorted with the agony of a violent death. He was then rowed back to his house, and not another word was ever said to him on the subject. The corse was that of a young man of amiable manner and great abilities, who had been his intimate friend, and the tutor of his children. In moments of familiar conversation, the senator had incautiously spoken of certain political matters of no great moment, which his auditor had afterwards repeated. That night he had been seized and strangled, while his protector was warned of his own indiscretion in the way narrated. A few years afterwards, Bonaparte put an end to the Venetian republic.

Having now obtained drawings, plans, and sections of the lazarettos of Marseilles, Genoa, Leghorn, Spezia, Naples, Messina, Trieste, and Venice, together with all the rules and regulations of the last named, and a minute and accurate account of the whole process of performing quarantine ; and having also procured, by paying handsome fees, replies to the series of questions with which he had been furnished in England, from the most competent physicians of Marseilles, Leghorn, Malta, Venice, Trieste, and Smyrna, Howard had done all that was possible, under the circumstances, to enlighten the West on this important topic. As soon as he was able to bear removal, he crossed the Adriatic to Trieste, and going thence to Vienna, entered the imperial city with all the precautions which he had formerly observed at St. Petersburg. He still continued in a state of great debility, and was quite unable to resume his homeward journey. Letters reached him here, confirming the terrible suspicions which were entertained as to the failing of his son's reason, and reporting the further progress of the Howardian Fund. He at once wrote to the committee, thanking them for their good opinion, but peremptorily refusing to sanction their scheme, and praying that it might be at once abandoned. In another letter, dated Vienna, December 17th, 1786, he says: — "I stayed a week after I left the lazaretto, at Venice, and in three days crossed the sea to Trieste. I found at the former, as at this place, the slow hospital fever creeping over me by my long confinement — the whole air of the lazaretto being infected. Mr. Murray, our last ambassador from Constantinople, died there of the putrid fever. But the sub-governor of Trieste spared me his good and easy carriage, and I came hither last Tuesday, in four nights and five days; three of the former I travelled, but one night, I was forced to stop. I am much reduced by fatigue of body and mind. I have great reason to bless God that my steadiness of resolution does not forsake me in so many solitary hours. If my night-fever keep off, I will go the long stride to Amsterdam. Pray, let me there receive a letter from you; give me your advice, fully and freely. Is my son distracted? Is it from the probability of his vice and folly at Edinburgh? . . . What I suffered in the lazaretto, I am persuaded I should have disregarded, as I gained useful information; the regulations are admirable, if better kept; Venice is the mother of all lazarettos; but oh! my son! my son! . . P. S. The post not going out till this evening, the 19th, I just add, that I had a poor night, and much of my fever, though it is quite off now — six o'clock; yet I must stop two or three days longer. The mountain air, I hope, will take it off, and I shall get on by the light nights. I only want a month's rest; for indeed nobody knows what I have suffered this journey; many weeks having only had dry biscuits and tea; often have I wished for a little of my skimmed milk."

Howard was obliged to stay longer in Vienna than he wished. On Christmas-day, he had an interview with the Emperor, Joseph II., at whose earnest desire it was brought about. On his side, our countryman, after seeing his majesty in his residentiary city, where he threw off much of the state and ceremony common to royalty, and especially to the house of Hapsburg, was disposed to think better of him; while the Emperor's interest in the subject of hospitals and prisons could not fail to create a certain sympathy between them. Of this singular interview, many interesting particulars are preserved in Howard's letters, and in his verbal communications to private friends — being in substance as follows:

On his arrival in Vienna, *incog.*, Howard, wishing to remain unknown, had taken up his abode in a small lodging in a by-street of the inner city, up three pair of stairs; and in this humble apartment, he received a visit from his Highness, Prince Kaunitz, the old and wily minister of Maria Theresa, who brought a message from the Emperor, to the effect that he would be pleased with a visit from the Philanthropist. The latter replied, that he would have waited upon his Majesty, had not his arrangements for leaving Vienna early on the following morning prevented it. Kaunitz could not prevail on him to alter his refusal, though, in order to smooth the way, he was prepared to waive every court ceremony which he knew would be displeasing to the Englishman. Recourse was then had to Sir Robert Keith, the English ambassador, and a valued friend of Howard, who was further empowered to state, that the Emperor would receive his visitor at any — even the earliest hour in the morning, so as not to interfere with the arrangements for his intended departure. The earnestness of Joseph, indicated by these concessions, must have been flattering to Howard. "Can I do any good by going?" he asked Sir Robert; adding, "for I will not accept the invitation unless it can be made to answer some useful purpose; and as I have some objections to the arrangements of the Emperor's pet hospitals and prisons, I shall freely speak my mind, if interrogated concerning them." On the ambassador's assuring him that good must result from the interview, Howard consented to wait upon his Majesty, and named nine o'clock next morning for that purpose.

Ever scrupulously exact as to his appointments, just as the clock struck nine, our countryman was announced at the palace, where the Emperor received him with every mark of personal respect in a small cabinet fitted up like a merchant's office, a secretary being the only other person present. At that period, it was customary at the Austrian court for all persons, whatever their rank, to approach the sovereign on bended knee, a piece of servile etiquette which Howard had peremptorily refused to comply with, and which had therefore been waived. Prince Kaunitz, a man of infinite tact, probably suggested the manner of the interview; and it was so arranged, that while the German Emperor did not appear to sacrifice his imperial dignity, there was nothing to offend the stern principles of the English democrat. On being introduced, Howard was requested to step into an inner cabinet, in which was neither chair nor stool. The Emperor immediately followed him. Both were compelled to stand the whole of the time — two hours — which their interview lasted; and this was done in order that the Philanthropist might not be forced to feel that a subject was not permitted to sit in the imperial presence.

His Majesty opened the conversation, after some preliminary small-talk, by asking his visitor's opinion of his new Military Hospital. Before he replied to this question, Howard desired to know whether he might speak freely what he thought, and on that assurance being given, went on to say: "Then I must take the liberty of saying, that your Majesty's Military Hospital is loaded with defects. The allowance of bread is too small; the apartments are not kept clean, and they are in many respects ill constructed. One defect particularly struck me: the care of the sick is committed to *men* — and men who are very unfit for their office, especially when it is imposed upon them as a punishment, as I understand to be the case here." Joseph observed that the allowance of bread in the hospital was the same as to every other soldier — a pound a day. To which Howard replied, that a pound a day was not sufficient for a man who was expected to work, or was recovering from sickness, being barely adequate to the support of life. They next spoke of the Great Hospital of Vienna, and afterwards of the Lunatic Asylum; the defects of both of which establishments the Philanthropist pointed out very copiously and freely, going into various details, for which he had carried his notes with him. On these points he spoke so strongly and plainly, that when his Majesty directed the conversation to the subject of prisons, his fearless monitor paused for a moment, as if to indicate that what he had to say thereon might prove still less palatable. Comprehending the sign, the Emperor pressed his hand cordially, and desired him to go on, and speak without fear.

"I saw in them," resumed the Friend of the Prisoner, "many things that filled me with astonishment and grief. They have all dungeons. The torture is said to have been abolished in your Majesty's dominions; but is only so in appearance, for what is now practised is in reality worse than any other torture. Poor wretches are confined twenty feet below the ground, in places just fitted to receive their dead bodies, and some of them are kept there for eighteen months. Others are in dungeons, chained so closely to the walls that they can hardly breathe. All of them are deprived of proper consolation and religious support——" Here the Emperor, annoyed at this severe censorship on his darling institutions, abruptly exclaimed: "Why, Sir! in your country they *hang* men for the slightest offences!" "I grant," said Howard, turning aside from his argument for a moment, to notice this explosion—"I grant that the multiplicity of her punishments is a disgrace to England; but as one fault does not excuse another, so neither in this case is the parallel just; for I declare that I would rather be hanged, if it were possible, ten times over, than undergo such a continuance of punishment as the unhappy beings endure who have the misfortune to be confined in your Majesty's prisons." The Emperor accepted the rebuke, and remained silent, while our countryman resumed his observations at the point where they had been interrupted. "Many of these men," he said, "have not yet been brought to trial, and should they be found innocent of the crimes laid to their charge, it is out of your Majesty's power to make them a reparation for the injuries you have done them; for it is now too late to do them justice, weakened in their health and deranged in their faculties as they are by their long confinement." Joseph admired the honesty and fearlessness of these remarks, even where he could not bring himself to admit their justice. He then asked his visitor's opinion of his workhouses. "In them too," was the spirited answer, "there are many defects. In the first place, the people are compelled to lie in their clothes, a practice which in the end never fails to produce distempers. Secondly, little or no attention is paid to cleanliness; and, thirdly, the allowance of bread is too small." "Where," asked his imperial majesty, with an air of conscious triumph, knowing the miserable state of all such institutions at that time existing in Europe, — "Where did you ever see better institutions of the kind?" "There *was* one better," said Howard, significantly, and the thrust went directly home, — "There was one better at Ghent; but not so now! not so now!" The Emperor winced sensibly, as well he might; but his stern monitor had not come thither to flatter his vain-glory, already too vast for his soul's good, but to lay before him the naked truth — perhaps for the first time in his life — and to speak to him of his doings with the judicial impartiality of history. It is but seldom that words like these are addressed to kings; still less frequently are they listened to and understood. At parting, the Emperor of Germany pressed the hand of the English gentleman with much cordiality, and thanked him repeatedly for his visit and his counsels. The next day he told Sir Robert Keith that his countryman was not much given to ceremony or compliment, but that he liked him better for that, and was much pleased with their interview; adding, that in some particulars he should certainly follow his advice, in others he should not.

The length of this interview prevented Howard from leaving Vienna as he had originally intended; and he was moreover induced to remain a few days longer, to see if any effect would be produced by his appeals on behalf of the suffering. His gracious reception at court of course rendered him an object of interest to the swarm of parasites who surrounded it. All who wished to be in the fashion found their way up the three pair of stairs, to offer our disdainful countryman their fulsome or impertinent attentions. One day he received a visit from a newly appointed governor of Upper Austria, and his vain and pompous countess. These courtly personages surveyed the humble lodging in which, to their astonishment, they found the Philanthropist, with profound contempt, and evidently looked upon its occupier only as a part of the furniture which they had come to inspect. Amongst other things, the gentleman condescended to inquire what was the condition of the prisons in his province. Howard half amused, half provoked at their petty impertinence, replied: "The very worst in all Germany, particularly in the condition of the female prisoners; and I recommend your countess here to visit them personally, as the best means of rectifying the abuses in their management." "I!" exclaimed the lady, with an indignant toss of the head. — "I go into prisons!" and, burning under the intolerable insult to her state and dignity, bounced out of the room, followed quickly by her lord. "Remember, Madam," said Howard, with solemn pleasantry, as she rapidly descended the stairs, "that you are yourself but a woman, and must soon, like the most miserable female prisoner in a dungeon, inhabit only a small space of that earth from which you are equally sprung!"

In a few days our traveller quitted Vienna, and making a rapid journey through the heart of Europe, reached England early in February, 1787. He at once went down to Cardington, — where he found his son a raving maniac! It would be vain to attempt to describe the agony of this sight to the devoted parent. There are emotions which are too profound for words to render them — feelings which sympathy can alone communicate. Everything which affection could suggest, or skill conceive, had been done for the unhappy youth from the moment when his malady had unequivocally shown itself; but to no purpose. He failed to recognise his father, and exhibited a malicious longing to rush upon and tear to pieces his friends and dearest relatives. Under these circumstances, Cardington could no longer be endured; the house was given up to the maniac boy and his keepers, and the afflicted father returned to his now desolate home in London.

The committee to the testimonial fund still persisted in their design, urging that Howard had no right to veto the project, and that he would at length be brought to respect a decision which he found himself unable to control. He thought otherwise, and wrote to the subscribers generally, through the public press, a strong letter, thanking them for their kind intention, but declaring his fixed repugnance to the proposed scheme, and prohibiting the fund collected from going any longer by his name. This produced the desired effect. The money, amounting to 1,533*l.* 13*s.* 6*d.*, was advertised to be returned, and about a third of it was refunded. The other contributors refused to receive back their donations; consequently, 200*l.* of the residue was expended in the liberation from gaol of fifty-five poor debtors, and the remainder of the fund invested in stock, which was used after his death for the purchase of the noble statue that now adorns St. Paul's Cathedral.

This source of annoyance off his hands, Howard applied himself to a new, and, as it proved, final inspection of all the gaols of the British islands, which was not completed until the end of September the following year — occupying more than eighteen months, though he was employed upon it with hardly an hour's intermission. When completed, the results were given to the world along with all his recent observations upon the plague and its provisions in his great work on the Lazarettos of Europe. Of his final observations upon the prisons and prison-system of England, only one emphatic remark requires to be given. Some of the vices of the newly adopted transportation scheme had begun to appear. After describing the horrors of a prison where convicts were kept, waiting deportation, he says: — "Such dreadful nurseries have been a principal cause of the increased number of crimes, and the shocking destruction of our fellow-creatures. I am persuaded that this would have been in a great measure prevented, if penitentiary houses had been built on the salutary spot at Islington, fixed on by Dr. Fothergill and myself. The gentlemen whose continued opposition defeated the design, and adopted the expensive, dangerous and destructive scheme of transportation to Botany Bay, I leave to their own reflections upon their conduct."

CHAPTER XII.

THE MARTYRDOM.

In a former part of this history, the unfortunate issue of young Howard's education was pointed out, and the fact that his father had been charged with contributing, by his severity, to that deplorable result, was noticed. Sufficient evidence was then adduced to show the groundlessness of such a charge; it now remains to give some account of the real causes of this dreadful malady. This duty is painful; but truth must be told — all real history is darkly streaked with vice and folly. It is a melancholy task to follow the career of this last scion of the race of Howard; but his fate is a solemn warning to those whom opportunity and fiery passions tempt into courses of profligacy, of the dangers which, unseen like serpents under flowers or poison in the wine-cup, beset their paths. There is now no longer doubt but that this ill-starred youth fell a victim to his own excesses. The great care which his father had taken with his education was neutralized by other influences. We have already spoken of the way in which Thomasson, Howard's favorite servant had obtained his notice. This young man was a useful attendant, but a most dangerous companion: and from playing with his young master, as a child, he had grown up with him more as a friend than as a menial. Whenever the Philanthropist was at Cardington, or in London, they were left together. Thomasson was of a restless, roving disposition, and anxious to see what the young call *life*. He was a country lad with strong animal energy, to whom dissipation had the inexpressible charms of novelty and excitement. Now, whether these qualities were his recommendation or not — whether man seduced master, as has been said, or master seduced man, which is quite as probable — we do not, and cannot know; this, however, is certain, that together, but in secret, they frequented the worst places of resort in London — whilst the unsuspecting Philanthropist was engaged in his own labors. Howard's peculiar habits of order and abstemiousness lent themselves readily to screen the imprudent debauches. All day long, when in London, he was absent from home on his errands of mercy; and his custom was always to retire to bed at an early hour. Then commenced the ruinous saturnalia. As soon as all was quiet in the house, the youths would leave their bed-rooms — steal noiselessly down stairs — and sally out to the theatres; whence, in due time, they would adjourn to cider cellars, gaming-places, hells, and night houses of the most infamous kind — in which they would pass the greater part of the night in drunkenness and debauchery. This they thought seeing life!

Before the last of the Howards was seventeen, he had been initiated into every scene of licentiousness which a great metropolis like London could afford, and had contracted that habit of vice which subsequently ruined his health, shattered his fine intellect, brought his noble parent to a premature grave, led to the extinction of his family name, and left in his track nothing but misery and desolation.

At the age of eighteen, when he was sent to study at Edinburgh, under the charge of Dr. Blacklock, this habit was confirmed, and his dissipations were continued. There the fatal effects of his vicious indulgence first began to appear. Man cannot violate the moral law without paying the penalty. Promiscuous intercourse produced its fruits in the shape of a loathsome disease; but, as the youth was not yet lost to all sense of shame, he imprudently attempted to conceal from his friends the consequences of his misconduct — and, finding himself growing worse from day to day, in his despair he took a large dose of powerful medicines, which acting upon a frame already rendered highly susceptible, affected the brain and the whole nervous system. A physician who lodged in the same house, was the first to observe the symptoms of the terrible disease which afterwards prostrated his mind and carried him to a permature grave. He at that time exhibited an hypochondriacal humor; was easily excited or depressed; and to the discerning eye showed marks of undoubted men tal aberration.

With the seeds of this incurable malady planted in his frame, he went to Cambridge, where he gradually lost all power of controlling his erratic fancies; and there his passions so overcame him at times, as to render his company highly disagreeable and even dangerous to his fellow Cantabs. When his father departed for the Cities of the Plague, he was left sole master of the house at Cardington; and being uncontrolled, his disease only the more rapidly developed itself. The mischievous tricks which he played the villagers soon alarmed the whole neighborhood — the more so as no person except the Rev. Thomas Smith could exercise the slightest influence over him. He began to entertain the most absurd notions. While at Cambridge, he had charged more than one person with attempting to poison him; he now conceived a ferocious hatred to his old friend Thomasson, and began to revile his father. At length his conduct grew so outrageous, that his relatives, Mr. Whitbread, Mr. Tatnall, and the Messrs. Leeds, his maternal uncles, judged it necessary to place him under restraint. Two keepers from a private lunatic asylum in London were engaged, and under their charge he remained at Cardington until his father's return.

On his arrival from Vienna, it was proposed to remove him to a regular asylum; but this the Philanthropist would not hear of. He thought it likely that familiar scenes, the home of his infancy, would have a tranquillizing effect upon his mind — which still had its lucid moments, though at long intervals — and resolved to give the house entirely up to him; himself in the meanwhile — as a relief from a parent's harassing anxiety during that interval in which his son's ultimate chance of recovery must of necessity be doubtful — entering upon a long and final inspection of the prisons and hospitals of Great Britain and Ireland. In these labors, and in preparing his last publication for the press, Howard consumed nearly two years; but at the end of that long period of heart-sickness and hope-deferred, no sign of amendment appeared; and at the earnest solicitation of the medical men, he at length consented to his son's removal to a celebrated asylum for lunatics at Leicester, under the care of Dr. Arnold. And here this sad recital may be closed; for he left it not again alive. Dead to himself and to the world, he lingered on, an incurable maniac, until April 24th, 1799, when he finally expired, — but still gave no sign!

His removal thence enabled Howard to revisit Cardington once more. With a mournful tenderness the old man now retrod the scenes of so much happiness and so much sorrow. The last terrible affliction had opened all his former wounds afresh; and in the closing scenes of his laborious life, he saw the clouds gathering in darkly from every quarter of the horizon.

This was his last leave-taking of his favorite home!

He had already arranged the plan of another continental tour, and he came amongst his Bedfordshire friends and dependants, deeply impressed with the idea that it was to be the last time he and they would ever meet on earth. In this his heart was only too prophetic. Death was already busy in his frame. The last shaft from the Chastener's hand had fallen on his hearth in such a shape, through wilful sin and folly, that the stricken father — who had already borne his ample share of suffering, still fondly nursing the delusive hope, that after a time of trial and of righteous expiation the veil which had descended on his house might be withdrawn, and his child's clear intellect again resume its vacant throne — felt at length his hold on life and its affections failing; yet still did he hope on — still did he dream of the penitent's recovery and restoration, the boy's physicians kindly encouraged this idea: but — as they urged—time was necessary for the trial. Two or three years must at least elapse before a cure could be effected: and in that dreary interval of hope and fear, the father could not sit down to brood upon his heart, and fall the silent prey of a devouring thought. On every ground it was wise for him again to travel and to act. Busy he must be; and, having done all that man could do in his own country, he resolved to go abroad again and visit some lands, especially in the east and south, which as yet he had not seen, and extend his inquiries on the subject of the plague. The proposed route now lay through Holland, Germany, Russia, Poland, Hungary, Turkey, Anatolia, Egypt, and the States of Barbary; if no fatality intervened, this journey was calculated to occupy from two to three years; at the end of which time it was thought that his son's malady would either have abated or proved itself a case of confirmed and hopeless insanity. Such was his programme — such his hope!

By this time, Howard's experience had shown him, that his tours in foreign countries could be made as useful to their inhabitants as to his own countrymen; and although the wish to be employed as a refuge from his domestic miseries, and the expectation of gathering knowledge of vital importance to Western Europe, had their influence in causing this last journey to be undertaken, it was nevertheless chiefly prompted by the hope of being able to carry the light of science and civilization into lands where they were as yet but little known. This resolution had been taken before the "Lazarettos of Europe" was given to the world, and was thus announced at the conclusion of that work, in the last words which Howard formally addressed to the public: — "To my country I commit the result of my past labors. It is my intention again to quit it for the purpose of revisiting Russia, Turkey, and some other countries, and extending my tour into the

East. I am not insensible of the dangers that must attend such a journey. Trusting, however, in the protection of that kind Providence which has hitherto preserved me, I calmly and cheerfully commit myself to the disposal of unerring Wisdom. Should it please God to cut off my life in the prosecution of this design, let not my conduct be uncandidly imputed to rashness or enthusiasm, but to a serious, deliberate conviction that I am pursuing the path of *duty*, and to a sincere desire of being made an instrument of more extensive usefulness to my fellow creatures, than could be expected in the narrower circle of a retired life."

To those who know the fatal issue of this tour, these words have a mournful and impressive dignity, which they would lack before the sad event which they foreshadowed; especially as it is now known more fully than could then be thought, that in the mind of the missionary, underneath all these projected and avowed designs, there lay a profound but secret consciousness that life would not be spared him to complete them. He felt that his race was almost run — that his great career was drawing rapidly to a close; but, like the gallant knight of old who scorned to die upon his silken couch, and, as he found his end approaching, rose, and caused himself to be encased in mail that he might die as became a soldier — *he*, rejecting the paradise of eider-down, prepared to be faithful to his trust unto the end, and not give up his work till all was finished. That this would be the concluding act of his varied drama he was well convinced. There could in fact be no mistake about it. The signs of his approaching dissolution were physical as well as mental. Often prostrated by the most violent shocks; accidents, fevers, infections — want of rest, food and shelter —privations on the roads — hunger and cold — confinement in lazarettos — perils and sufferings at sea — the whole wreck and waste of a life of almost unparalelled activity, had sapped the foundations of a constitution never remarkable for its strength; and when to these destroying elements are added the wearing excitement of heart and mind which he had to endure, — the loss of his dear wife, and the sickening consciouness that her son, the hope of his house, had fallen a victim, not to any of those imperious laws of nature to which the wise can always submit in silence, but to a disgusting vice that almost divested his misfortune of the pity of the good; considering these things deeply, it is really marvellous that the old man's frame should have maintained its vigor, and his mind its tone, so long. Howard never juggled with himself, and now he had become convinced that the sap was drying up — that the shaft had been struck into the core. His health was breaking up faster than it appeared, because his spirits, naturally inclined to depression, had been educated in the course of many years of trial and self-discipline into a state of habitual calmness and serenity. And this exterior composure not only served to deceive his friends as to the strength and soundness underneath, but of itself contributed to hold the dissolving elements for a time together. Howard, however, knew his state too well to be deceived.

When he went down to Cardington, it was to take a last farewell of scenes and friends so dearly loved and honored. He took a tender interest in going for the last time over the grounds which he had trodden in happier years — in standing, in the silent eve, beside the grave of his lost wife—in thinking over all those schemes, so full of pride and hope, which young and happy lovers build up for themselves in the phantom future. Standing one evening with his old gardener in the grounds behind his house, and talking of the past with that affectionate familiarity which most men would imitate at such a moment, the wayfarer observed, in a tone tremulous with emotion, that after many years of planning and altering he had at length got everything into the state which Harriet would have best liked — and now he was about to leave it forever!

The indulgence of these sweet and troubled memories did not divert him from his more active duties. There were many calls upon his attention at the moment of separation forever. He carefully inspected all his schools and model cottages — and took such means as he thought most likely to perpetuate a provision for the education of the villagers of Cardington. By his will, which bears date the 24th of May, 1787, he bequeathed the whole of his real estate in trust to his son, in case of his recovery, failing which it was to descend to the next heir, Howard Channing, son of his maternal uncle; and, as he also died without issue, the property then devolved upon C. Whitbread, Esq., second son of the well-known politician, who still resides upon the estate of his illustrious relative. A considerable portion of the personal property was left (1) to the poor of Cardington and Croxteth, the latter the place where he was married to Henrietta — a delicate instance of his affection for his wife — and (2) in trust for the benefit of a certain number of poor debtors and prisoners confined in houses of correction. The elder Whitbread was made chief executor of the will; and to him, and to his family, Howard confidently committed the sacred charge of maintaining his schools and other charitable institutions in vigorous life.

The parting of the good man with those humble friends who, as we have seen, were never absent from his thoughts, however far away, and however deeply involved in his own private troubles, was extremely pathetic and interesting. It was like the parting of a father from his children. He visited every family separately, made some kind present to each, and gave to all his last counsel and advice. And long and proudly, were those parting words remembered by the simple-hearted creatures to whom they were addressed. Honest John Prole he settled in a farm, and made his wife — Harriet's favorite maid — a present of a handsome tea-caddy and his own miniature of her former mistress. At first he intended to have gone this tour alone, as he had done the last, but the strong entreaties of Thomasson moved him at length to accept his services.

Howard's farewell interviews with his private friends were solemn and affecting. The last words spoken by him upon many of these occasions have been religiously preserved. To one he said: — "I am going to the Mediterranean and elsewhere (naming some other places). I have had several malignant disorders: yet I am persuaded that I shall not return and be permitted to lay my bones in my native land. If, however, I should, I think I shall then have done all my duty can require of me; and I shall most probably seek a peacefnl retirement for the rest of my days." To another he said: — "You will probably never see me again; but, be that as it may, it is not matter of serious concern to me whether I lay down my life in Turkey, in Egypt, in Asia Minor, or elsewhere. My whole endeavor is to fulfil, according to the ability of so weak an instrument, the will of that gracious Providence who has condescended to raise in me a firm persuasion that I am employed in what is consonant to his Divine will." In parting with one friend, he observed: — "We shall soon meet again in heaven;" and as he thought it most likely that he would fall a victim to the heat or the plague in Egypt, added, after a pause, "The way to heaven from Grand Cairo is as near as from London." Dr. Aikin, from whom he parted with tender regret, has described the farewells of a friendship of still longer standing,—"He and his very intimate and highly respected friend, Dr. Price, took a most affectionate and pathetic leave of each other. From the age and infirmities of the one, and the hazards the other was going to encounter, it was the foreboding of each of them that they should never meet again in this world, and their farewell corresponded with the solemnity of such an occasion. The reader's mind will pause upon the parting embrace of two such men, and revere the mixture of cordial affection, tender regret, philosophical firmness, and Christian resignation which their minds must have displayed." Such was the grave and tender serenity of mind with which the good man bade his friends farewell—such the temper in which he walked to his appointed martyrdom!

On the 5th of July, 1789, he quitted England to return no more. Arriving at Amsterdam on the 7th, he proceeded by slow stages through Germany and Prussia into the empire of the Czar, which he entered at Riga. At this town we find him making the following memoranda:—"I am firmly persuaded, that as to the health of our bodies, herbs and fruits will sustain nature in every respect far beyond the best flesh meat. . . . The Lord planted a garden for mankind in the beginning, and replenished it with all manner of fruit and herbs. This was the place ordained for man. If these still had been the food of man, he would not have contracted so many diseases in his body nor cruel vices in his soul. The taste of most sorts of flesh is disagreeable to those who for any time abstain from it, and none can be competent judges of what I say but those who have made trial of it." It is curious to see a dogma like this advocated so earnestly by minds so great and yet so different as Shelley's and Howard's. While at Riga, as again at Moscow, whither he went directly from St. Petersburg, he reviewed his life, and read over and renewed that solemn covenant which he had made at Naples three-and-twenty years before. From Moscow he sent a letter to his friend Dr. Price, dated September 22d; and as it is the last he wrote, contains several particulars of his journey, it must be given entire. "My dear friend: Your kind desire of hearing from me engages me to write. When I left England, I first stopped at Amsterdam. I proceeded to Osnaburg, Hanover, Brunswick, and Berlin; then to Konigsberg, Riga, and St. Petersburg; at all of which places I visited the prisons and hospitals, which were all flung open to me, and in some the burgomasters accompanied me into the dungeons, as well as into the other rooms of confinement. I arrived here a few days ago, and have begun my rounds. The hospitals are in a sad state: upwards of 70,000 sailors and recruits died in them last year. I labor to convey the torch of philanthropy into these distant regions, as in God's hands no instrument is weak. I go through Poland into Hungary. I hope to have a few nights of this moon in my journey to Warsaw, which is about 1,000 miles. I am pure well — the weather clear — the mornings fresh — thermometer 48°, but we have not yet begun fires. I wish for a mild winter, and shall then make some progress in my European expedition. My medical acquaintance give me but little hope ef escaping the plague in Turkey; but my spirits do not fail me; and, indeed, I do not look back, but would readily endure any hardships and encounter any dangers to be an honor to my Christian profession. I long to hear from my friend, yet I know not where he can direct to me, unless at Sir Robert Ainslie's, Constantinople. I will hope all things. Remember me, &c."

Circumstances prevented him from following the route here indicated — and in fact he was destined never more to quit the soil of Russia. The tremendous destruction of human life to which the military system of that country gives rise, had not then, as it has since, become a recognized fact in Western Europe; and the unconceived and inconceivable miseries to which Howard found recruits and soldiers exposed in Moscow, induced him to turn aside for a moment from his main design, and devote his attention to them and to their cause. In these investigations horrors turned up of which he had never dreamt, and impressed him still more profoundly with a sense of the hollowness of the Russian pretence of civilization. In the forced marches of recruits to the armies over horrid roads, being ill-clothed and worse fed, he found that thousands fell sick by the way, dropped at the road-side, and were either left there to die of starvation, or transferred to miserable hospitals, where fever soon finished what fatigue had begun. This waste of life was quite systematic. An hospital for the reception of the poor wretches had recently been erected at Krementschuk, a town on the Dnieper, which contained at that time 400 patients in its unwholesome wards. Thither Howard repaired to prosecute his new inquiries. The rooms he found much too full; many of the soldiers were dreadfully ill of the scurvy, yet they were all dieted alike, on sour bread and still sourer quas, alternated with a sort of water-gruel, which if not eaten one day was served up again the next. From this place, Howard went down the Dnieper to Cherson, where he examined all the prisons and hospitals, and made various excursions in the neighborhood for the same purpose. The hospitals were worthy of the evil which they were designed in part to alleviate. Our countryman thus sums up his observations upon them: — "The primary objects in all hospitals seem here neglected — namely, cleanliness, air, diet, separation, and attention. These are such essentials, that humanity and good policy equally demand that no expense should be spared to procure them. Care in this respect, I am persuaded, would save many more lives than the parade of medicines in the adjoining apothecary's shop."

While at Cherson, Howard had the profound gratification of reading in the public prints of the capture and fall of the Bastille; and he talked with delight of visiting its ruins and moralizing upon its site, should he be again spared to return to the West. But however moved by that great event, so important for all Europe, he did not allow it to divert him from his own more especial work; the sufferings of poor Russian soldiers in the hospitals of Cherson, Witowka, and St. Nicholas, had higher claim upon his notice at that moment than even the great revolution making in the faubourg St. Antoine at Paris. In one of the papers brought to England after his death, he says: — "Let but a contemplative mind reflect a moment upon the condition of these poor destitute wretches, forced from their homes and all their dearest connections, and compare them with those one has seen cheerful, clean, and happy at a wedding or village festival; let them be viewed quitting their birth-place, with all their little wardrobe, and their pockets stored with roubles, the gifts of their relations who never expect to see them more. Now joining their corps in a long march of one or two thousand wersts; their money gone to the officer who conducts them and defrauds them of the government allowance; arriving, fatigued and half naked, in a distant dreary country, and exposed immediately to military hardships, with harassed bodies and dejected spirits; and who can wonder that so many droop and die in a short time, without any apparent illness? The devastations I have seen made by war among so many innocent people, and this in a country where there are such immense tracts of land unoccupied, are shocking to human nature!"

A fortnight after this affecting picture was drawn, the hand which painted it was stiff and cold; the heart which had so long beaten for the woes of others, had ceased to beat at all — the troubled soul had found its everlasting rest!

The reader will recall to mind, that, at the time of Howard's residence at Cherson, a desperate war was raging between the Sultan and the Autocrat. The strong fortress of Bender had just fallen into the power of Russia, but as the winter was already too far advanced to allow the army to push forward until spring, the commander of the imperial forces gave permission to such of his officers as chose to go and spend the Christmas with their friends in Cherson. That city was consequently crowded with rank and fashion. All the city was in high spirits. The victories of the imperial troops produced a general state of jubilation. Rejoicing was the order of the day, and dancing and revelry the business of the night. But in the midst of these festivities, a virulent and infectious fever broke out — brought, as Howard believed, by the military from the camp. One ot the sufferers from this disorder was a young lady who resided about twenty-four miles from Cherson, but who had been a constant attendant at the recent balls and routs. Her fever very soon assumed an alarming form ; and as a last resource her friends waited upon Howard — whose reputation as a leech was still on the increase — and implored him to ride over and see her. At first he refused, on the ground that he was only a physician to the poor; but their importunities increasing, and reports arriving that she was getting worse and worse, he at length acceded to their wish — being also pressed thereto by his intimate friend, Admiral Mordvinoff, Chief Admiral of the Black Sea fleet, — and went with them. He prescribed for the lady's case; and then leaving word that if she improved they must send to him again, but if she did not, it would be useless, went to make some visits to the sick of an hospital in the neighborhood. The lady gradually improved under the change of treatment, and in a day or two a letter was written to Howard to acquaint him with the circumstances, and requesting him to come again without delay. Very unfortunately this letter miscarried, and was not delivered for eight days — when it was brought to him at Mordvinoff's house. When he noticed the date, Howard was greatly alarmed — for he had become interested in the case of his fair patient, and thought himself in a manner responsible for any mishap which might have befallen her. Although, when the note came to hand, it was a cold, wintry, tempestuous night, with the rain falling in torrents, he did not hesitate for a moment about setting off for her residence. Unfortunately, again, no post-horses could be had at the time ; and he was compelled to mount a dray-horse used in the Admiral's family for carrying water, whose slow pace protracted the journey until he was saturated with wet and benumbed with cold. He arrived, too, to find his patient dying ; yet, not willing to see her expire without a struggle to save her, he administered some medicines to excite perspiration, and remained for some hours at her side to watch the first signs of the effect produced. After a time, he thought the dose was beginning to operate, and, wishing to avoid exposing her to the chance of a fresh cold by uncoverring her ams, placed his hand under the coverlett to feel her pulse. On raising it up a little, a most offensive smell escaped from beneath the clothes ; and Howard always thought the infection was then communicated to him. Next day she died.

For a day or two, Howard remained unconscious of his danger; feeling only a slight indisposition, easily accounted for by his recent exertions; which he nevertheless so far humored as to keep within doors; until finding himself one day rather better than usual, he went out to dine with Admiral Mordvinoff. There was a large, animated party present, and he stayed later than was usual with him. On reaching his lodgings, he felt unwell, and fancied he was about to have an attack of gout. Taking a dose of sal volatile in a little tea, he went to bed. About four in the morning, he woke, and feeling no better, took another dose. During the day he grew worse, and found himself unable to take his customary exercise ; towards night, a violent fever seized him, and he had recourse to a favorite medicine of that period, called "James's Powders." On the 12th of January, he fell down suddenly in a fit — his face was flushed and black, his breathing difficult, his eyes closed firmly, and he remained quite insensible for half an hour. From that day, he became weaker and weaker; though few even then suspected that his end was near. Acting as his own physician, he continued at intervals to take his favorite powders; notwithstanding which, his friends at Cherson — for he was universally loved and respected in that city, though his residence had been so short — soon surrounded him with the highest medical skill which the province supplied. As soon as his illness became known, Prince Potemkin, the princely and unprincipled favorite of Catherine, then resident in Cherson, sent his own physician to attend him ; and no effort was spared to preserve a life so valuable to the world. Still he went worse and worse.

In one of his intervals from pain — probably on the 15th or 16th of the month, he wrote the following pious reflections : — "May I not look on present difficulties, or think of future ones in this world — as I am only a pilgrim and wayfaring man, that tarries but a night. This is not my home; but may I think what God has done for me, and rely on his power and grace — for his promise, his mercy, endureth forever. I am faint and low, yet I trust in the right way — pursuing, though too apt to forget, my Almighty Friend and God. Oh! my soul, remember and record how often God has sent an answer of peace — mercies in the most seasonable times; how often, better than thy fears, exceeded thy expectations! Why should I distrust this good and faithful God? In his Word He hath said, 'In all thy ways acknowledge Him, and He will direct thy path.' Lord, leave me not to my own wisdom, which is folly, nor to my own strength, which is weakness. Help me to glorify Thee on earth, and finish the work Thou givest me to do; and to Thy name alone be all the praise!"

On the 17th, that alarming fit recurred; and although, as on the former occasion, the state of complete insensibility lasted only a short time, it evidently affected his brain, and from that moment, the gravity of his peril was understood by himself, if not by those about him. On the 18th, he went worse rapidly. A violent hiccuping came on, attended with considerable pain, which continued until the middle of the following day, when it was allayed by means of copious musk drafts.

Early on the morning of the 20th, came to see him his most intimate friend, Admiral Priestman — a

Russianized Englishman in the service of the Empress. During his sojourn at Cherson, Howard had been in the habit of almost daily intercourse with his gallant ex-countryman. When taken ill, not himself considering it at first serious, no notice of it had been sent out; but not seeing his friend for several days, Priestman began to feel uneasy, and went off to his lodgings to learn the cause. He found Howard sitting at a small stove in his bedroom—the winter was excessively severe—and very weak and low. The Admiral thought him merely laboring under a temporary depression of spirits, and by lively, rattling conversation, endeavored to rouse him from his torpidity. But Howard was fully conscious that death was nigh. He knew now that he was *not* to die in Egypt; and, in spite of his friend's cheerfulness, his mind still reverted to the solemn thought of his approaching end. Priestman told him not to give way to such gloomy fancies, and they would soon leave him. "Priestman," said Howard, in his mild and serious voice, "you style this a dull conversation, and endeavor to divert my mind from dwelling on the thought of death; but I entertain very different sentiments. Death has no terrors for me; it is an event I always look to with cheerfulness, if not with pleasure; and be assured, the subject is more grateful to me than any other." And then he went on to say, "I am well aware that I have but a short time to live; my mode of life has rendered it impossible that I should get rid of this fever. If I had lived as you do, eating heartily of animal food, and drinking wine, I might, perhaps, by altering my diet, have been able to subdue it. But how can such a man as I am lower his diet, who has been accustomed for years to live upon vegetables and water, a little bread, and a little tea? I have no method of lowering my nourishment, and therefore I must die;" and then turning to his friend, added, smiling, "It is only such jolly fellows as you, Priestman, who get over these fevers." This melancholy pleasantry was more than the gallant sailor could bear; he turned away to conceal his emotion; his heart was full, and he remained silent, whilst Howard, with no despondency in his tone, but with a calm and settled serenity of manner, as if the death-pangs were already past, went on to speak of his end, and of his wishes as to his funeral. "There is a spot," said he, "near the village of Dauphiney — this would suit me nicely; you know it well, for I have often said, that I should like to be buried there; and let me beg of you, as you value your old friend, not to suffer any pomp to be used at my funeral; nor let any monument, nor monumental inscription whatsoever, ever be made to mark where I am laid; but lay me quietly in the earth, place a sun-dial over my grave, and let me be forgotten."

In this strain of true Christian philosophy did Howard speak of his exit from a world in which he felt that he had done his work. The ground, in which he had selected to fix his everlasting rest, situated about two miles from Cherson, on the edge of the great highway to St. Nicholas, belonged to a French gentleman who had treated him with distinguished attention and kindness during his stay in the vicinity; and having made his choice, he was very anxious to know whether permission could be obtained for the purpose, and begged his gallant friend to set off immediately, and ascertain that for him. Priestman was not very willing to leave his friend at such a time and on such a gloomy errand; he fancied people would think him crazy in asking permission to make a grave for a man still alive, and whom few as yet knew to be ill; but the earnestness of the dying martyr at length overcame his reluctance, and he set forth.

Scarcely had he departed on his strange mission, when a letter arrived from England, written by a gentleman who had just been down to Leicester to see young Howard, giving a highly favorable account of the progress of his recovery, and expressing a belief that when the Philanthropist returned to his native land, he would find his son greatly improved. This intelligence came to the death-bed of the pious Christian like a ray of light from heaven. His eye brightened; a heavy load seemed lifted from his heart; and he spoke of his child with the tenderness and affection of a mother. He called Thomasson to his bed-side, and bade him tell his son, when he went home, how long and how fervently he had prayed for his recovcry, and especially during this last illness.

Towards evening, Admiral Priestman returned from a successful application; with this result Howard appeared highly gratified, and soon after his arrival retired to rest. Priestman, conscious now of the imminency of the danger, would leave him alone no more, but resolutely remained and sat at the bed-side. Although still sensible, Howard had now become too weak to converse. After a long silence, during which he seemed lost in profound meditation, he recovered for a moment his presence of mind, and, taking the letter which had just before come to hand — evidently the subject of his thoughts — out of his bosom, he gave it to the Admiral to read; and when the latter had glanced it through, said, tenderly: — "Is not this comfort for a dying father?" These were almost the last words he uttered. Soon after, he fell into a state of unconsciousness, the calm of sleep, of an unbroken rest — but even then the insensibility was more apparent than real, for on Admiral Mordvinoff, who arrived just in time to see the last of his illustrious friend, asking permission to send for a certain doctor, in whom he had great faith, the patient gave a sign which implied consent; but before this person could arrive he had fallen off: —

Howard was dead!

This mournful event took place about eight o'clock on the morning of the 20th of January, 1790, — 1,500 miles from his native land, with only strangers round about his bed; strangers, not to his heart, though their acquaintance with his virtues had been brief — but to his race, his language, and his creed. He, however, who was the friend of all — the citizen of the world in its highest sense — found friends in all. Never perhaps had a human being such funeral honors. Never before, perhaps, had a human being existed in whose demise so universal an interest could be felt. His death fell on the mind of Europe like an ominous shadow: the melancholy wail of grief which arose on the Dnieper, was echoed from the Thames, and soon re-echoed from the Tagus, and the Neva, and the Dardanelles. Everywhere Howard had friends — more than could be thought till death cut off restraint, and threw the flood-gates of sympathy wide open. Then the affluent tide rolled in like the dawn of a summer day. Cherson went into deep mourning for the illustrious stranger; and there was hardly a person in the province who was not greatly affected on learning that he had chosen to fix his final resting-place on the Russian soil. In defiance of his own wishes on the subject, the enthusiasm of the people improvised a public funeral. The Prince of Moldavia, Admirals Priestman and Mordvinoff, all the general and staff officers of the garrison, the whole body of the magistrates and merchants of the province, and a large party of cavalry, accompanied by an immense cavalcade of private persons, formed the funeral procession.

Nor was the grief by any means confined to the higher orders. In the wake of the more stateyl band of mourners, followed on foot, a concourse of at least three thousand persons — slaves, prisoners, sailors, soldiers, peasants — men whose best and most devoted friend the hero of these martial honors had ever been; and from this, after humbler train of followers, arose the truest, tenderest expression of respect and sorrow for the dead. When the funeral pomp was over, the remains of their benefactor lowered into the earth, and the proud procession of the great had moved away — then would these simple children of the soil steal noiselessly to the edge of the deep grave, and with their hearts full of grief, whisper in low voices to each other of all that they had seen and known of the good stranger's acts of charity and kindness. Good indeed he had been to them. Little used to acts or words of love from their own lords, they had felt the power of his mild manner, his tender devotion to them, only the more deeply from its novelty. To them how irreparable the loss! The higher ranks had lost the grace of a benignant presence in their higher circle; but they — the poor, the friendless — had lost in him their friend — almost their father. Nature is ever true; they *felt* how much that grave had robbed them of. Not a dry eye was seen amongst them; and looking sadly down into the hole where all that now remained of their physician lay, they marvelled much why he, a stranger to them, had left his home, and friends, and country, to become the unpaid servant of the poor in a land so far away; and not knowing how, in their simple hearts, to account for this, they silently dropped their tears into his grave, and slowly moved away — wondering at all that they had seen and known of him who was now dead, and thinking sadly of the long, long time ere they might find another friend like him!

The hole was then filled up — and what had once been Howard was seen of man no more. A small pyramid was raised above the spot, instead of the sun-dial which he had himself suggested; and the casual traveller in Russian Tartary is still attracted to the place as to one of the holiest shrines of which this earth can boast.

Words cannot depict the profound sensation which the arrival of this mournful news produced in England. The death-shaft cut the withes which had kept his reputation down. All at once the nation awoke to a full consciousness of his collossal fame and his transcendent virtues. Howard was now — history. Envy and jealousy were past: rivalry had ended on the brink of the grave. Death alone sets a man on fair terms with society. The death of a great man is always a calamity; but it is only when a country loses one of its illustrious children in a distant land, and under peculiar circumstances, that the full measure of the national calamity is felt. Every possible mark of honor — public and private — was paid to the memory of Howard. All orders of men vied with each other in heaping honors upon his name. The court, the press, parliament, the bar, the pulpit, and the stage — each in its different fashion, paid the well-earned tribute of respect. The intelligence of his demise was publicly announced in the official Gazette — a distinction never before accorded to a private individual. The muses sang his virtues with innumerable voices; the churches echoed with his praise; the senate and the judgement-seat resounded with the tribute to his merits; and even at the theatres, his character was exhibited in imaginary scenes, and a monody on his death was delivered from the foot-lights.

Nor was a more enduring memorial wanting. The long dormant Committee of the Howardian Fund was resuscitated, and the sculptor Bacon was employed to make a full-length marble statue of the Philanthropist. At that time it was in contemplation to make St. Paul's serve the double purpose of a cathedral and a Walhalla; and this design was inaugurated by placing there, as the first great worthy of England, the statue of John Howard. It stands immediately on the righ hand of the choir-screen; it is a handsome figure, tolerably faithful, and is illustrated by emblems of his noble deeds, and by the following inscription: —

THIS EXTRAORDINARY MAN HAD THE FORTUNE TO BE HONORED
WHILST LIVING,
IN THE MANNER WHICH HIS VIRTUES DESERVED;
HE RECEIVED THE THANKS
OF BOTH HOUSES OF THE BRITISH AND IRISH PARLIAMENTS,
FOR HIS EMINENT SERVICES RENDERED TO HIS COUNTRY AND TO
MANKIND.
OUR NATIONAL PRISONS AND HOSPITALS
IMPROVED UPON THE SUGGESTION OF HIS WISDOM,
BEAR TESTIMONY TO THE SOLIDITY OF HIS JUDGMENT,
AND THE ESTIMATION IN WHICH HE WAS HELD.
IN EVERY PART OF THE CIVILIZED WORLD,
WHICH HE TRAVERSED TO REDUCE THE SUM OF HUMAN MISERY;
FROM THE THRONE TO THE DUNGEON HIS NAME WAS MENTIONED
WITH RESPECT, GRATITUDE, AND ADMIRATION.
HIS MODESTY ALONE
DEFEATED VARIOUS EFFORTS THAT WERE MADE DURING HIS
LIFE, TO ERECT THIS STATUE,
WHICH THE PUBLIC HAS NOW CONSECRATED TO HIS MEMORY.
HE WAS BORN AT HACKNEY, IN THE COUNTY OF MIDDLESEX,
SEPT. IId, MDCCXXVI.
THE EARLY PART OF HIS LIFE HE SPENT IN RETIREMENT,
RESIDING PRINCIPALLY UPON HIS PATERNAL ESTATE
AT CARDINGTON, IN BEDFORDSHIRE;
FOR WHICH COUNTY HE SERVED THE OFFICE OF SHERIFF IN THE
YEAR MDCCLXXIII.
HE EXPIRED AT CHERSON, IN RUSSIAN TARTARY, ON THE
XXth OF JAN. MDCCXC.
A VICTIM TO THE PERILOUS AND BENEVOLENT ATTEMPT
TO ASCERTAIN THE CAUSE OF, AND FIND AN EFFICACIOUS REMEDY
FOR THE PLAGUE.
HE TROD AN OPEN BUT UNFREQUENTED PATH TO IMMORTALITY
IN THE ARDENT BUT UNINTERMITTED EXERCISE OF
CHRISTIAN CHARITY:
MAY THIS TRIBUTE TO HIS FAME
EXCITE AN EMULATION OF HIS TRULY GLORIOUS ACHIEVEMENTS.

THE END.

www.ingramcontent.com/pod-product-compliance
Lightning Source LLC
LaVergne TN
LVHW021143110826
845150LV00005B/1116

* 9 7 8 1 4 2 5 5 4 7 7 9 0 *